The Beautiful Animal

The Beautiful Animal

Sincerity, Charm, and the Fossilised Dialectic

Michael Lewis

ROWMAN &
LITTLEFIELD
——— INTERNATIONAL ———
London • New York

Published by Rowman & Littlefield International Ltd.
Unit A, Whitacre Mews, 26–34 Stannary Street, London, SE11 4AB
www.rowmaninternational.com

Rowman & Littlefield International Ltd.is an affiliate of Rowman & Littlefield
4501 Forbes Boulevard, Suite 200, Lanham, Maryland 20706, USA
With additional offices in Boulder, New York, Toronto (Canada), and Plymouth (UK)
www.rowman.com

Copyright © 2018 by Michael Lewis

All rights reserved. No part of this book may be reproduced in any form or by any electronic or mechanical means, including information storage and retrieval systems, without written permission from the publisher, except by a reviewer who may quote passages in a review.

British Library Cataloguing in Publication Data
A catalogue record for this book is available from the British Library

ISBN: HB 978-1-7866-0754-6
       PB 978-1-7866-0755-3

Library of Congress Cataloging-in-Publication Data Is Available

ISBN 978-1-78660-754-6 (cloth)
ISBN 978-1-78660-755-3 (pbk)
ISBN 978-1-78660-756-0 (electronic)

To the Mog, whose name never quite fitted,
and who for that reason has remained all the more an animal.

Le Chat

Dans ma cervelle se promène,
Ainsi qu'en son appartement,
Un beau chat, fort, doux et charmant.
Quand il miaule, on l'entend à peine,

Tant son timbre est tendre et discret;
Mais que sa voix s'apaise ou gronde,
Elle est toujours riche et profonde.
C'est là son charme et son secret.
— Baudelaire

In my brain there walks about,
As though he were in his own home,
A lovely cat, strong, sweet, charming.
When he mews, one scarcely hears him,

His tone is so discreet and soft;
But purring or growling, his voice
Is always deep and rich;
That is his charm and secret.
— trans. Aggeler

Les Chats

Les amoureux fervents et les savants austères
Aiment également, dans leur mûre saison,
Les chats puissants et doux, orgueil de la maison,
Qui comme eux sont frileux et comme eux sédentaires.
— Baudelaire

No one but indefatigable lovers and old
Chilly philosophers can understand the true
Charm of these animals serene and potent, who
Likewise are sedentary and suffer from the cold.
— trans. Dillon

Contents

Introduction 1
  The perfect, beautiful animal: Philosophy, sincerity, and charm 1
  Shaving, painting, weeding: Bad infinity against bad infinity 2
  Historical and cultural variance in the bad infinite 4
  Humans alone with a washing cat sneezing 4
  Hegel's two infinites 6
    a) Bad infinite 6
    b) True infinite 7
  Spirit and history, nature and time 9
  The cat and the fish 11
  Reading philosophy as animals 14
  The interest of the charming: Kant's *Critique of Judgement* 16
  Animal philosophy and the useless world 18

1 The Animal's Sincerity: Wittgenstein, Levinas, Lacan 21
  Sincerity: Wittgenstein, Levinas, Lacan 21
    a) Wittgenstein 21
    b) Levinas 22
      Llewelyn on Levinas and animal sincerity 23
      Bobby, the literal dog 24
      The speechlessness of the Sphinx 28
    c) Lacan 30
      i) The 'metaphysical' strand in Lacan 30
      ii) The 'non-metaphysical' strand in Lacan 33
      The sincerity of being without a symbolic order 34

2	**Kant and the Animal's Charm**	**37**
	Kant before Hegel: On charm	37
	Kritik der Urteilskraft: Beginning German Idealism	38
	Beauty and the beast: The two halves of the *Critique of Judgement*	39
	On a collapse of the distinction between beauty and charm in the face of nature's diversity	40
	a) Determinative and reflective judgements: Beauty	40
	b) The diversity of nature and the potential for intelligibility: Nature's purpose	42
	c) Beauty and the freedom of free-play	45
	d) The judgement of the charming	47
	e) Charm and beauty	47
	f) Kant, birdsong, and the diversity of nature	48
	g) Kant and the impossible beauty of animals	53
	h) The animal and purpose	55
	i) The transcendental quality of the teleological judgement	56
	j) The irrepressible biologist in us	57
	k) Beyond Kant. Hegel.	59
3	**Hegel and Nature**	**61**
	Hegel's Philosophy of Nature	61
	Science and philosophy	62
	I. Nature's necessity	63
	Nature as teleological: Purpose and the concepts in nature	63
	Glimpsing concepts in hindsight	64
	Realist and idealist interpretations of the *Philosophy of Nature*	65
	From the collapse of the opposition to the restoration of distinctness	67
	II. Nature's contingency	67
	The odyssey of the concept: Alienation in nature and its supersession	67
	Contingency and the remnant alienation	71
	Nature's impotence — idealism — nature's shortfall	72
	The richness of nature and a divergence on the subject of beauty	73
	A monstrous failure to fall under the concept	74
	The beautiful animal in nature. Two lives: Nature to spirit, on the line.	75
4	**Beauty in Nature — Hegel's *Aesthetics***	**81**
	Hegel's *Aesthetics*: Beauty in nature	81
	The organism and beauty	81

	The distinction between beautiful and ugly animals: Animation	82
	Breath, spirit, and birdsong	84
	The perfect animal	86
	Hegel's sublation of the beautiful animal	88
	Natural and spiritual beauty	88
	Transition: Leaving behind	90
5	Fossils and the Fossilisation of the Dialectic	93
	The fossil of the dialectic	93
	Fossil-writing	94
	The formation of fossils	97
	Fossil-writing, metaphysical writing, and archi-writing	98
	The fossil beyond deconstruction and metaphysics	102
	Fossil writing and Hegelian writing	104
	The two places of writing in Hegel's dialectic: Dialectic and history	105
	Petrified life	108
	Hegel's Fossils I — the inorganic earth 'organism' and 'natural history'	110
	Hegel's Fossils II	114
	The immortality of stone after the second death	118
	Three forms of undeath: Horror, comedy, and fossil	121
	The beautiful fossil: Contingent encounter of man and animal	122
	Fossilised dialectic	126
	Dialectics at a standstill. The fossilisation of the dialectic.	127
	Man petrified	129
	Madness and the frozen dialectic: Derrida, Hegel, and Genet	130
	Fixation on a part, alienation, and the neurotic body	131
	Habit as the cure for madness	133
	The psychoanalytic reading: Madness and death drive	134
	The Levinassian inflection	135
	The difference between desire and charm	137
Conclusion		139
	Learning philosophy from animals	139
	On bad reading habits — detaching the bad infinite from 'bad faith'	140
Notes		143
Bibliography		207
Postscript		221
Index		223
About the Author		231

Introduction[1]

THE PERFECT, BEAUTIFUL ANIMAL: PHILOSOPHY, SINCERITY, AND CHARM

Can philosophy conceive of a perfect animal? Will it ever have considered the animal to be anything more than an imperfect human being?

Perfection appears to us in the form of beauty: can philosophy, in its Kantian and post-Kantian guise, make sense of the idea of a 'beautiful animal'?

When philosophy finds itself face to face with such an animal, what happens?

But first of all, we should ask ourselves: why do we find certain animals beautiful?

Animals are sincere — this is their charm: our conjecture is that these two characteristics, sincerity and charm, are related, and that together they explain the especial beauty of the living being. It is the sincerity, charm, and beauty of the animal that we shall here attempt to understand. But in order to do so we must first simply *describe* the experience of animal sincerity.

The animal is sincere. It dedicates itself entirely to one thing, whether playful or serious, without the slightest distraction or doubt, and it returns to the object of its devotion again and again, without variation — never imagining that it might pursue something else or that its activity should be turned towards some other, more productive end.

The animal is also sincere in that it does not conceal its desires: the cat's tail beats so hard that it frightens away the bird she was stalking. The animal does not mask its wants with the politeness of circumlocution; it simply insists, to the point of shrillness, with an absolute straightforwardness. In a manner quite analogous to its eternally repetitive behaviour, the animal reiterates exactly the same demand time after time, without in either case betraying the slightest hint of lethargy or boredom. Its enthusiasm remains forever undimmed by the least trace of ironic detachment.

The animal never learns, but it also never tires. It is absolutely sincere at the level of both word and deed — in the insistence of its demand and in the unflagging pursuit of its quarry.[2]

This eternal return of the same, this sincerity, may ultimately be what those who love animals find so charming about them. And yet, when similar behaviour is observed in *human beings*, it inspires a quite different response: tedium, or even disgust.

SHAVING, PAINTING, WEEDING: BAD INFINITY AGAINST BAD INFINITY

Let us consider several interrelated examples of gestures which we experience very differently when they are made by humans rather than animals, in order steadily to find our way into the problem at hand.

The protagonist of Jean-Paul Sartre's first novel, *Nausea*, laments the repetitive nature of the ritual of washing, and, most significantly for our purposes, shaving: 'this morning I took a bath, I shaved. Only, when I think back over all those careful little actions, I can't understand how I could bring myself to perform them. They are so futile. It was my habits, probably, which performed them for me' (Sartre 2000 [1938], 224/222).

The natural process of regrowth, like the periodic cycles of sleeping and waking and the passage of the day during which one gathers dirt, necessitates a series of cultural rituals to prevent the accumulation from becoming hypertrophic. Nature must be kept at bay, although the reasons why this is the case are often opaque to us: they have become self-evident through repetition, or they were never clear.

Shaving in itself is a curious gesture, and above all it seems to us a gesture of humanisation, a quotidian procedure which participates in our daily 'anthropogenesis' in an illuminating way. Man's fur is already deficient, in that it neither protects him from the cold nor shields his skin from sun and thorn. But shearing off what little remains, fully to reveal the face in all its nudity, makes the situation even worse. The human being's sparse pelt is thus prevented from making even the slightest incursion into an area where in any case it would not have done much good. Thus the already considerable distance that separates the human from the animal in this particular regard is re-emphasised, day in, day out, by the negation of something which was already nugatory.

In the diurnal ablution we find an example of what the German philosopher G. W. F. Hegel calls a 'bad infinity', an indefinite series of repetitions of exactly the same thing, without development or progress, without beginning or end.

In Britain, one example of the bad infinite which has become proverbial is the process of painting the Forth Bridge. The structure has so many surfaces, all susceptible to the natural processes of rusting and decay, all needing to be painted red over and over again, and so extensive is its span that no sooner has one reached the end than one immediately has to start again from the beginning. Even a temporary stasis is beyond us, let alone progress.[3]

Wayne Martin has provided us with another excellent example of the bad infinite: the endless task of weeding a garden (Martin 2007, 179). The maintenance of a flowerbed is precisely an act of *cultivation* — 'horticulture', the tending of gardens (*hortus*, in Latin). Nature would grow wild without the (horti)cultural act of cutting it back: hence the cruel, unnatural acts of the gardener, guardian of the boundary between nature and culture, kin to the shaver and the painter.[4]

All three of these activities — shaving, painting, weeding — attempt to maintain the opposition between nature and culture in all of its strictness, and yet one of their most curious features is that each of them involves a gesture of ceaseless repetition that we associate with the *other side* of the opposition, against which their acts are a defence. These humanising, cultivating activities deploy a structure which characterises *natural* processes and which we have already associated with the *animal*: the bad infinite. Each of them operates on a different kind of object: shaving, painting, and weeding work respectively on a human object, an artificial object, and a natural object. They are cultural activities designed to keep nature in check, and yet they *mimic* nature, for, generally speaking, it is in *nature* and not in culture that we seem to encounter the bad infinite — this, in any case, is what *philosophy* will have taught us.[5]

These human gestures involving the bad infinite take place in a borderland between nature and culture, a margin which must — it seems — be kept clear of detritus, free from natural excesses and ingressions. Perhaps one way in which we might reconcile these examples with the Hegelian-philosophical tendency to assign the bad infinite to nature rather than culture, is to say that these acts, despite being in accord with the bad infinite, are designed to protect a space in which the *true* infinite might take root. Weeding the garden is necessary in order to create a plot of land where cultivated species may begin to flourish. One keeps nature at bay by fighting like with like, bad infinite on bad infinite, repelling the incessant incursions of natural life time and again.

And one wages such a war only in order to ensure that processes which accord with the true infinite will find room to unfurl.⁶

We shall expand upon the nature of these processes only once we ourselves have cleared sufficient space for an explanation.

HISTORICAL AND CULTURAL VARIANCE IN THE BAD INFINITE

For this is not the most distinctive feature of the cultural bad infinite: the natural means which man employs in the battle against nature *change* over the course of history. Thus, the tactics which dictate precisely how we are to resist natural excess are historically and geographically *variable* in the case of man. This is not so in the animal world.

Perhaps man is the only animal able to grow a covering that serves no purpose, and then to remove it, or choose in place of its complete eradication an artificial modification of its appearance according to the customs of the particular culture and epoch of history in which it has sprung up. (And let it be noted that the rebellion *against* such fashions is just as much determined by its time and place as unreflecting or deliberate conformity.) Perhaps it is a certain weariness (*ennui, Langeweile*), even that of an entire age, which leads us to make such changes in our manner of cultivation. ('They are so futile . . . [let us therefore have a change . . .]')

Thus the conflict stirred up by pitting bad infinite against bad infinite can assume various guises in the human being — it can form a certain *culture*. Thus, even the apparently *natural* gesture of the repetitious bad infinite becomes *historical* when carried out by man. The technology and fashions of shaving have a history, indeed many histories — as does painting, as do the design of gardens and our relation to them as well as to the wilderness of nature.

HUMANS ALONE WITH A WASHING CAT SNEEZING

Before moving on to draw the outlines of our problem from these examples, we might wonder whether there is in fact anything *truly* human about the gestures we have picked out. Painting is a relatively clear-cut case, although one can find examples of animal adornment; but non-human animals certainly preen and crop the grass; squirrels nibble the shoots which threaten the integrity of their acorn, as nature attempts to actualise the potential oak that slumbers *in embryo* at its heart. Do animals not commit natural crimes against nature in just the way human beings do?

Let us consider a creature more furry than man, washing itself: a privileged example for us — the cat. A domestic animal, and yet by no means fully domesticated, for the feline sits athwart a curious threshold between wild nature and civilised culture, insisting that it not be confined to the house, but allowed out (and then in) whenever it sees fit, as if demanding the freedom to be either feral or tame.[7]

What is striking, for our purposes, is that the animal equivalent of, for instance, washing, the licking of one's fur, is not just functional, but at the same time, if we explicitly include the human onlooker who was in any case already implicitly presupposed, a spectacle of some charm.

We are not perhaps as surprised as we should be by this fact — that the sight of an animal applying its tongue at great length, repeatedly, to its own body should be charming. Indeed, all of the most natural instinctual and practical behaviours, which can go so far as to provoke either *ennui* or repulsion when they occur in humans, become delightful in animals such as the cat. The appeal seems to involve the fact that these actions, while necessary, are not in the least treated as drudgeries, but are carried out with a devotion which is utterly sincere, quite indefatigable and without a trace of reluctance or complaint.[8]

Consider another natural process: sneezing. Cats sneeze. They might have undergone this trembling and explosion every day for a lifetime, but the cat demonstrates genuine surprise at such an eruption, the natural necessity of evacuating a potential blockage or hazard, each and every time. Momentarily flummoxed, the cat's dignity is seamlessly restored as, without concern for any veneer of sophistication, it responds with absolute sincerity: it licks its nose.

We have yet to be as perplexed as we might by our response to this response.

Something is going on in these examples which troubles the opposition between the true infinite and the bad infinite. It seems to be the result of a splitting between two forms, or at least two uses, of the bad infinite: the human use and the animal use.

The fact that we respond so differently to these functional activities when they occur in humans demonstrates a certain difference that we have yet to think. Our task here is to gather together the concepts which are necessary for us to do so. These conceptual tools will help us to relate together systematically those other differences which we have identified in the examples of shaving, painting, and weeding — human peculiarities which, even if in certain cases they may also be said to characterise animals, we react to in a curiously disparate way.

HEGEL'S TWO INFINITES

The first conceptual tool we have taken up in order to weigh it in our hands is Hegel's notion of infinity. We have seen already that the human being deploys the bad infinite against itself to reaffirm the border between the bad infinite and the true infinite, nature and culture, and yet, in doing so it reveals that there is another kind of difference between the human and the animal, distinct from the one we had been led to expect. The human being demonstrates this in the fact that it grows *weary* of the reassertion of this border, while the animal's actions are tireless, charming, and sincere. This, we might say, is why the latter never changes, and the animal never becomes historical. For Hegel, this is a flaw, an evidence of imperfection; but to us, the animal's use of the bad infinite, and indeed the animal itself, seem to be in a certain way *superior* to man, and in precisely that respect in which Hegel thought the animal our inferior.

Now that the notion of the bad infinite has been introduced by means of our examples and we have alighted upon the notion that it may help us to make sense of the animal's charm, the time is ripe to explore what the bad infinite and the true infinite are more fully. They stand at the heart of our problem and are among the richest resources that the history of philosophy affords us with regard to the experience of animal sincerity and its charm. But we have already come to suspect that they also stand in need of some modification.

a) Bad infinite

In our vulgar, pre-philosophical understanding, we assume that there is an opposition between the finite and the infinite, the limited and the unlimited, relative and absolute. But Hegel shows that this way of conceiving the infinite is false because on this account the 'infinite' *lacks* something, and the infinite should by definition lack nothing. What the infinite lacks here is precisely the *finite*, from which it is separated by a rigid boundary: 'The infinite as thus posited over against the finite, in a relation wherein they are as qualitatively distinct *others*, is to be called the *spurious* [*bad*] *infinite* [Schlecht-Unendliche], the infinite of the *understanding*, for which it has the value of the highest, the absolute Truth' (SL, 139/152). This is the understanding of infinity embodied by Kant's thing-in-itself (*das Ding an sich*), which is held apart from the thing 'for us', the thing as it appears within our sensuous experience. This is akin to the Jewish god's interdiction of 'iconoclasm', the refusal of its own representation, one of the ten commandments brought down by Moses from Mount Sinai — the Jewish god 'appears' only in the form of these very prohibitions, in the guise of the Law (cf. CJ, 135/274). Kant and Judaism provide us with two classic instances of a bad conception of the infinite.[9]

The bad infinite also describes the eternal recurrence of the same which characterises the cycles of nature and the behaviour of animals: in such an indefinitely long series of repetitions, each element remains resolutely finite, qualitatively the same as the last and the next, never achieving a perfect moment in which the sequence would be consummated. Thus the distinction between finite and infinite persists in the form of the distinction between the elements of the series and the indefiniteness of the process of counting, the eternal incompletion of the series itself. 'In this context [the logic of mathematics] Hegel's central example of Bad Infinity is not God but rather the number series' (Martin 2007, 170); 'we say, "they go on and on and on . . .", "there is no end to them"' (ibid., 171). Martin adduces the example of the labour of Sisyphus, pushing a boulder to the summit of a mountain only to have it tumble straight back down again, and this in unending punishment of the unfortunate fellow's attempt to transgress the limits of human finitude.

Thus, again, the infinite is conceived in such a way as to exclude the finite.[10]

This is a 'bad' understanding of infinity since, 'the infinite is not yet really free from limitation [*Beschränktheit*] and finitude; the main point is to distinguish the genuine [or 'true'] Notion of infinity [*wahrhaften Begriff der Unendlichkeit*] from spurious [or 'bad'] infinity [*schlechten Unendlichkeit*], the infinite of reason from the infinite of the understanding' (SL, 137/149).[11] Thus, by contrast, the *true* infinite will be 'the self-sublation [*Sichaufheben*] of this infinite and of the finite, as a *single* process' (SL, 137/149). In the *Philosophy of Nature*, Hegel offers a very clear statement of at least one possible understanding of such a 'sublation': 'The movement here is precisely this self-separation, [. . .] and the sublation [*Aufheben*] of this separation as the inclusion of itself with that opposed to it [*Entgegengesetzte*]' (PNIII, 123/451 §354A). Applying this to the notion of infinity, we can say that, '[t]rue infinity [*Das wahrhaft Unendliche*] is the unity of itself and the finite [*Endlichen*]; it is the category of philosophy' (PNI, 203/21 §246A).

b) True infinite

Beyond the bad infinite of mechanical repetition, quantitative sameness, and the infinitely remote Judaic god, Christianity provides us with a powerful image of the true understanding of the infinite. God cannot be just the father, in heaven, invisible and invulnerable; he must also be incarnated in the son, in the form of a finite man, on earth, in flesh and bone — visible representative of infinity. Some way must be found to reconcile these two instances *within* a broader and truer understanding of god in its totality, which in Christian theology is described as the 'Trinity' of father, son, and holy spirit. Hegel understands this spirit or ghost (*Geist*) as the love which binds the Christian community together, across the ages, a charitable love which originates in God's love for man as evinced by the sacrifice of Christ on the cross.

The crucifixion was the 'death of god' which allowed father and son, God and Christ, to be reconciled in the form of the latter's resurrection to eternal life.[12] Thus the (Judaic) border between the infinite and the finite — the father and the son — is overcome. This act of overcoming an opposition is described by Hegel as 'sublation' (*Aufhebung*). In sublation, the opposition is both preserved and cancelled.[13] The word 'sublation' is intended to capture the manner in which this opposition is respected while, at another level, the opposites themselves are reconciled, understood differently, as both are revealed to be dependent upon one another for their very definition. Neither half can establish its own identity without differentiating itself from the other. Thus at a higher level, it becomes clear that the two are not opposed but are rather 'moments' of a greater whole, a unity or a 'One'.

Once we are in the business of *defining* entities, we are involved in an attempt to construct their *concept*: we are trying to think them. A thought is understood to be *dialectical* if the entity which it conceives cannot properly *be* so conceived if that entity is not placed in 'dialogue' with its other or its opposite number (*dialegesthai*, the middle voice infinitive in Greek, means 'to enter into discussion or conversation', while *dialegein*, the active infinitive, means 'to classify or define'). If the two supposed opposites are to be *thought* then they must be understood as two moments of the *same* concept, and it is within this concept that the two entities are not simply opposed but also conjoined. Hence sublation is an 'idealisation' in that it raises material things to the level of the *ideal* — to the plane of rational thought and its concepts. Sublation endows entities with *meaning*, it 'recollects' the former state of things, in which these opposites were understood to be separate, and gathers them up into a single whole. This explains Hegel's use of the word '*Erinnerung*' to describe the act of sublation: 'memorisation' but also 'internalisation', taking a number of things into the shelter of a concept.[14]

We may think of sublation or internalisation as a process of emergence: in the case that interests us most, the second term of the opposition ('infinite') is produced only through the negation of the first ('finite' becomes '*not* finite' or '*in*-finite').[15] This type of negation is described by Hegel as 'determinate negation' (*bestimmte Negation*).[16] The conceptualisation we have just described, which contrasts a certain thing with whatever stands opposed to it, as if the other were a mirror image of the first, helps to explain Hegel's description of this dialectical mode of thought as 'speculative' (from the Latin, *speculum*, mirror). Truly to think an entity in its dialectical identity is to bring it into relation with that which stands opposed to it.

In Hegel's speculative dialectic, the identity of things is formed gradually by a process of bifurcation which invokes not just the entity in question but also its opposite; then, in a further development, the entity achieves its ultimate self-identity by way of a reflection in the other, as it becomes clear that it cannot be fully constituted without this detour. At the same time, the concepts used to think such an identity must also be in motion, in order to capture this differentiating process. They can only conceive that which they are attempting to grasp by negating its opposite, in such a way as to give rise to the determinate identity of that which is being conceptualised. But this is not the end of the process, for thought then discovers that the newly determined entity now stands opposed to something *else*, which must similarly be negated, and so on and so forth, until there is *nothing* that is not included in the totality within which the entity is individuated, defined, and conceived. Gradually, thought produces a more and more definite and, at the same time, inclusive concept, until one has a System which literally encompasses everything.

SPIRIT AND HISTORY, NATURE AND TIME

This ability to think dialectically, to determinately negate or sublate, belongs to rational thought, the most self-conscious form of which is *Philosophy*. Hegel understands philosophy as the highest form and most complete manifestation of 'spirit' (*Geist*). We have encountered something like spirit before, in the form of 'culture'.

The movement of sublation may be seen to operate everywhere, in thought, in nature, in culture, but the possibility of so discerning it becomes explicitly apparent only when spirit reaches a certain level of development. Spirit may be said to make progress when it advances towards self-consciousness, which amounts to a more explicit awareness of what precisely it is, and this knowledge transforms the very way in which spirit unfolds. When a dialectical movement becomes self-conscious, it is capable of understanding that each stage of its own genesis is constituted by the determinate negation of every preceding stage. One might therefore say that spirit's process of development is a *historical* one, with history itself amounting to the accumulation of its own earlier moments as strata upon which the present is seen to be built. Thus, a qualitative difference emerges between nature and culture, time and history, and the two forms of infinity which we are in the course of discussing.

What is history? It is time, but a time in which what has passed is not forgotten but rather understood in its passing as the negation upon which the present depends — the past is determinately negated rather than 'abstractly' negated, which is to say, consigned to oblivion. What has gone by is not lost but archived and thus used as a foundation upon which to build: for this reason, the past and its mistakes should never be repeated identically, and from the moment history begins there is — or can be — *progress*. History is dialectical and dialectic is *Bildung*, edification, education or acculturation: history teaches us lessons, and in learning them we pass beyond nature and into culture, from the bad infinite of an eternal repetition of the same to the true infinite of rational enlightenment. The latter characterises the realm of spirit and is the province of the human in contrast to the animal.

Time, nature, and the animal — as opposed to history, spirit, and the human — are characterised by the *bad* infinite. Time is a sequence of moments, each identical to the last, and no one of its moments retains the previous moments in their entirety. Time is here understood as a series of instants or 'nows' akin to the cardinal numbers. Like pulling up weeds, time's task is endless and without profit — it never draws to a halt in exhaustion or perfection. In nature one finds merely an endless repetition, without progress.

The bad infinite in nature is a cycle returning to the same spot (like the seasons), or an alternation (like the tides). In truth, neither the rotation nor the oscillation comprise a genuine infinity, and not least because none of their (finite) phases takes us any closer to infinity. What this sequence appears to stand in need of is a *single* element that would complete the series, by bringing it to perfection — an *exemplary* instance which would act as the model for every other instance, and thus transform the open-ended series into a totality, 'totalising' it. The perfect example of a type would be a finite element which nevertheless embodies infinity. This unique instance would thus unify the series — by exemplifying each and every one of its number — and represent true infinity by overcoming the separation between the finite (individual members) and the infinite (the perfect totality of the series), since it is both.

Thus the nature of 'examples' as such suggests a solution to the problem of the true infinite. Such a finite representative of infinity we find in the incarnate figure of Jesus Christ: for Hegel, Christ is a privileged 'example' or even the 'example of examples', a demonstration of what it means to *be* an example in the truest sense.[17] An example stands for the entire set of which it is also a member, but precisely by doing so it exempts itself somewhat from that series and elevates itself to an especial status enjoyed by no other.

There is, therefore, an intimate connection between the sublation which we find in the true infinite and the Christian notion of *resurrection*. Dialectic involves a certain relation to negation, to 'death': sublation is survival, but in a new, transfigured form.[18] In truth, the 'negation of negation' involved in dialectical progression, a sundering followed by a healing of the breach, might be understood as a philosophical translation of the 'death of death'.[19]

To overcome death in this manner means to transform the brute biological fact of mortality into a productive living possibility, a freedom which issues forth from nature but is not to be found there — the autonomous freedom of the rational *spirit*.[20]

On the Hegelian scheme, the animal does not die in this sense: the encounter with death does not raise it to a new spiritual plane; whatever glimpse of death it is vouchsafed does not rebound upon its understanding of its own potentialities. The animal does not become free: it is imprisoned within the cage of a bad infinity that limits it absolutely. The animal will not be resurrected and it cannot become more free. But things are quite different for the human being, since here death can elevate the individual to the life of the free spirit.

Perhaps it would be instructive at this point to examine the conception of death developed in the wake of Hegel by Martin Heidegger. The latter demonstrates most clearly that the encounter with death bestows upon human beings not just their freedom but their *individuality*; while for the animal, it only makes the individual's subordination to the species all the more clear.[21] The human being's death is the only possibility which we can envisage that would be 'non-transferrable' — no one can die in my place, and it is the same for each and every one of us. My death is unique (Heidegger 1962 [1927], 284/240). Thus, in the encounter with death, one's resurrection takes the form of the individual's rising up from the genus, or even, some have said, from the anonymous masses, to the acquisition of a name (even if the closest it gets to being inscribed in the annals of history is in the form of an epitaph).

This means that man can be individualised in a way that the animal cannot, remaining as it does subordinate to the transmission of its genes in the survival of its offspring, and indeed death's only function for the animal is to act as a boundary across which these genes — and hence the species — can pass. Perhaps this is why when we look into the eyes of an animal, or at its physical form — or rather when *it* looks at *us* or shows itself to us — we can sometimes discern *other* individual members of that species, as if the creatures we have encountered elsewhere were haunting that animal which is otherwise a stranger to us: this renders even the most unknown street cat loveable.[22]

In any case, the animal does not encounter anything that might carry it beyond its natural life and into the resurrection unto spiritual life. Paradoxically, only a human being can be a phoenix, or fly with the owls.[23]

THE CAT AND THE FISH

That the animal in its habits embodies the bad infinite we do not deny — nor does our experience contradict Hegel's assertion. Indeed the connection is essential to our thesis. But nothing in Hegel's account of the subordination

Illustration I.1.

of the bad infinite to the true, or the animal to the human, explains why the animal's cyclical performance of its natural functions should strike us as a sincerity which is infinitely charming.

This is why we need both to learn from Hegel and also to take a certain distance from him, so as to refine the tool he has placed in our hands. Thus to make our way towards a position from which we might make sense of this charming sincerity, let us turn to a particular example — a personal, autobiographical one — and the experience which it has engendered, to which we will have been attempting to do justice all along.

For fourteen years, every single day, our cat has attempted to maul our pet goldfish. The goldfish is quite safe, in its impenetrable plastic tank, and the cat has never once done more than startle the fish with a particularly abrupt lunge. A Hegelian might find in this an occasion to upbraid the cat and beseech it, 'why have you never learned? In five thousand attempts, you have come not one inch closer to the fish'.[24]

But here precisely is where we would put the Hegelian perspective in question. The cat knows full well that it has made no progress. It has not forgotten. Or more precisely, it never remembered, and has remained eternally indifferent to the opposition between progress and stasis, learning and not learning — aloof to the question of remembering and forgetting. Its continual attempts to harass the fish *are* the embodiment of a bad infinite, but it is a bad infinite which remains wilfully uninterested in the possibility of becoming good or true. We might even say that this opposition between two infinities can be posited only from the standpoint of the concept and thus of the *true* infinite — but this will mean viewing the animal *retrospectively*, from the human point of view and its inadequacy thereto.[25]

The cat and her fish compose something like the 'primal scene' of this book, a paradigmatic case of animal sincerity and charm which we are setting out to explain. The human, even the human child, will eventually grow out of this endless cycle of repetitions, and it must in order to avoid becoming tiresome and to complete the process of anthropogenesis to which it is destined. It needs to pass beyond the stage of what psychoanalysis calls 'drive' (the motivation for this automatic repetition, this machinic glee) on pain of being driven insane, or at least becoming ill with that noisome eternal puerility that Slavoj Žižek describes as the 'pathological narcissism' which has come ever more strikingly to characterise our culture. The child will — in non-pathological cases, if such there be — break out of this cycle, and move from straight repetition to memorialising progress; but the animal never will.[26] And yet the animal's repetitions are not tiresome; on the contrary, it is within the infinity of their recurrences that the secret of the animal's charm lies concealed: this, at least, is our hypothesis.

For an Hegelian, the animal has been hypnotised at a preliminary stage of the spiritualisation process, and this process can only lead *beyond* the animal in the direction of man — nature's crowning *opus*, the highest and most perfect animal. For a certain kind of Hegelianism at least, the animal remains constitutively unable to surpass itself, its dialectic remains 'at a standstill', frozen or petrified, and, since we are speaking of the living, we might even say 'fossilised'.

Hegelianism suggests that the opposition between the bad infinite and the good is purely and simply the difference between nature and culture, the animal and the human; but as we shall see throughout the present work, and as should already have become clear from our examples of shaving, weeding, and painting, the two infinites in fact form a threshold upon which the boundary between nature and culture is constantly guarded in a way that deploys the very methods of the realm whose encroachment is being guarded *against*. It is as if the only way man can prevent himself from being taken over by the animal is by becoming a little bit animalic himself, as if to become immune to the disease one had to inject one's self with a certain measure of its poison.

A bad infinite patrols the border between animal and man, but the latter must make surreptitious incursions into the animal realm in order to arm himself for the struggle. Thus the division turns out differently than we might have expected: the bad infinite is not merely something to be surpassed, but proves useful — and in the animal it is even charming. Indeed, we can become so bewitched that we forget we are engaged in a battle. Perhaps, today, it would be valuable if this experience could be relearnt. It is something which the Hegelian human has never understood, as if it were slightly too animalic itself, caught in its own kind of bad habit — the tendency to sublate everything. It may be that this lesson will allow a new kind of continuity to be installed between man and the animal.

READING PHILOSOPHY AS ANIMALS

In this book, our task is to delineate the theoretical resources which will allow us to make sense of the fact that the bad infinite takes such a different form in humans and animals, and to explain why it provokes such disparate responses in each case. At the same time, we shall attempt to clarify why the bad infinite nevertheless constitutes a threshold between the two kingdoms, which joins as much as it separates. We shall show how far philosophy can travel in this direction before it runs up against a limit and thereby reveals to us its beyond.[27]

We shall examine a number of philosophers, but the greater part of our time will be devoted to Immanuel Kant and G. W. F. Hegel, as we attempt to determine the extent to which we can, with their help, render the experience of the beautiful animal intelligible. It may be that these thinkers, for all the illumination they shed, reveal almost as much in those aspects of the experience which they are forced to leave in shadow. That said, this darkness will not always compel us to pass on to a completely different thinker, but will at times encourage us to focus more than is customary on certain obscure corners of the philosopher's own work. These minor strands within the text as a whole might espouse theses which do not necessarily cohere with the text's most readily apparent thread, but, if developed, they might tell us something about animals which the philosopher finds himself unable to say openly. These nooks will shelter certain hints which may be elaborated beyond the limits within which the philosopher's broader system confines them. But even this stretch has a breaking point which signals the need to move elsewhere, if we are to make progress.

Ultimately, we might wonder at the significance of the fact that philosophy has largely found itself *unable* to account for our experience of the beautiful animal, particularly in the case of Kant and Hegel, who remain the chief protagonists of our discourse, even though there are others pulling the strings behind the scenes and guiding our idiosyncratic passage through their works.

Kant and Hegel shed as much light as any on the progress that philosophy has made in the direction of understanding the animal in its charming sincerity, while at the same time bringing into sharp relief the problems it has encountered. In the end, perhaps this is to confirm to a certain extent Jacques Derrida's suggestion that philosophy — or 'metaphysics' — is constitutively anthropocentric, and that, even beyond the metaphysical account which assigns superiority to man on the basis of his possession of reason, language, or self-consciousness, in our culture we only ever treat the animal as an *object* of the human gaze, when we subject it to scientific scrutiny, or even when we consider our ethical duties towards it. Philosophy has never allowed the animal to be a *subject* — to do so it would need to let the animal cast its gaze upon *us*.[28]

Derrida, in his marvellous and intimate writing on animals, describes an encounter with his own cat in which he finds himself falling beneath the cat's gaze while naked and experiencing the perhaps perverse feeling of shame or embarrassment. This reversal of the traditional metaphysical relation between the human and the animal is in many ways akin to the task we have set for ourselves, but, despite all that we owe to Derrida, we are more interested in showing how philosophy may after all be able to admit the animal's look. *Prima facie*, perhaps the principal difference between our approach and Derrida's is that, for us, the *opposition* between man and animal, that at least in the first instance Derrida wishes to reject as metaphysical and unjustified in light of both advances in zoological knowledge and the deconstruction of the metaphysical understanding itself, is not to be erased altogether, but only *rethought*.[29]

And yet even this does not necessarily take us beyond Derrida, for deconstruction only *begins* by flattening out the field which metaphysics has furrowed, dividing it into two separate enclosures (in this instance, keeping the human and the animal altogether apart); it does not remain there. The next stage is to decide upon a *new* taxonomy of the field, which may indeed remain in this levelled state of indifference, or it might involve a multiplicity of differences, a number of different ways of dividing entities up into various groups; or indeed, it may take a third way and reinstall a certain opposition, for other reasons than metaphysics' and with other purposes in mind. We have opted for something like this final path.[30] But even so, and despite the immensity of our debt to Derrida's *corpus*, which is quite uncircumventable, we shall not reach exactly the same conclusions as he, even in the way that this new opposition is configured.

On our account, man and animal end up exchanging places in the metaphysical arrangement as the gaze is transplanted from man to animal — thus far we are in accord with Derrida. But this does not lead us, even in the first instance, to consider man and animal as utterly alike, the situation between them having been rendered symmetrical; the animal possesses a charm which man does not, and hence the animal is *superior* to man in this regard. That said, it is crucial to add that the human being also retains a certain privilege, which makes it unique in the entire animal kingdom and hence, despite everything, diametrically opposed to it. This is a privilege that metaphysics did not think to bestow upon man: the capacity for *appreciating* what the animal can do. Thus we shall arrive at a new definition of the human being: man is the (only) animal capable of being charmed by an animal.[31]

When we speak of the dialectic's 'fossilisation' as making possible a new philosophical discourse on the animal, an account which rescues it from the depreciation in which it has been left to languish by metaphysics, we are neither simply looking *at* the animal *nor* merely allowing ourselves to be looked at *by* the animal; we are restoring a gaze to the animal in the sense that we ourselves are attempting to look at *philosophy* from the animal's perspective — to see philosophy through the eyes of an animal, and to view dialectics as it might. This means to render ourselves indifferent to the distinction between the true infinite and the bad, which in turn allows us to imagine a dialectic that *would* attribute an inherent value to the animal and *could* admire its perfection.

Thus, in our own way, without perhaps following Derrida to the end, we are responding to his critique of the omission of the animal gaze from philosophy, while at the same time combining Derrida's insight with that of Oxana Timofeeva, in her exceptional book on philosophy and animality, the *History of Animals*. As a result of this, we are also implicitly confronting Derrida's texts with certain philosophical accounts of animality with which for the most part he does not engage, and certainly not in *The Animal That Therefore I Am* — Hegel, as Timofeeva and Žižek have tacitly insisted upon, but also Kant, and in particular his theory of the organism from the *Critique of Judgement*. This theory, along with its development in Hegel's *Philosophy of Nature*, is largely absent from Derrida's work. We shall see what happens when we bring it back.

THE INTEREST OF THE CHARMING: KANT'S *CRITIQUE OF JUDGEMENT*

Therefore, it is in the works of Kant and Hegel, albeit amongst others, that we shall seek the conceptual resources to make sense of these unique properties of the human and the animal — that the latter is charming in ways that, for the most part, human beings are not, and yet we are capable of being charmed by them.

We shall take our departure from a certain privileged moment in the history of philosophy, when the notion of charm is addressed before being almost immediately deposed by the category of *beauty*. This is Kant's *Critique of Judgement* (1790), where a *necessary* connection between freedom and nature, man and animal — or at least the necessity of *presupposing* such a connection — is described.

Eventually, we shall be forced to put in question Kant's suppression of charm in the name of beauty. Kant supposed beauty to be an experience of 'disinterest' — without desire for possession and thus without a personal interest in the *reality* of the beautiful object. The charming differs from the beautiful in that it is precisely of interest to us, in the literal etymological sense of the word, *inter-esse*: it entwines itself in the fabric of our existence — we are the two of us involved in each other's being.[32] If it is a living thing that bewitches us, then this charm will interweave human being with animal being, in a new relationship, after metaphysics, but still in opposition to one another, the one charmed by the other without reciprocation. Thus we make few claims as to the inherent nature of man or animal in their independence from one another — absolutely rather than relatively. 'Charm', and in this it resembles 'beauty', is after all a relation.

Although he replaces charm with beauty, Kant nevertheless brings this relation to light. In the *Critique of Judgement* he presents us with two analyses which he is compelled to keep distinct: the first concerns beauty and the second, animality. Both constitute moments at which the opposition between nature and reason is ameliorated. Kant juxtaposes these moments without being able to think them together in a manner that is truly convincing. Therefore, we move on to examine the way in which Kant's analyses are taken up and transformed by Hegel, who develops an account of organic nature which is able to bind beauty and animality together more tightly than Kant's manner of posing the question allowed. The animal is beautiful to the extent that it embodies the concept which will achieve perfection in man.

But in the case of both Kant and Hegel, the presence of beauty within nature reveals the latter to be intelligible to humanity, and not as alien to our freedom and rationality as it might first, in its chaos, have seemed. The beautiful animal, then, testifies to the presence of a necessary connection between man and nature.

And yet we shall not stop there: passing on from Hegel, and on the basis of an account of *charm* rather than *beauty*, we shall demonstrate that while there is indeed a conjunction between man and nature, revealed in these experiences, it remains *contingent* rather than *necessary*, and all the more special for that. Charm institutes a *continuity of being* (an 'inter-est') between man and the animal, and hence between freedom and nature, which demonstrates that if there is such a continuity, it is based on a presupposition of the most radical difference: the human being's possession of freedom and spirit. Man is not alienated from nature, and this thanks to the very feature which makes of us a stranger in this wilderness: the root of our capacity to be charmed by the animal in its indifference to our world.

Both Hegel and Kant attempt to posit between man and nature *both* an opposition *and* a continuity: indeed, bridging this gulf that philosophy itself had opened up (and for which Kant's first two Critiques, Pure and Practical Reason, are partly responsible) is the prime task of the philosophy of German Idealism (which we take to include Kant's final critique, along with the work of those post-Kantians customarily included in this designation: J. G. Fichte, F. W. J. Schelling, and Hegel himself).

The kind of continuity we wish to propose is not quite the same as that posited by either Kant or Hegel, and indeed the difference is related to Kant's surreptitious replacement of charm with beauty. In an attempt to understand this usurpation, we shall ultimately advance a new understanding of the human being, or at least one which for the most part exceeds the definition employed by Kant and Hegel. What defines humanity on our account is the ability to redeem the bad infinite that we encounter in the animal, and to see it not as failure but as charm. This capability stems from the refusal to understand the bad infinite solely in terms of its relation to the *good* infinite which would supersede it.[33] The eternal return of the Same constitutes not an inferiority to the dialectical learning process of the human spirit, but the animal's very charm. The bad infinite and the infinitely sincere return to the same activities and haunts, over and over again, which is precisely what appeals to us in the animal. Man is the entity capable of dialectical philosophical thought, but he is also endowed with the capacity to remain indifferent to it, and in that he is akin to the animal. We hope in the course of the present work to show that the human being might learn to *actualise* this potential for indifference *from* the animal.[34]

ANIMAL PHILOSOPHY AND THE USELESS WORLD

In our being charmed, it is as if we become one with the animal and glimpse something of its world — or else it dawns on us that this is where we will always have lived. In any case, we learn to see the world through their eyes. It is as if the cat sees through us: the animal can strip the human world of its specific functions through the mere indifference of its gaze and comportment, as when a cat sits on a keyboard we had previously understood to be intended solely for typing, or a book for reading. This is how an animal looks upon our philosophy.

When we witness such indifference, we may be forced to confront the contingency of the significance with which we have endowed our precious 'equipment'. The animal has its own purposes, which it pursues sincerely, and they are often rather at odds with our own. Perhaps this is why we find it charming when a cat sneezes, scratches, or washes itself, and the actions themselves more than merely functional and mundane.

This relativity of function, once revealed, can hardly be prevented from spiralling: the animal's vision of things in the world, thanks to the disparity which separates it from our own, can lead us eventually to catch sight of a world that is not simply endowed with other functions but lacking in functionality altogether — a world without purpose, without the seriousness of productive work, of which dialectical thought — the 'labour of the negative' — is a theoretical analogue. The dialectic has stopped working for animals.

The question of the 'beautiful animal' will allow us to stroll at our leisure through the history of philosophy, taking in certain of its avenues and pathways, and settling down for a while in those parts we find most commodious. We shall take our time over those passages which captivate our interest and bewitch us with their charmed and sometimes perplexed descriptions of the philosopher's encounters with animals. Perhaps in the course of our amble we shall come to realise that we are approaching philosophy as an animal would, while producing a work that is really no work at all, having little purpose, and remaining somewhat indifferent to this fact.[35]

Chapter One

The Animal's Sincerity: Wittgenstein, Levinas, Lacan

SINCERITY: WITTGENSTEIN, LEVINAS, LACAN

The charming is an experience which, on our account, links man and animal together in a new way; but before we can consider charm itself we need first to clarify that quality which we find charming: the animal's sincerity. When we try to speak of such a thing philosophically, we immediately encounter an obstacle: the animal has been said by the likes of Ludwig Wittgenstein, Emmanuel Levinas, and Jacques Lacan *not* to be sincere.

a) Wittgenstein

For Wittgenstein, it is a question of the correct use of language: we cannot be described as 'sincere' if we do not also have the capacity to be *in*sincere: 'A child has much to learn before it can pretend. (A dog cannot be a hypocrite, but neither can he be sincere [*Ein Hund kann nicht heucheln, aber er kann auch nicht aufrichtig sein*])' (Wittgenstein 1999 [1953], 229).[1] One must be capable of shuttling between both poles of a dichotomy in order for the ascription of either quality to make sense. An opposite is formed by the negation of that which it opposes: if the negation is to be genuinely informative then the negated must be a state in which the entity could potentially find itself. To describe a stone as 'immortal', we are told, is senseless because rock cannot under any circumstance die. Because an animal cannot be 'hypocritical' — deceptive or insincere — it becomes illegitimate to describe the *lack* of that insincerity as 'sincerity'.

b) Levinas

That much we might have granted, but then Levinas opens up a way beyond the Wittgensteinian position. He does this by locating a moment of sincerity *prior* to the opposition between insincerity and sincerity in their usual senses.

For Levinas, to be sincere is to respond immediately, without the slightest ambiguity or indirection, to an appeal from another entity, or to make such an appeal. This would be a sincerity that precedes any determinate use of language, any proposition or word actually enunciated, which Levinas calls 'the Said' (*le Dit*) — the realm of language or the 'signifier'. His concern is a more original sincerity, essentially earlier than the oppositions which structure the Said and hence more primitive than the opposition between sincerity and insincerity upon which Wittgenstein considered the attribution of either to depend. This would be a sincerity which reflexively indicates the very fact that something is being said (by us, here and now, in response to the presence of another), or that the entity facing us is *capable* of speaking, without our having translated this speaking or *Say-ing* (*Dire*) into some particular proposition that is *said* (*dit*).

Sincerity is a saying without a said, a *Dire* without a *Dit*, a speech (*parole*) in some way prior to language (*langue*) and all of its oppositions. It is the address that we make to the Other (*Autrui*) whom we encounter, in the merest pre-linguistic gestures that acknowledge their presence and humanity, the fact that we respond to another 'speaking animal', irrespective of what might eventually be said. Sincerity is an entirely straightforward welcoming of the other that cannot but remain utterly frank, even if our actual words are ultimately hypocritical or insincere.

According to Paul Davies, one of the most insightful commentators on the notion of sincerity,[2]

> Levinas does, it seems, want to suggest that being sincere is not simply one type of linguistic behaviour among myriad others. The uttered (said) 'Yes' and 'Hello', once learnt, do not bring affirming and greeting into the language, nor do they only denote mastery of the language games of affirming and greeting, thereby adding to the stock of games at the speaker's disposal [contra Wittgenstein]. Rather, in Levinas's hands, they tell us about all language, any language game whatsoever. They provide (phenomenological) insight into what it is for there to be any *said* at all. 'Sincerity' is, perhaps, Levinas's last word on what he calls the saying of the said, the saying of all the — *de jure* and *de facto* — systematisable, theorisable and describable saids. It permits us to speak of the sincerity of the always unsaid 'yes' or 'hello' presupposed in everything that is said. The subject thought in relation to the saying, and exposed *as* this relation, cannot avoid a sincerity that makes of every said,

however violent or thoughtless, a bearer of the trace of its saying, a sign of the giving of signs. (Davies 2002, 163)

And yet, for the animal? Even in this sense, beyond Wittgenstein's ken, sincerity as the enunciation of speech in its very taking place, prior to the assertion of any determinate proposition, remains beyond the animal. It is as if the beast's vocal signals were restricted to a fixed and finite code, a determinate set of quasi-propositions emitted mechanically in response to a stimulus. The animal's squeaks and chitters would always lack the infinite expressive range of the human voice which is somehow related to its reflexive ability to curve back upon itself and express the pure and unlimited *potential* to say, the *signifiance* prior to signification: 'the philosophical thematising of signification [such as Wittgenstein seems to propose] is derived from [i.e., is derivative *of*] a thought of signification in its *signifiance*, its signifyingness — otherwise said, its sincerity' (Davies 2002, 164).

The animal can never merely and sincerely *welcome* the Other and thus falls short of the most elementary gesture of *ethics*; it can *react*, but never truly *respond*. The latter is reserved for human beings alone.

And yet, despite the appearance of a rather traditional anthropocentrism on Levinas's part, about which Derrida, among others, has expressed reservations, the most fundamental thrust of Levinas's discourse is perhaps pushing in the opposite direction. Levinas has removed sincerity from the realm of language proper, which is to say from the province traditionally reserved for human beings — the house of language from which Wittgenstein's dog was shut out. This opens up the possibility of assigning the sincerity of a spontaneous welcome not just to *humans*, caught up in the web of oppositions that constitutes language, but also to *animals*. And sure enough, a great advocate of both Levinas and dogs, John Llewelyn, has attempted to chart this very route, with and beyond Levinas himself.

Llewelyn on Levinas and animal sincerity

In *The Middle Voice of Ecological Conscience*, in a chapter titled, '*Who* Is My Neighbour?', Llewelyn ascribes to Levinas, at least temporarily and hypothetically, a position quite on a par with Jeremy Bentham's when it comes to the animal's right not to suffer through human instrumentalisation and whim, to the point of comparing animal slaughter with genocide:[3] 'he [Levinas] all but proposes an analogy between the unspeakable human holocaust and the unspoken animal one' (Llewelyn 1991, 50).

Let us, then, introduce Levinas's most renowned animal: a dog, Bobby by name, of whom Llewelyn and, in turn, Derrida, will speak, with the aim of demonstrating the presence in Levinas of something which he himself never fully develops: the animal's sincerity understood as an ethical welcoming of the Other. The dog's textual home is 'The Name of a Dog, or Natural Rights' (1975) from *Difficult Freedom*, and apart from the question of vegetarianism and the killing of living things, the precise problem addressed by the text is whether the animal must be confined to such a home.

Bobby, the literal dog

In an interpretation of a verse from Exodus (22:31), regarding the eating of animal flesh — in the King James edition, 'And ye shall be holy men unto me: neither shall ye eat *any* flesh *that is* torn of beasts in the field; ye shall cast it to the dogs' — Levinas investigates the tenuous possibility of understanding a figure from a biblical text in a *literal* fashion, free of 'theology' (DF, 151/214) and 'allegories' (DF, 152/214). A literal, straightforward which is perhaps to say a *sincere* reading. Not unlike ourselves, Levinas appears to be engaged in a pursuit which is attempting to live up to the sincerity of its quarry.

In any case, this figure is a dog. The importance of the arduous nature of the journey from the metaphoric to the literal, as well as the ultimate impassibility of the path, will steadily become apparent, but if there is one definite conclusion to be drawn from this attempt, it is that dignity and a certain sincerity can — for Levinas — be attributed to animals only in an *analogical* sense, however doggedly one might probe the limits of these notions.

And yet Levinas initially asserts quite forcefully — though in whose voice is as yet unclear — that the dog is here being spoken of in a literal fashion, and not as a metaphor for anything else: 'this biblical text, troubled by parables, here challenges the metaphor: in Exodus 22:31, the dog is a dog [A locution we shall encounter elsewhere, as if the animal encouraged it. The dog referred to here is the beast unholy enough to be a carnivore]. Literally a dog!' (DF, 152/214).

Levinas goes on to state that '[h]igh hermeneutics', with its 'word-for-word' approach, will uncover another invocation of the canine, in Exodus 11:7, where 'forgotten dogs' lie, Egyptian dogs which fall silent in honour of Jewish slaves, once subhuman, now freed and restored to their humanity. 'But against any of the children of Israel shall not a dog move his tongue, against man or beast: that ye may know how that the LORD doth put a difference between the Egyptians and Israel'. These apparently more *analogical* dogs, in recognising the humanity of the human, show themselves to be capable of *ethical* behaviour or at least teach us a lesson regarding what it means to be human (DF, 152/214–15).

According to a venerable Hegelian tradition, to be free one must be *recognised* as free by another who is as free as we are (but who therefore stands as much in need of recognition as we do). Is the animal's recognition worth as much as a human's recognition? Does this recognition amount to anything more than a metaphorical anthropomorphisation, read into the dogs' behaviour in order to convey an ethical teaching; or do the dogs in fact assume a dignity of their *own* precisely in the act of giving this recognition, or as a precondition of the ability to grant it? Do the dogs in the Levinassian text surpass the position of the slave to which Hegel would confine them, and adopt the role of a master?

That the Egyptian dogs are not literally real, but merely characters in a parable suggests that the ability to recognise human beings is in fact attributed to them only by analogical transference. And as if suggesting that the biblical text fails to reach the level of pure literality, Levinas asks whether 'perhaps the subtle exegesis we are quoting gets lost in rhetoric?'

But then, instead of definitively answering this question, he immediately supplements it with another: 'Indeed?' (DF, 152/215), as if to weaken the force of the first question's gentle prodding in the direction of the answer 'yes' and to reiterate that the rhetorical character of the animal is still an open question, even if we remain more tempted by the affirmative response. The second question mark is all important, since it does not finally concede the non-literality of the biblical text. This is all the more clear in Levinas's original French where the syntagm is not a question at all: '*Voire*.' Full stop.

Indeed, the possibility of a *literally* ethical dog is what Levinas goes on to probe still further by moving on to an instance of canine dignity in his *own* experience. The scripture seems to lack something, but to test rather than merely confirm this lack, Levinas recounts a (presumably) literally true tale of his time with Bobby, a 'cherished' dog (*un chien chéri*). This stray came temporarily to frequent the prisoner of war camp in which Levinas was interned: it 'would appear at morning assembly and was waiting for us as we returned, jumping up and down and barking in delight. For him, there was no doubt that we were men' (DF, 153/216). The dog was a 'wanderer' (*errant*) and hence affiliated in some way not just with human beings but with Jews in particular or at least with the prisoners in their homeless exile (DF, 153/216).[4]

Here Levinas describes a case in which there is 'no doubt' that a man is being recognised as such by an animal, *literally*. Bobby's recognition and Bobby himself seem to be much more unequivocally real than the dogs of the bible. The animal seems to perform a function which might have been considered the exclusive preserve of the human being: to restore the bestialised Jews to their humanity.[5]

However metaphorical this Kantianism might have remained — as for Kant *himself* it would need to — and even if this recognition were only a hopeful delusion on the part of the prisoners, Bobby's actual effect on the camp was to humanise its inhabitants in a way that the prison guards had refused, treating the inmates simply as animals, if not worse: 'the other men, called free [. . .] stripped us of our human skin. We were subhuman [*quasi-humanité*], a gang of apes [*une bande de singes*]' (DF, 151–52/215).

Placing in doubt Eichmann's later testimony in Jerusalem, as well as Kant's own reservations about attributing an ethical status to animals in the sense of decreeing that we have 'direct duties' towards them, '[t]his dog was the last Kantian in Nazi Germany', the only one to treat these human beings *as* human, recognising the dignity of their rationality and freedom (DF, 153/216).

Thus, Bobby occupies an analogous position to those dogs of Egypt who perhaps assumed and almost certainly bestowed a similar dignity upon the Hebrew slaves. Apart from the fact that 'Bobby' has received from the prisoners a *name*, unlike the anonymous mass of Egyptian dogs, what distinguishes the latter is that these still too rhetorical dogs ironically remain silent, while Bobby the wandering dog *speaks* or rather emits his welcoming bark to the Other.

The *status* of the dog's eloquence is decisive in answering the question of whether a dog can be an ethical subject in Levinas's sense. Is the animal sound merely an instinctual *reaction* or is it a spontaneous and sincerely given ethical *response*? As if finally to decide on the question of whether the Levinassian dog can only *recognise* dignity or whether it may also be *described* as 'dignified', Llewelyn affirms that, '[t]here are grounds for believing that Levinas would consider it crucial for his account whether Bobby merely barks or whether in doing so he can say *Bonjour*' (Llewelyn 1991, 56), and that is to say, whether the dog can only make noises, automatically, in response to triggers, or whether it can also be *sincere*.

In general, Llewelyn avers that the question of 'whether animals talk and, if so, which if any can talk to us' is for Levinas to be answered in the negative (Llewelyn 1991, 56–57). Levinas certainly makes a point of comparing the silence of the Egyptian animals with Bobby's loquacity: 'He [Bobby] was a descendant of the dogs of Egypt' (DF, 153/216), 'his [Bobby's] friendly growling, his animal faith, was *born* from the *silence* [*naquit dans le silence*] of his forefathers on the banks of the Nile' (DF, 153/216, emphases added). The point stands even if an initial reading would more naturally place the emphasis on *Egypt*, since the primary intention of the passage in question is to distinguish these ancestors from a certain *Greek* relative: 'the dog that recognised Ulysses [or rather, Odysseus]', a symbol of Ancient Greece which Levinas associates with Modern Germany, as he is wont to assimilate the recursive trajectory of Homer's *Odyssey* with the circular character of Hegel's *Encyclopædia*, a journey that returns to its starting point only to find it transformed. Genetically, Bobby is not a Homeric or philosophical dog.

But we should remember that these potential forefathers of the literal dog are not *literally* ancestors. Levinas's affirmation of Bobby's affiliation with *rhetorical* dogs may in the end be intended to suggest that, for all his apparent reality in flesh and blood, Bobby himself is not deployed in this text as a literal empirical entity — a literal animal could not literally *be* a 'Kantian', as Bobby is in fact described. It is as if any understanding of animals which assigns them an ethical status can do so only because it is — inextricably? — affiliated with a scriptural figure. No, the dog, however singular, however named, is not literally ethical.

We might conjecture that the dog's failure literally to be Kantian is marked by Levinas in his extremely *non*-Kantian reference to something as empirical as a *bodily organ*, the brain, as the space in which Reason might have inhered — not to mention the animal 'drives': Bobby would be a *literal* dog that was only *metaphorically* Kantian, since he lacks 'the brain [*cerveau*] needed to universalise maxims and drives [*ses pulsions*]' (DF, 153/216). Levinas indicates a similar absence on the part of the more silent dogs of the Nile, 'with neither ethics nor *logos*', but this is not attributed to the lack of an organ (DF, 152/215).

It is as if the process of reading through, proposing and then retracting, saying and unsaying that which has been said, legibly erasing what is written, withdrawing every possible (non-literal) way of interpreting these Exodic dogs does not altogether succeed in leaving us finally in the full presence of a substantial 'literal' referent. Perhaps this is because even the literal account of Bobby cannot — or does not — do without reference to the scriptural dogs of Egypt and their avowed affiliation with Bobby, at least in the way that the dog functions in Levinas's own *text*.

It is as if Kantianism were ultimately something like an Egypticism, as Hegel pointed out in the context of Kant's *sublime* (cf. A, 362ff/466ff). The Egyptians were the creators of artworks belonging to what Hegel calls the 'symbolic' moment in art's history, products in which form and content are related in the way of the finite and the infinite. But this particular instantiation of the infinite is none other than the *bad* infinite which Kant's epistemology stands accused of employing — just like the formalism of his ethical imperative, all too indifferent to the concrete, particular situations in which it is to be applied.[6]

In the end, we should not forget that Bobby is invoked in the overall context of an interpretation of verse — a literary arena that does not need to be surpassed for Levinas's purposes. But if that is the case, then this particular work would not in the end be the most apposite when it comes to deciding whether or not Levinas can bestow an ethical status upon the animal in the literality which would ultimately be our concern — since here it is not his. Like Llewelyn, we have been compelled to focus on this work because it is the closest Levinas gets to an extended account of the animal as an ethical subject. It seems to us — as it does to Llewelyn — that the ultimate difference between animal and human which Levinas will not relinquish here, the failure of the dog *truly* to be a Kantian, ethical and logical, ethical *because* logical, is related to the enduring necessity of metaphoricity in the biblical context. This metaphoricity explains the recourse to the biblico-rhetorical dogs of Egypt *even* in the description of the supposedly literal dog of the camp. Elsewhere Levinas suggests that, in the final analysis, to describe the animal as having a 'face' and therefore as an ethical subject capable of making demands and responding to them, is possible only by virtue of an 'analogy' with human beings. It involves a secondary metaphoricity rather than a primary literality which would still be reserved for man alone. Hence any attempt to describe animals as ethically responsible or dignified with personhood would be stained with the residue of metaphor, marked by the textual memory of the fabulous canines of the Old Testament:

> When asked about our responsibilities toward non-human sentient creatures, he [Levinas] is inclined to reply that our thinking about them may have to be only analogical or that the answer turns on whether we can discern in the eyes of the animal a recognition [. . .] of its own mortality [which it has been suggested, on a Hegelian-Heideggerian account to which Levinas would likely still be affiliated, we cannot], on whether, in Levinas's sense, the animal has a face. (Llewelyn 1991, 56–57)

With a mouth that can sincerely say (in response *to* another, in recognition of them, or by way of an appeal *to* the Other) and eyes which can, in their direct and steadfast gaze, announce the literal presence of subjectivity (to be responded to *by* another), the face is the opening in which sincerity manifests itself: the face looks and speaks with sincerity. The Other — the other subject, who makes ethical demands upon us — has to be able to speak, at least in the sense of 'the silent saying of the discourse of the face', which can simply mean that '[t]he Other has to look at me' (ibid., 58). As Llewelyn insists, '[i]n the metaphysical ethics of Levinas I can have direct responsibilities only towards beings that can speak, and this means beings that have a rationality' (ibid., 58).

The speechlessness of the Sphinx

Beyond the letter of Levinas's text, Llewelyn wishes to interrogate this absolute dependence of ethical status upon a certain kind of rational-linguistic ability: '[o]ur main problem in this chapter has been and still is to understand why Levinas gives so much ethical weight to the ability to speak' (ibid., 63). This weight risks prejudicing us against animals from the start, since according to the traditional metaphysical-Aristotelian determination, the animal has no *logos*, and so all animals would be judged in advance by philosophy to be essentially Egyptian — Nile dogs and Pharaohs' cats.

But even accepting the hypothesis that the animal would have inherited the Sphinx's muteness, Llewelyn is still able to inquire into the reasons why ethical speech might not be a speech on *behalf* of the speechless, — the animal without language just as much as the human robbed of its voice — a witnessing for the Drowned of which Primo Levi was the most prominent author: 'If calling or claiming are to be understood in such a way that they do imply speech, why cannot the speech be that of persons who speak on behalf of those that cannot speak for themselves?' (ibid., 63).

But Llewelyn goes even further, and puts in question just that metaphysical account of animality which leaves it bereft of speech in the first place: 'in the case of at least some non-human animals it is only on an extremely exacting definition of language that it is plausible to hold that such a response is ruled out [for them]' (ibid., 64).

Llewelyn, in general, goes as far as possible in granting Levinas, according to the letter of his text, an ethical attitude towards animals on the part of man: 'in reply to the question whether we have obligations to animals, he answers, as we have never doubted for one moment that he would, Yes we do' (ibid., 64). And yet, not only do these obligations not belong to the same order as those duties which we owe to other human beings, but the *reason* for this is that animals can never experience *themselves* as being placed under such obligations: 'Despite his granting that we are under ethical obligations to animals, these obligations appear on Levinas's account to have a lower status than obligations to human beings because the latter, but not the former, are clearly expressions of proto-ethical responsibility' (ibid., 66). We *are* responsible strictly speaking only to those who *have* responsibility, which is to say, other human beings.

Llewelyn ends the chapter we have been reading by suggesting that his quest remains unfinished, since his aim was to challenge any account of man's relation to the animal which would deprive it of responsibility, irrespective of whether or not it is granted speech: 'if, as Levinas maintains, ethics can escape violence or permit more than a second-best sort of obligation only if it is not severed from proto-ethical responsibility, can the latter be described in such a way that it does not restrict proto-ethical responsibility to the human?' (ibid., 67).[7]

In the end, Llewelyn will have shown us how to take advantage of those moments in Levinas's work, regarding the animal, where the author leaves certain points ever so slightly open. But despite Llewelyn's best efforts, we may conclude that Levinas does not ultimately grant sincerity to the animal, not wholeheartedly, and certainly not in the supreme sense we are advocating. But the least we can say is that Levinas has charted the territory we must traverse if we are to move beyond the Wittgensteinian denial of sincerity to animals. Our final guide across this landscape, to lead us home, is Jacques Lacan.

c) Lacan

Levinas has shown us that we might find a certain sincerity *before* the opposition between sincerity and insincerity, and indeed prior to the system in which *all* oppositions are ultimately contained — language (*langue*). Sincerity is then attributed to an elementary speech (*parole*) more primitive than '*parole*' in the sense given to the term by structural linguistics which understands it to be the act of enunciating diachronically a determinate string of signifiers extracted from the synchronic language-system. Sincerity for Levinas would be that moment of speech prior to this determinacy, something like its necessary condition — an affirmation that speech is going on and language taking place.

Levinas will have delineated this threshold of the house of language but he will not have been inclined to allow the animal to repose there. Cats must either come in or stay out.

Lacan's attitude to his animals is subtly different from both Wittgenstein's and Levinas's. Unlike Wittgenstein, Lacan is willing to assign pretence and deception to the animal: beasts are quite capable of insincere gestures, but what they lack in comparison with the human being is the ability to *pretend* to pretend, to *double* bluff, which means to tell the truth in the anticipation that the other will assume we are *not* telling the truth, as in the classic Freudian joke: 'Why are you telling me you're going to Krakow when you are *really* going to Krakow?'[8]

i) The 'metaphysical' strand in Lacan

The reason for this difference is to be found in the dimensions to which Lacan confines the animal and the human being respectively: the 'imaginary' order and the 'symbolic' order. It is commonly assumed that this parcelling out of territory is ultimately akin to positing a metaphysical opposition between animal and man. The evidence most frequently cited in support of this metaphysical reading is a passage from 'The Subversion of the Subject and the Dialectic of Desire in the Freudian Unconscious'. This passage, deriving as it does from one of the few pieces of Lacan's work which may be said to have been widely read, forming as it does a prominent part of Lacan's 1966 *Écrits*, has for some time lent substance to the predominant reading of Lacan's position on humans and animals. This is a reading at least partly advocated by Derrida, and on this account the Lacanian animal is locked within an 'imaginary' relation, which is to say a 'narcissistic' duality made up of two spitting images or counterparts (*semblables*). The animal experiences the world only in terms of its own needs and 'projects', which structure its very perception into a set of gestalt images which, when recognised in the external world, stimulate an automatic response, as if the animal were looking into a world of its own devising, and so into a kind of mirror.

Lacan's two orders of the imaginary and the symbolic (if we ignore the third dimension of the 'real', which is comprised of whatever remains distinct from either) involve two different kinds of 'otherness': (1) the relatively insignificant difference between an entity and its own likeness. Here the only significant difference is that, to speak in part metaphorically, right and left have exchanged positions; and (2) the radical otherness of the symbolic order of language, the realm of conventions and laws which can absolutely contradict our natural instincts despite having only a symbolic efficacy rather than a physical force of constraint. This order stands absolutely apart from the natural animal and is therefore capable of separating the ego (our imaginary self-image) from itself: it alienates the ego by constructing something which will remain utterly inaccessible to it — the unconscious. The arbitrary signifiers of the symbolic order need bear no resemblance to that which they signify, any more than the law must be akin to that which falls under its sway. Hence, we find here a much more extreme form of otherness than was present in the imaginary: that of nature and culture. The symbolic law of culture and that to which it ordains us may well be utterly distinct from anything that we find in nature and towards which our (animal) instincts direct us.

The symbolic order is the domain of the signifier and the particular kind of prohibition which it makes possible: it is the system of language and everything that may be considered analogous to it, which for structuralists such as Saussure and Lévi-Strauss includes the entire realm of human culture. Lacan distinguishes between symbolic otherness and imaginary otherness by means of a capital letter in the word 'Other' (*Autre*), the symbolic Other which he often calls 'the big Other' (*le grand Autre*) — a locution which also refers to the parental adult who first embodies the order of prohibition for the child finding its way in(to) the (symbolic) world.

The symbolic order is what allows us to speak and makes possible the contingent, historical, non-natural conventions which regulate intercourse between (what were once) animals, and, in particular, sexual relations. In the symbolic order, only *human beings* are immersed. This impersonal Other, truly different from our animal bodies, is a 'third thing' or *tertium datur*, an 'excluded middle' that intervenes between two animals locked in an imaginary relationship, forever separating man from the simplicity of an animal coupling.

The symbolic order is what allows the human being to transform the pretence into a mere *pretending* to pretend, the feigned feint. It lets us deploy a signifier which can be effaced in such a way as to leave *traces* of this effacement, or a signifier which is not hidden at all but may be left in plain sight precisely in order that it be passed over. Only in the Symbolic can the *truth* be mistaken for something that is *shielding* the truth, truth's effacement. The symbolic order not only allows us to lie by way of concealment, but also opens up an intersubjective realm in which the other is given the chance to 'see through' our 'subterfuge' and make their own (erroneous) judgement (that the other is insincere, not acting in good faith, concealing the truth, when in fact he or she is manifesting it quite openly, as in the avowed trip to Krakow — a truth supposedly designed to be perceived as a falsehood):

> this Other [*Autre*], distinguished as the locus of Speech [*Parole*], nevertheless emerges as Truth's witness. Without the dimension it constitutes, the deceptiveness of Speech would be indistinguishable from the feint, which, in fighting or sexual display, is nevertheless quite different. Deployed in imaginary capture, the feint is integrated into the play of approach and retreat that constituted the first dance [*la danse originaire*] [. . .]. Moreover, animals show that they are capable of such behaviour when they are being hunted down; they manage to throw their pursuers off the scent [*dépister*] by briefly going in one direction as a lure and then changing direction [*en amorçant un depart qui est de leurre*]. [. . .] But an animal does not feign feigning [*ne feint pas de feindre*]. It does not make tracks [*traces*] whose deceptiveness lies in getting them to be taken as false, when in fact they are true — that is, tracks that indicate the right trail [*la bonne piste*]. No more than it effaces its tracks [*n'efface ses traces*], which would already be tantamount to making itself the subject of the signifier. (Lacan 2006 [1966], 683/807)[9]

The absence of the higher order of the signifier (the Symbolic) means that the animal can only feign and never redouble this feint in the feigning to feign or pretence at pretence, which one finds in the more cunning examples of human deception.[10]

And yet, animals can pretend, they can feign or be 'hypocritical', as Lacan emphasises at the beginning of this passage, even if only to distinguish this rigorously from the duplication involved in pretending to pretend. If the animal is capable of pretence, perhaps it is also capable of sincerity.

To establish whether or not Lacan might allow that the animal has the potential not only for indirection but also for straightforwardness, let us turn to another strand in his work. Here we shall witness Lacan, *avant la lettre*, turning Levinas's account of a Saying without a Said back on Levinas himself. He does so by attributing this type of saying to an entity from which Levinas withheld it: the animal. This gesture forms part of a *non*-metaphysical seam in Lacan's thought which at times seems to elude Derrida, even during the unusually expansive reading he pursues in *The Animal That Therefore I Am*. In the end, Derrida's account here, for all its interest, arrives at conclusions that are near identical to those of his earlier work: while there are non-metaphysical openings in Lacan, the predominant strain is notably traditional.[11]

ii) The 'non-metaphysical' strand in Lacan

In his ninth seminar, on 'Identification', Lacan states that the animal (in particular, his dog, female this time, unlike Levinas's and Wittgenstein's), while it may lack the symbolic order of language, nevertheless has a capacity for speech — for *parole* but not for *langue*. A speech without language is precisely what Levinas described as 'a Saying without a Said':

> My dog has speech, and it is incontestable, indisputable, due not only to the fact that the modulations which result from these properly articulated decomposable efforts may be inscribed *in loco*, but also because of the correlations between the moments at which these phonemes are produced, namely when she is in a room where experience has taught the animal that the human group gathered around a table should be there for a good while [. . .]: *it must not be believed that all of this is centred in need*. There is no doubt a certain relationship with this element of consumption, but the *communing* element of the fact that she is eating with the others is present in it.
> What is it that distinguishes this usage of speech, which is in short very much successful as regards the results that for my dog it is a question of obtaining, from human speech? [. . .] What distinguishes this speaking animal from what happens because of the fact that man speaks is the following [. . .], contrary to what happens in the case of man [. . .], *she never takes me for another* [. . .], contrary to what in all your experience is there to testify to what happens in the measure that, in the analytic experience, [. . .] *by taking you for another, the subject puts you at the level of the Other* with a big O.
> It is precisely this which is lacking for my dog: for her there is only the small other [the imaginary other]. As regards the big Other, it does not seem that her relationship to language gives her access to it. [. . .]
> [//] I am very sorry to appear, with this reference, to be re-establishing the cut between the canine species and the human species. I am saying this to signify to you that *you would be completely wrong* to believe that the privilege I give to language is some sort of pride which hides this sort of prejudice which would make of man precisely some sort of summit of being. (Lacan, *Seminar IX*, 1961–62, 29th November 1961, emphases added, translation modified)

In this passage we witness a very characteristic gesture, which seems to us largely to have escaped Derrida's attention: Lacan *appears* to institute a very traditional opposition between man and animal, but then gives it a twist of such novelty that it slips the bonds of this tradition even while it retains the skeleton of one of its structures.

At the same time, there is a clear movement beyond the traditional schema at the very beginning of this passage, which might be taken as a trap intended to distract us from the real difference between Lacan and metaphysics, an obvious truth whose glare conceals a more subtle light. The metaphysical tradition — along with Lacan himself in that seam of his work which is most frequently mined — would assign *need* to the animal and *desire* to the human. The human being would ultimately be driven by an infinite, insatiable, and unconscious desire, pursuing objects which the symbolic order (*logos*) will have rendered eternally unattainable. On the other hand, the Aristotelian animal makes sounds (*phōnē*) only to indicate its pleasure and pain, expressive of the satisfaction or otherwise of its survival needs. And yet here, in the most glaring departure from metaphysics, we find the animal *speaking*, with a voice detached from need, which seems to involve the animal in a certain sociality with human beings — an intersubjective conversation of sorts.

The sincerity of being without a symbolic order

This distinctly non-traditional disjunction between an animal's speech and its natural need may be contrasted with Lacan's more traditional assertion, later in the same passage, that this speech cannot rely on the symbolic order of language for its enunciations, for the animal is barred from this order or remains on its threshold. *Prima facie* this seems to return us to a traditionally metaphysical view of the animal as lacking language in the strictest sense. Lacan's dog would seem to be let off the leash briefly — or admitted to the house of language for the space of a particularly convivial meal — only to be confined once again at the end of festivities to the Imaginary. It is ultimately this lack with respect to the Symbolic that prevents the animal from pretending to pretend, concealing the truth in plain sight, like one special letter among others pinned to a mantelpiece.

But the lack of a symbolic order has another effect, besides the foreclosure of the double feint, and this transforms the entire aspect of Lacan's apparently metaphysical gesture. This will return us to our topic, sincerity, for the animal knows nothing of politeness, of purely conventional rituals the efficacy of which are purely symbolic — those mores by which desires approach satisfaction indirectly or even delicately refrain from such satisfaction in the name of something 'higher', by sublimation; or else these desires might simply be stifled and frustrated by the conventions and laws that govern human interaction. In speaking to us and to each other without language, in a pure speech without indirection and deceit, the animals speak sincerely.

We need only translate Lacan's vocabulary of *parole* and *langue* into the Levinassian *Dire* and *Dit*, to turn Levinas's discourse against itself: the dog's well-timed bark is a saying without a said. When it comes to voicing its desire to the Other, and particularly to its 'owners', the animal can only speak sincerely, and with a sincerity of a Levinassian rather than a Wittgensteinian kind. This is particularly true of domestic animals, which lap the shores of the symbolic order but remain frozen there.[12] The beseeching of house pets captures the event of language *in embryo* as a permanently fossilised abortion. Their importunate demands for food, and for a passage either way across the domestic threshold, express the opening of speech prior to any determinate signification, signifying the very possibility of signifying — 'Saying', 'sincerity'.

Lacan allows a female Bobby to slip the leash of her Egyptian owners and enter a literality which Levinas found it necessary ultimately to deny her — and him.

So, in the end, we may allow that the animal is indeed sincere. But is this what charms us? Certainly what would be importunate vulgarity — or hopeless naivety — in a human being delights us in the animal.

Chapter Two

Kant and the Animal's Charm

KANT BEFORE HEGEL: ON CHARM

Lacan has allowed us, beyond Wittgenstein and Levinas, to make sense of the idea that an animal may be described as sincere; but why should this sincerity be charming? What indeed is charm?

We have established a connection between sincerity and the bad infinite. Animals are restrained at the threshold of the symbolic order, the regime of human thought and language, the arena in which dialectical gymnastics are on display. This means that an animal, in its sincere speech, can only repeat its desires, demands, and actions indefinitely, without variety, without ever learning the double bluff or disingenuousness that the signifier allows. This would transport the attempt to satisfy desire onto another level altogether, strictly intersubjective as it anticipates the manner in which this demand will be received by the other, in such a way as could occur only if speaker and hearer were bound together by a symbol (*symbolon*).

We have suggested that the Hegelian philosophy tends overwhelmingly to supplant the bad infinite with the good or the true, and thereby subordinates the animal to the human in a gesture which we have repeatedly called 'metaphysical'. For Hegelianism, the animal would either be utterly wild, standing altogether outside the human realm, or be fully domesticated; but can it account for those animals, like cats, which sit upon the very threshold of the house?

In any case, the general tendency of the dialectic to surpass the animal in the name of the human suggests that if we wish to revise the Hegelian evaluation we would do well to return to a moment prior to Hegel. We shall in fact return to Immanuel Kant who in Hegel's own estimation represents a more primitive stage in the history of philosophy where the thing in itself stands distinct from the multiplicity of its apparitions in just the same way that the bad infinite remains separate from the finite. For this reason, Kant is said by Hegel to occupy a position not dissimilar to the animal, in comparison with which Hegel would be a mature adult human being. Kant remained caught in a dialectical machine that had snagged at a certain point and become lost in the alternation of unresolvable 'antinomies', just as the animal remains captivated by the object of its demand just shy of dialectical thought. Thus in both Kant and the animal the same machine perpetually rotates, without ever thinking to leave the orbit of its natural cycle: the dialectic is frozen and we remain transfixed at the door.[1] The subtitle of the present work is intended to indicate that we ourselves are attempting wilfully to stand in precisely this position, to find those moments within philosophy which might be said to think and see as animals do, and to philosophise as they might.

From a Hegelian point of view, and that is to say the perspective of the true infinite, the human or spiritual standpoint, the bad infinite which the animal's behaviour embodies appears to be idiotic. Therefore we shall perhaps have more luck in moving beyond this evaluation if we return to Kant and ask whether he allows us to make any headway in our attempt to understand the animal's sincerity as not cretinous but charming.

We are using the word 'charming' to translate the German term, '*reizend*', and 'charm' for '*Reiz*', in accordance with the version of Kant's *Critique of Judgement* rendered by Werner Pluhar.[2] It is a word invoked by Kant in his attempt to define 'beauty'.

Our hypothesis is that the 'charming' alludes to something which lets us read both Kant and Hegel against themselves and that Kant, while giving us crucial insight into the notion, nevertheless hurries through it with telling haste.

KRITIK DER URTEILSKRAFT: BEGINNING GERMAN IDEALISM

Let us open the *Critique of Judgement*.

This book forms the lynchpin, the pivotal text of German idealism, the most prominent way-marker in the transition from Kantian to post-Kantian philosophy, a passage which begins to unfold within Kant himself. It is the moment at which Kantianism itself begins to transcend its own system, and in particular the opposition between nature and freedom which defines the first two Critiques. Or perhaps the third Critique reveals both the necessity *and* the impossibility of such a transcendence. A double impasse — one cannot and one cannot *not* — this is described in philosophy, particularly after Derrida, as an 'aporia', the absence of any way (*poros*, in Greek). An aporia is the impassibility of either of two contradictory paths, or of any third route which might bisect them. Some, like Martin Heidegger, have suggested that the abyss between nature and freedom (or *being* and freedom) should in fact be left open *as* an aporia rather than being bridged in the way German idealism *stricto sensu* (Fichte, Schelling, and Hegel) at the beginning of the nineteenth century is said to have done (Heidegger 1997 [1929], 137ff/195ff).

This second option is important to us because here a certain anti-Hegelianism enters philosophy and attempts to reverse the evaluation of Kant that derives from Hegel himself. Anti-Hegelianism more generally so often returns to Kant for this very reason and thus sets a precedent for our own gesture.

In general, we might say that this transition beyond Kant — or rather this oscillation between the need to surpass the aporia of nature and culture and the insistence upon dwelling within it — is a turbulent movement we are caught in the midst of, today just as much as yesterday and perhaps forever, as long as time itself. The movement describes a swaying between the true infinite and the bad infinite, and constitutes a position which Derrida himself suggests cannot but be occupied by philosophy.[3]

Indirectly, the present work might suggest a certain approach to this question.

BEAUTY AND THE BEAST: THE TWO HALVES OF THE *CRITIQUE OF JUDGEMENT*[4]

The *Critique of Judgement* is divided into two parts: the critique of aesthetic judgement and the critique of teleological judgement. The first concerns the beautiful (and the sublime),[5] while the second treats of the organism or the animal. According to Kant, we can understand the latter only if we consider it to be designed for a certain purpose (*telos*, in Greek). The parts of an animal are disposed in such a way as to serve the purposes of the whole: hence we must conceive of a teleology in nature, a final totality that guides the construction of its parts in the manner of what the philosophical tradition calls a 'final cause'. In a physical world seemingly without purpose, the organism thus restores some measure of meaning, rendering nature amenable to the concepts of our understanding. In being to some extent liberated from efficient causality, the animal represents the incursion of a certain freedom within nature.

We make an aesthetic judgement when confronted with a beautiful object, and a teleological judgement when we confront an animal. So what happens when we encounter an entity which is both — when we come across a *beautiful animal*?

'A beautiful animal': this phrase might be said to encapsulate the totality of Kant's work and the still mysterious nature of the connection between the two halves of the third Critique. The two divisions of this text deal with two different types of judgement, each bringing together two elements which the rest of the Kantian philosophy, if not the whole of metaphysics, has kept firmly apart: in Kant's terms, nature and freedom, or nature and reason.[6] We shall have to say a little about what these involve, but the differences which exist between them suggest that Kant might have some difficulty in bringing together in one entity the topics that each division addresses: the beautiful and the animal, beauty and the beast.

The link between nature and freedom, the topic of the first and second Critiques respectively, is not just a problem internal to Kant's philosophy; it is the enigma of the human being itself as metaphysics construes it — that conjunction of free rational thought and the animality of a sensory body; and its pertinence extends further than the human, to the universe as a whole, for the relation between body and soul captures in microcosm the relation between the real world and the ideal, the sensible and the intelligible, phenomenon and noumenon, the physical and the metaphysical, or beings and being (*Seiende* and *Sein*, in Heidegger's German). Much, therefore, is at stake in this question.

Let us investigate whether Kant has any difficulty in making sense of the notion of a 'beautiful animal', and if so, what progress does he nevertheless allow us to make in our search?

And what of the charming?

ON A COLLAPSE OF THE DISTINCTION BETWEEN BEAUTY AND CHARM IN THE FACE OF NATURE'S DIVERSITY

a) Determinative and reflective judgements: Beauty

The first Part of Kant's *Critique of Judgement* begins with a Book (*Buch*) titled the 'Analytic of the Beautiful'. In it Kant attempts to isolate what is peculiar about the judgement according to which a certain entity is beautiful. A 'judgement' (*Urteil*) in Kant's technical sense means the application of a predicate to a subject — these days a judgement is more commonly referred to as a 'proposition'. It adjudges precisely what attributes may be assigned to a certain substance, and thus it bestows a certain identity upon whatever has entered our experience.

But the aesthetic judgement of beauty is a judgement of the most curious kind — while taking the form of a proposition, it nevertheless refrains from predication. In the experience of beauty, the predicate that would identify the subject *as* some particular thing is suspended before application. 'Beauty' is the 'predicate' that names this suspension of predication: the beautiful is whatever reveals itself to be susceptible of conceptualisation without lending itself to any one concept in particular. The beautiful object has the *potential* to be many. Thus while we are unable or unwilling to recognise an identifiable object in what presents itself to us, all the same we find reflected back to us our own ability to cognise, the very possibility of nature's intelligibility. And this experience is a joyful one.[7]

The reason for applying a determinate predicate to a subject and thus identifying it in its 'being', is so as to *know* it — to *comprehend* what the entity *is* by taking cognisance of some or all of its properties. A judgement which results in such cognition, because it determines the identity of the subject under consideration, is deemed by Kant a 'determinative judgement' (*bestimmend Urtheilskraft*).

The aesthetic judgement of beauty, on the other hand, is rather a '*reflective* judgement' (*reflectirend Urtheilskraft*) (CJ, 18–19/179). It does not aim at knowledge. It is a judgement made on the basis of a 'feeling', the pleasure or enjoyment we have just alluded to, which is supposedly shared by *all* judging subjects. For this is what the judgement of beauty must assert: a certain universality which is based not on anything objective but on something subjective, shared by every subject capable of knowledge, as a necessary condition *for* such knowledge. The judgement of taste *reflects back* upon the judging subject itself — it tells us something about that subject, but not about the object.

The reason for this feeling of pleasure that wells up inside us in the presence of the beautiful is that one's subjective (cognitive) faculties have come to 'harmonise' with one another. This harmony — between our sensory intuition, which receives data from the outside, and our understanding, which applies concepts to these sense-data, lending 'form' to this 'matter'[8] — arises because the sensory material given to us is manifestly something which *could* be conceptualised. The very profusion of the entity's sensible matter is indeed what hinders any ultimate application of a unique concept that would be absolutely adequate: because this conceptualisation could happen in so many different ways, a determinate concept is held in suspense, as if in delightful anticipation. Therefore, in the experience of beauty, our cognitive capacities remain in a state of potential prior to the application of a concept, in advance of knowledge and its determinate judgement, and what is more they *feel* their own power. This is the 'reflection' that stands at the basis of a 'reflective' judgement: the object resists a determinate conceptualisation but precisely thereby refers us back to our own power of conception.

The possibility of euphony among the cognitive capacities, along with the capacities themselves, must be shared by all subjects capable of knowledge, for they are to be counted among the very conditions for the possibility of this knowledge (*Erkenntnis*) — necessary conditions, conditions *sine qua non*, which Kant had identified in the *Critique of Pure Reason*, the 'transcendental' conditions of any experience which may be said to be of *objects*. Thus we can say that the precognitive harmony achieved in the aesthetic judgement is 'subjectively universal' (CJ, 54/212).

In this judgement we do not rush ahead to achieve the certainty and gratification of a particular knowledge, but rather we hold back, and in this abstinence there dawns upon us a certain subjective state and even a subjective faculty which might otherwise have been overlooked, particularly if one were intent solely upon knowledge (as for instance Kant himself was in the first Critique: often, this faculty goes by the name of 'imagination' (*Einbildungskraft*), the work of which is 'schematism'.

An aesthetic judgement is not a cognition. It does not tell us *what* something is: it does not provide us with knowledge, but it is related to the process of cognition, for it constitutes one of its stages. But this stage was never truly revealed in its own right in the earlier work, at least not fully — perhaps it was unveiled briefly only to be eclipsed later on[9] — for there the purpose was to understand how knowledge was possible, and hence the activity of the imagination in itself, prior to and apart from its termination in a determinate 'cognitive' judgement, had to blush unseen. The autonomous operation of the capacity for fantasy is what we experience in the beautiful. The experience of beauty in the aesthetic judgement is the revelatory enjoyment of the imagination.

b) The diversity of nature and the potential for intelligibility: Nature's purpose

The problem addressed by the third Critique is the relation between nature and reason. This is also described by Kant as the problem of the 'diversity of nature'.

The first Critique had established that, if the subject were to acquire any objective knowledge from experience, this experience had to be characterised by certain necessary and universal structures or 'transcendental' characteristics. This was essential if the flux which became apparent in the deliverances of the senses was to constitute an enduring *object* rather than a merely subjective 'representation' (*Vorstellung*), and the latter way led only to scepticism, which Kant was bent on avoiding.

These transcendental conditions for the possibility of objective *knowledge* were understood to be necessary features of *nature*, for this is how Kant describes the sum-total of the phenomenal objects of our experience, which we receive through the senses. Since attributing these features to an object outside of ourselves would presuppose what it was intended to prove (the possibility of the existence and knowledge of objects and object*ivity*), these features were to be sought in the *subject*. But this did not mean the *empirical* subject, which was potentially different for each individual, but the 'transcendental' subjectivity which every experiencing subject must embody insofar as its subjective representations are to constitute the experience of an *object* and hence *knowledge*. Kant's name for the world that we thereby experience is 'nature', and therefore we can say that the subject 'legislates' for nature, supplying the most basic laws to which nature must conform.

And yet Kant does not claim that the transcendental subject determines *all* of nature's laws, only the most general. The way these general laws of nature are actually specified, in all their variety, *cannot* be rationally deduced since, 'as far as we can see', the particular forms which these laws take are 'contingent' (CJ, 23/183). Contingency, the unnecessary and irrational, that of which philosophy cannot provide a logical account, creeps in through the smaller nooks and crannies of the natural world.

This is what we might call Kant's 'philosophy of nature'. But here a problem arises: if contingency is allowed into nature, this threatens to introduce a degeneration in which the natural laws, genera, and species become so chaotic and numerous that nature would cease to be intelligible. A gulf would yawn once again between nature and human intelligence. Contingency introduces the risk of nature running riot and generating a diversity so wild that human reason simply cannot make sense of it, whereupon objectivity itself begins to fall apart:

> it is quite conceivable that [. . .] the specific differences in the empirical laws of nature, along with their effects, might still be so great that it would be impossible for our understanding to discover in nature an order it could grasp — that is, impossible for it to divide nature's products into genera and species, so as to use the principles by which we explain and understand one product in order to explain and conceive another as well, thereby making coherent experience out of material that to us is so full of confusion (though actually it is only infinitely diverse and beyond our ability to grasp it). (CJ, 25/185, translation modified)

What these laws are cannot be known in advance and so the subject must have recourse to other means to moderate the risk of unintelligibility: it must treat nature *as if* it had been created by an *intelligence*. If this were the case, the physical world would be rationally structured down to its minutest components: 'since universal natural laws have their basis in our understanding [. . .], the particular empirical laws must, as regards what the universal laws have left undetermined in them, be viewed in terms of such a unity *as* they would have *if* [*als ob*] they too had been given by an understanding (even though not ours)' (CJ, 19/180, emphases added).

The phrase 'as if' here indicates that this judgement of nature's intelligibility is not a determinative judgement which asserts a state of affairs to be the case *objectively*. Rather than asserting something about the object, this judgement asserts something about the *subject*: namely, that the subject needs to understand the variegation of specific empirical laws to be 'as if' they were created *rationally*, just as the more general structures of nature really *were*. It speaks, then, of a *transcendental* necessity, which is to say that it is a matter of the conditions that make knowledge possible (CJ, 24–25/185). As Kant puts it, we are 'attributing to nature [. . .] a concern, as it were, for our cognitive power' (CJ, 33/193). This type of judgement is thus a *reflective* judgement, in which 'judgement gives a law only to itself, not to nature' (CJ, 20/180).

The assumption that things are intelligently — and so intelli*gibly* — ordered is necessary if our experience of nature is to be coherent: 'we must necessarily presuppose and assume this unity, since otherwise our empirical cognition could not thoroughly cohere to form a whole of experience' (CJ, 23/183). We assume that such order is 'necessary'.

The orderliness of nature which follows from this attribution of rational design is described by Kant as 'the *purposiveness* [Zweckmäßigkeit] *of nature*' (CJ, 20/181). If Nature was created by Reason then it must have a purpose, an end-goal, a 'finality' or 'telos'. Kant defines 'purpose' in general in the following way: 'insofar as the concept of an object also contains the basis for the object's actuality, the concept is called the thing's *purpose*' (CJ, 20/180). In this case, the mere concept is sufficient for the object of that concept to become real: the concept encapsulates the goal to be achieved, the end-point to be realised, and thus, in such cases, the ideal outcome of a process acts causally to motivate the very process itself. Philosophy's name for a *telos* that guides the unfolding of an object's potential into actuality is the 'final cause' — quite opposed to the 'efficient causality' which we in the modern age have progressively come to think of as coextensive with causality itself.

If we presuppose the origin of the purpose to reside somewhere beyond nature, 'transcending' it, then we would speak of god's *fiat*, in which He merely has to entertain a concept of something in order for that thing to be created, just as a human artificer would entertain the idea of something they were about to make before skilfully producing it. In a purely immanent nature, without creator or human intervention, this final cause would simply be the full potential of an object that inherently demands to be actualised as the entity develops.

This demand becomes most apparent in the natural thing which can *only* be understood in terms of purpose, and that is the living thing, the animal or organism. For the living thing grows, spontaneously and naturally, and it grows into something which it was preordained to. The animal organism contains the potential to become something — its adult form. Although in truth this teleological causality operates in the organism both synchronically and diachronically: the function of each part of the whole is to ensure the survival of the organism as a totality — this is the *purpose* of the organs and members which make it up. For Kant, we can understand neither the whole organism nor any of its parts without the assumption of teleology within nature.

If nature is understood to be purposive, which is to say, if things function under the guidance of *concepts*, then the chasm which threatened to open up between man and world is closed once again and held fast. It is the concept of purposiveness which allows this to happen: the reflective judgement that nature is 'as if' conceptual 'provides us with the concept that mediates [*vermittelnden Begriff*] between the concepts of nature and the concept of freedom: the concept of a *purposiveness* of nature' (CJ, 36–37/196). Nature appears to us as possessed of a finality that seems to resemble conceptuality so closely as to be unintelligible to us without the presupposition that animals are in fact a kind of living and breathing concept.

Thus the teleological judgement, just like the aesthetic judgement, implies that mind and nature might not after all be so radically opposed. Indeed, ameliorating or even forestalling this opposition is the overall purpose of the third critique, which avowedly sets out to bridge '[t]he great gulf that separates the supersensible from appearances' (CJ, 35/195).

c) Beauty and the freedom of free-play

It is not that this harmony between reason and nature can certainly be *known*; rather, it is necessary for us to *presuppose* it. In reality — so far as we can tell — it is only contingent that this harmony prevails, and this gives us all the more reason to be delighted when we happen upon something in the external world which reassures us of it (cf. CJ, 23–24/184). One instance of this chance harmony is the experience of *beauty*, and another is the experience of *animals*.

In the experience of beauty, we do not apply a determinate concept to the beautiful entity but merely bask in the pleasant feeling that nature, in all its diversity, is not altogether chaotic and recalcitrant to thought. The beautiful is the promise that there might yet be room for reason and freedom in nature. This is why it is not accidental that Kant should speak of the harmony of the faculties and particularly of the imagination which hovers between sense and the understanding as possessed of *freedom*, in 'free play' (*freien Spiels*) (CJ, 62/217):

> Here we presuppose no concept of any purpose for which the manifold [of sensory data] is to serve the given object, and hence no concept [as to] what the object is [meant] to represent; our imagination is playing [*der Einbildungskraft ... spielt*], as it were, while it contemplates the shape, and such a concept would only restrict its *freedom*. (CJ, 77/229–30, emphasis added)

The imagination is free in not being restricted by any particular concept. This freedom is the leeway of its play, and the occasion for this free ranging is a moment of beauty within nature. If there is room for reason within nature, there is also room for freedom, a liberty which depends upon the autonomy and freedom *from* external determination which reason provides.[10]

The beautiful gives pleasure ultimately because it delightfully confirms our hypothesis that nature was made in order to be understood, that the assumption we were compelled to make was not far off the mark.

In a beautiful entity, the two halves of the Kantian system, nature and freedom, approach a moment of interpenetration, as if attempting to surpass the bad infinite of a rigid division between the thing-in-itself and the thing-for-us, since here a certain (beautiful) moment within the sensible comes to embody the intelligibility of nature as a whole. A *natural* entity thus acquires *spiritual* stature in the radiance of its beautiful apparition.

In conjunction with this *objective* matter, the understanding feels itself *subjectively* to be mightier than it might otherwise have thought, and the power it finds itself wielding is of a new kind: the experience of beauty is an experience of the power to postpone satisfaction, the enjoyment of renouncing enjoyment, wallowing in a means without an end.[11] Aesthetic judgements of taste unveil reason's ability to render nature intelligible and display this power playing freely within its leeway, clearing whole swathes of nature's unruly chaos, overgrown with weeds. Only in the suspension of the concept is the process of cognition itself revealed and the experience of beauty undergone.

Because of its relation to the cognitive process, as a 'subjective condition' necessary for cognition, the state of mind in which we judge the beautiful must be characteristic of all subjects capable of knowledge: in a word, universal. It is by dint of this subjective universality that the judgement of taste stands midway between the subjectivity of feeling and the objectivity of knowledge, equidistant from a mere 'pathological' liking that is absolutely peculiar and relative to us as individuals, and a cognition which should by rights be shared universally. This allows Kant to distinguish the aesthetic judgement from various other kinds with which it might easily be confused, including the judgement that something is *agreeable* (which is wholly subjective) and the judgement that something is *good* (which is entirely objective). The judgement of beauty occupies an intermediate position between the 'too subjective' and the 'too objective'. Since we have already sufficiently distinguished reflective judgements from determinate cognitive judgements and remain less interested in ethics than aesthetics, we shall focus on the former — the agreeable, the subjective. And indeed, it is here that the notion of the 'charming' appears for the first time. The charming is, it seems, most certainly 'too subjective'.

d) The judgement of the charming

For Kant, it is necessary to separate the feeling associated with the beautiful from any purely personal pleasure. The judgement of taste is 'disinterested' in the literal sense of 'interest' which is to be bound up with the existence of an object. It means that we do not need the object of the judgement actually to exist, to touch us and be tactile. We have no need of this because we take no sensuous, desirous interest in the beautiful object — after all, the freedom which one's straying imagination here encounters is a matter of the 'as if' and the experience of beauty is ultimately internal to the mind. We do not depend upon the object's existence because we do not intend to put this object to any practical use, as a means to some end, which is to say the satiation of some need or desire of our own, in which case it would be necessary for it actually to exist. Our attitude towards the work of art and indeed any instance of beauty is disinterested because, to us, the object is useless.

It is by way of this disinterest that Kant distinguishes the beautiful from the charming. In the case of the charming, as the German words '*Reiz*' and '*reizend*' suggest, we need to be *touched*, and we shall be touched only if the object can actually impinge upon our senses in its very materiality. The 'matter' of an entity is the business of sensibility and it is that which speaks to us as individuals since it impacts in a unique way upon our particular 'sensibility'; while it is only the 'form' of an object which should concern judgements of taste. In order to count as 'beautiful', the object has to display the general structure of something conceptualisable and nothing more. This distinguishes the beautiful from the charming: 'A *pure judgement of taste* is one that is not influenced by charm or emotion [*Reiz und Rührung*] [. . .] and whose determining basis is therefore merely the purposiveness of the form' (CJ, 69/223).

e) Charm and beauty

And yet, while attempting to maintain a rigorous distinction between charm and beauty, Kant is forced to admit that the charming and the beautiful are often to be found together in natural things: 'what I mean here is actually the beautiful *forms* of nature, while I continue to set aside the *charms* that nature tends to connect so plentifully with them' (CJ, 166/299).[12]

The charming and the beautiful are indeed 'analogous' to one another:

> We *linger* [weilen] in our contemplation of the beautiful, because this contemplation reinforces and reproduces itself. This is *analogous to (though not the same as)* the way in which we linger over something charming [*ein Reiz*] that, as we present an object, repeatedly arouses our attention, though here the mind is passive [*das Gemüth passiv ist*]. (CJ, 68/222, emphasis added)

The two are analogous but 'not the same', for it seems that in the case of the beautiful the mind is actively synthesising, while in that of the charming it only passively enjoys itself. The initial analogy is stressed only more subtly to delineate the differences between the two, and Kant seems to think that reiterating the opposition between disinterest and interest, form and matter, will be enough to hold the beautiful and the charming apart.

And yet, twenty-five pages later, in a concluding 'General Comment' on the Analytic of the Beautiful, the gap between the charming and the beautiful seems to narrow to a point at which they become indiscernible. The moment arrives just before the Analytic of the Sublime begins, and it involves a charming little animal.

f) Kant, birdsong, and the diversity of nature

At the end of a relatively arduous tract — the treatise on the beautiful — his mind perhaps straying ahead to the apparently yet more unruly matter to come, where nature's diverse profusion threatens once again to wreak havoc and overwhelm our finite faculties, Kant finds himself distracted by the twittering of birds (CJ, 94–95/243–44). It is a seemingly unimportant coda, but in fact heavy with consequences.

For Kant, beauty in nature involves a certain kind of orderliness: there must be order and a certain kind of finitude if the mind is to be capable of making sense of what it encounters. But here Kant suggests that it may be possible for there to be *too much* order: too great a regularity will soon pall on the taste. Nature must be intelligible, but within limits — it must *remain* natural, which is to say a little bit wild. If the beautiful object is manmade then it must not flaunt its artifice by displaying too rigorous an order: it must retain some reserve of 'nature' in the narrow sense.

And so Kant calls to mind an example which we have met with before, in the context of weeding: he contrasts an overly neat and tidy *garden* with the wildest of the Wild, the forests of Sumatra: '*nature* in those regions, extravagant in all its *diversity* to the point of opulence, subject to no constraint from *artificial* rules, can nourish [. . .] [man's] taste permanently' (CJ, 94/243, emphases added). The artificial would seem here to conceal the natural and strip it of its beauty, as if an excess of weeding and trimming had amortised the growth essential to nature and the profusion necessary for its beauty. It is as if one had taken the extreme measure of suppressing natural flourishing altogether with a particularly noxious weed-killer. Nature moves from being 'as if' designed by an intelligence to *really* being so, and is fitted with so rigid a template that it becomes choked.

When it comes to the uncivilised Indonesian wilds, we find a nature altogether free of culture, luxuriating in its untrammelled 'extravagance'. But the overwhelming diversity of nature is precisely the problem which the *Critique of Judgement* was designed to solve, and it aims to do so by demonstrating the (necessity of presupposing) the compatibility of nature and reason. An *infinite* diversity among the species of nature would place an insuperable barrier in the way of this — this wild diversity must therefore be tamed.

But what is strange about the example of the pristine forest is that it seems *so* wild and *so* diverse that it becomes difficult to see how it can be treated 'as if' it were created by an orderly rational mind. Would this vast, unmanageable, perhaps uninhabited chaos not rather more naturally be presented as an example of the *sublime*, which exceeds the power of the understanding altogether? The sublime is precisely what is preparing to make its entrance in the very next chapter of Kant's text. And yet he clearly intends these verdant and luxuriant forests to stand as an example of the *beautiful*.

Let us see what unfolds here, in this enforced lull before the storm of nature erupts in the Analytic of the Sublime.

In this sheltered corner of the text, we find a quite untamed diversity which is nevertheless to our liking — the unspoilt rainforest of Sumatra as against the fussily cultivated European garden. This diversity in all its unruliness Kant compares to the singing of birds: 'Even bird song, which we cannot bring under any rule of music, seems to contain more freedom and hence to offer more to taste than human song [. . .] because we tire much sooner of a human song if it is repeated often and for long periods' (CJ, 94/243).

The chaotic twittering of the birds is deployed here as an intriguing metonym for the vast intricacy of the natural forest, in which these birds might indeed be perching or have taken flight. But this sylvan immensity is one which, even though it seems to lack all cultivation and to exceed the design and grasp of intelligence, nevertheless — for Kant — proves more beautiful than the human artifice of music and the immaculately pruned hedge.

This apparent absence of intelligence is mirrored in a curious reversal of predicates: Kant assigns a greater freedom to that part of nature which is without reason than he does to the 'rational animal' ('Even bird song, which we cannot bring under any rule of music, seems to contain *more freedom* [. . .] than human song'). By rights, freedom should remain strictly the preserve of the human or at least of rational entities, and mechanical repetition the province of the animal; and yet here it seems that a repetition carried out by man, at least in the very particular case of his song, accords with the bad infinite. But when the birds take over, the chorus soars and becomes free. It seems that we are to understand as the birdsong's freedom its capacity to break with the eternal sameness of repetition and generate novelty in its iterations. It is as if a machine were to break its programming and become more free than its inventor — an animal-machine which metamorphoses into something beautiful, while the human being reverts to the level of the machine, boring us to death with the tune it is endlessly grinding out.

Kant then likens the diversity of nature (the rainforest) and its metonym (birdsong) to 'the changing shapes of the flames in a fireplace or of a rippling brook' (CJ, 95/243). In birdsong, the self-consumption and regeneration of fire, the ceaseless rippling of the brook, one witnesses a kind of repetition in which difference is produced, an infinite number of infinitesimal novelties. This ingenious repetition seems compatible neither with the bad infinite, in which everything stays the same, nor with the true infinite, in which there is accumulation and progress. When it comes to birdsong, flame, and water, we find an eternal sameness which partakes of an unchanging natural cycle, in which endless variation is introduced. Perhaps this implies a new sense of 'diversity', a limitless variety which is not a hindrance to beauty. This variant diversity for Kant seems to constitute a kind of *freedom* which allows the wild animal and its landscape to strike us as beautiful.

But here Kant stops us in our tracks, shying away from a leap in pursuit of the free and beautiful animal, as if something in that notion were ultimately repugnant to him. Despite everything, even the explicit reference to 'taste', Kant feels compelled to assert that we are in fact 'confused' in our estimation that birdsong is beautiful — 'probably': 'in this case we *probably* [*vermuthlich*] confuse [*vertauschen*] our participation in the cheerfulness of a favourite little animal with the beauty of its song [*unsere Teilnehmung an der Lustigkeit eines kleinen beliebten Thierchens mit der Schönheit seines Gesanges*]' (CJ, 94/243, emphasis added).

The notion that this animal is favoured by us and therefore particularly touching, implies that the animal has *interested* us and so merely *charmed* us. In the confusion which this charm has induced, we have erroneously attributed a free beauty to its song — mistaking interest for disinterest.[13] In the end, for Kant, the wild animal and also, by extension, the wild forest, must be charming but not beautiful.

To warn us against this indistinction between the charms of something that we love, and genuine beauty, Kant insists that taste does *not* in fact discover beauty in such things but rather takes delight in 'the occasion they provide for it to engage in *fiction* [dichten], i.e., [. . .] the actual fantasies [*eigentlichen Phantasieen*] with which the mind entertains itself as it is continually being aroused by the diversity that strikes the eye' (CJ, 94/243). How this phantasy is distinct from the imagination in its schematisation is not immediately clear. Nevertheless, Kant could hardly be more direct: he concludes the entire Analytic of the Beautiful by reaffirming that the manifestations of nature's diversity which we discover in flame and brook, to which the wilderness of nature and the animal have been directly assimilated, are in fact *charming* rather than *beautiful*: 'neither of these are beauties [*keine Schönheiten sind*], but they still charm the imagination [*aber doch für die Einbildungskraft einen Reiz bei sich führen*]' (CJ, 95/243–44).

And yet if this is charm, it is of a very unusual kind. It does not concern our personal sensibility and the matter of the entity which happens to appeal to our peculiar 'pathological' liking (*pathos*, feeling, in Greek). Kant himself says that the reason why these multifarious and disorderly profusions charm the imagination is 'because they sustain its *free play* [*freies Spiel*]' (CJ, 95/244, emphasis added).

With the description of that which is akin to birdsong and in particular this final allusion to 'free play', the experience of the charming draws so near to the beautiful as to make it extremely difficult to see how Kant can any longer distinguish the two, save by a blunt stipulation.

In the experience of beauty, freedom makes its otherwise incongruous presence known within nature, but here things go further. It seems as if Kant cannot accept the idea of a beautiful animal or a genuine kind of natural freedom, an animal repetition which ceases to be mechanical and becomes free variation. When such a thing occurs, man and animal have exchanged places.

But perhaps this experience occurs *only* when the animal is beloved and touches us in its reality. In which case, it would be beautiful and charming at once, and the line separating charm from beauty could hardly fail to become blurred.

At the very least, we can say that the animal seems to be a special case when it comes to beauty and one which Kant's system finds it difficult to encompass. To clarify the problem, let us turn to the second half of the *Critique of Judgement*, since this will begin to tell us exactly what the animal is for Kant. To anticipate this definition we can say that in the experience of the organism, the subject ascribes not just purposiveness or conceptualisability to nature, but an actual *purpose* or *concept*.

And this has consequences. Not only will this definition make it difficult for the Kantian philosophy to account for a specifically *animal* form of *beauty*, but also and for precisely the same reason, in the case of the animal we experience an entity which actually exists, conceptually and intuitively individuated, an entity which is then the potential subject of *interest* rather than *dis*interest. And if charm is associated with interest then it might well prove to be the case that, with a beautiful animal, beauty and charm become inextricable — as a consequence of Kant's own theory of the organism, this time.

The entwinement of the beautiful and the charming and a curious exchange of places for man and animal is what takes place in the experience of the beautiful animal. Perhaps charm and beauty *must* be intertwined because man himself cannot but be interested, involved in his very being in this encounter, since he is himself, as the passage we are about to read states, situated in a perhaps novel way on the plane of nature *insofar as* he undergoes the experiences of beauty and animality. Perhaps we shall then have to rethink the human as the animal which is capable of perceiving in the non-human animal what the charming reveals, and as the animal which is also capable of re-evaluating the bad infinite of repetition in a way that Hegel hardly suspected, whether that endless instinctual repetition results in free variation or not.

To conclude this part of our trek, let us get ahead of ourselves and simply read this mysterious passage from the Critique of Teleological Judgement, full of promise, which affirms the objective purposiveness one finds in the animal kingdom whilst also placing man himself within nature, and in almost the same breath associates beauty and charm with one another. It is as if Kant could not but suspect these latter of some illicit collusion in the experience of the animal, or as if the animal cannot but be loved, since it is after all something like a gift from heaven or a divinely granted 'favour' (*Gunst*):

> once nature has been judged teleologically, and the natural purposes that we find in organised beings have entitled us to the idea of a vast system of purposes of nature, then *even beauty in nature*, i.e., nature's harmony with the free play of our cognitive powers [*dem freien Spiele unserer Erkenntnisvermögen*] as we apprehend and judge its appearance, can similarly be considered an *objective* purposiveness, namely, of the whole of nature [regarded] as a system that includes man as a member [*worin der Mensch ein Glied ist*]. We may regard nature as having held us in favour [*Gunst*] when it distributed not only useful things [*das Nützliche*] but a wealth of *beauty and charms* [*Schönheit und Reize*] as well; and we may love [*lieben*] it for this, just as its immensity may lead us to contemplate it with respect [*Achtung*] and to feel that we ourselves are ennobled in this contemplation [in the experience of the *sublime*] — just as if [*als ob*] nature had erected and decorated its splendid stage quite expressly with that aim. (CJ, 260/380, emphases added)

This is the moment of the great crossover between teleological and aesthetic judgement, and not only do we find beauty and charm conjoined, we find ourselves inclined to *love*, as with our favourite little animal, the songbird — and finally yet another 'as if', protesting perhaps a little too much that none of this is strictly 'real'.

g) Kant and the impossible beauty of animals

Yet despite what these rather obscure corners of the Kantian text allow us to glimpse, Kant himself may be said to display great difficulty in fully assuming and directly stating what his text reveals in its most unguarded moments. Despite everything, Kant still finds it hard to assign beauty to an animal, for animals are too easily subsumed under a particular concept, and as we shall see in a moment, when we come to read the *Critique of Teleological Judgement* in earnest, they can *only* be subsumed under a particular concept, making the case of beautiful animals particularly intractable. To bring under a concept is the task of determinative judgement, the judgement which brings to light the *object* rather than the *subject*, as is the case with reflective judgements, which reveal the subjective conditions that make the object as such possible.

And yet, once again, despite the *spirit* of Kant's text, the *letter* betrays something different: the very first examples of 'free beauty' that Kant gives are taken from nature, not art, and include that irrepressible little creature, the bird — and this one even hums:

> Flowers are free natural beauties. Hardly anyone apart from the botanist knows what sort of thing a flower is [meant] to be; and even he, while recognising it as the reproductive organ of a plant, pays no attention to this natural purpose when he judges the flower by taste. [. . .] Many birds (the parrot, the humming-bird, the bird of paradise [a bird that speaks, a bird that sings, and a bird that has descended from Eden — as human as can be]) and a lot of crustaceans in the sea are [free] beauties themselves [and] belong to no object determined by concepts as to its purpose. (CJ, 76/229)[14]

Kant compares these 'free beauties' to 'the foliage on borders or on wallpaper, etc. [which] mean nothing on their own: they represent [*vorstellen*] nothing, no object under a determinate concept' (CJ, 76–77/229). It seems from the preceding passage that our birds and crustaceans might even *in themselves* be somehow recalcitrant to concepts, just as much as the wallpaper patterns that infinitely suggest an object without ever quite resolving into one, as our childish eyes play across them at nightfall or in ennui. What else can it mean that, '[m]any birds [. . .] belong to no object determined by concepts [*keinem nach Begriffen in Ansehung seines Zwecks bestimmten Gegenstande zukommen*]'?[15]

This we must leave in suspense for now, but it points towards the fact that if animals are to be considered beautiful, then the conditions they will have to meet are perhaps exorbitant: either they would have to forego a concept altogether, or — and this alternative is perhaps closer to Kant's intention, if one considers the example of the botanist, who knows full well what the plant is, scientifically speaking — they should be considered absolutely apart from the concept which identifies them. But even if the more prosaic option is the true one, the very fact that Kant chooses to give specific examples suggests that there are some elements in nature which *lend themselves* to a relinquishing of concepts and encourage by their very essence a free play of conceptuality. Avian and marine creatures seem to fall into this category.

That said, whichever option we choose — the speculative or the more sedate transcendental — we can say of animals what Kant would have us say of anything: *insofar as they are animals*, belonging under a particular concept, they are not beautiful. Animals are not beautiful for Kant. They possess a form which is too familiar to us — even if the unearthly abstract shapes of shell-fish and the patterns traced by darting birds, like their song, do not form objects that are as immediately recognisable as all that. Nevertheless when it comes to the creatures themselves, our minds still too readily impose on them a particular concept.

In fact, Kant makes a distinction here between two kinds of beauty: a more Platonic and Hegelian kind which involves the application of a concept in conjunction with 'the object's perfection in terms of that concept' (CJ, 76/229), and a form of beauty which does not involve a concept or which requires its very subtraction. Thus, our proneness to apply concepts to animals relegates their beauty for the most part to a *subordinate* type: Kant calls it 'adherent beauty', and the more perfect form, 'free beauty'. Thus, Kant tells us that, 'the beauty of a horse, or of a building (such as a church, palace, armoury, or summer-house)[16] does presuppose the concept of the purpose that determines what the thing is [meant] to be, and hence a concept of its perfection, and so it is merely adherent beauty' (CJ, 77/230). Thus one can imagine finding a perfect horse but it would not be beautiful in the strictest sense of the term because it presupposes a prior *determinative* judgement, while the true judgement of taste would *precede* such a judgement and would not even need to be destined for such an act of cognition.

For Kant, one cannot in general be a beautiful instance *of* something, for what is beautiful in the highest sense is conceptualisability *without* a concept ('purposiveness without a purpose'), and not something that has already been conceptualised, which is to say, assigned to a particular type. Beauty is a suspension of conceptualisation; it is prior to identity and representation, prior to the 'as', prior to the entity as such. No 'thing' is beautiful.

This is not to say that being in possession of a concept actually prevents us from finding something beautiful, but, *if* we are to adjudge it beautiful, we must abstract the entity from its concept, like a botanist resting from his work to admire the daisies. Thus Kant admits that a determinate concept is no hindrance to beauty; we just need to take some distance from our conceptual work.

But how far must we take this abstraction? Do we need to extract the entity from *all* of the concepts which have been applied to it? How far must we climb up Porphyry's tree before we catch sight of something beautiful? Once we have stripped the entity of the concept of its species do we then move on to liberate it from all of its higher genera? We (perhaps) have a concept of an organism, a living thing as such: will we have to abstract from the fact that we recognise an *animal* here before us, bellowing out its chorus from the branches? Should we go so far as to say that we are confronted simply with an 'object' or a 'being' without any further determination, a being 'as such'?

But in the beautiful we encounter something even less than that, for we cannot see the 'entity' 'as' anything at all: it lacks the elementary identity of the merest entity. The beautiful is less than being, dis-inter-ested in a more literal sense than we might have suspected. It remains at the level of possibility, an as yet unactualised object, perhaps never to be actualised.

h) The animal and purpose

In any case, this might explain why Kant does not speak of beautiful animals very often, without reservations and retractions. And yet, as the very structure of the Critique makes clear, there is a privileged connection between the beautiful and the animal. Indeed, broadly speaking, they comprise the very subject-matter of the two halves of the *Critique of Judgement* itself. They are connected by the central concept of the Critique — 'purpose' or 'purposiveness', 'the concept that mediates between the concepts of nature and the concept of freedom' (CJ, 36–37/196). Beauty and the beast constitute moments within experience at which nature and freedom are shown to be compatible, thanks to the presumed existence of a purposiveness which both share.

In the first part of the book, devoted to beauty, we find a *subjective* purposiveness, the judgement that nature was made for the purposes of our understanding; and in the second half, centred on the organism, we are compelled to adjudge that there is an *objective* purpose at work in none other than the animal — an actual organism, whose functioning can be rendered intelligible only if we assume that it embodies a final cause.[17]

In the case of the organism, we have an actual, individual entity before us, to which our understanding has applied a determinate concept: unlike the experience of beauty, when faced with an animal our experience is no longer that of a mere conceptualisability or purposiveness *without* a purpose; here we encounter a living and breathing concept, a determinate purpose embodied in the creature itself. Purposiveness *with* a purpose: 'where we attribute to nature our concept of a purpose in order to judge its product[,] in that case we present not just a *purposiveness* of nature in the form of the thing, but [we] present [*vorgestellt*] the product itself [the organism] as a *natural purpose*' (CJ, 33/193). We are confronted not with *beauty* but with an *animal*.

The organism organises itself in the sense that the purposes of the whole explain the organisation of its parts. The whole and that potential to which it is destined are represented by us as a concept which gathers and gives sense to the multiplicity. In its own way, the animal is *self-caused*, as if some kind of 'ontological argument' could prove not the existence of an infinite being but that of a finite sensate animal, for the mere concept of the organism's totality is sufficient to bring into actual existence the parts of the animal in their vital coordination.[18]

The existence of a final cause in nature, an entity causing itself spontaneously to function, amounts to the existence of a primitive form of autonomy or *freedom* within nature. Thus the radical difference between nature and freedom is diminished, and this coincidence of the two broken halves of the Kantian worldview, nature and humanity, takes place in the animal, or at least, in our experience of it.

i) The transcendental quality of the teleological judgement

The 'teleological' judgement asserts that this object facing us is a living thing, an organism. It applies a concept to the object and thus bestows an identity upon it: it therefore stands closer to the determinative judgement of cognition than the aesthetic judgement does. Beauty is judged by taste and imagination, but the animal is judged by understanding and reason.[19]

Despite the affirmation of a 'real' purposiveness and even a 'real' purpose, we must be careful not to assume that these teleological judgements tell us anything about the inherent nature of the animal substance in itself: they stop just short of a determinative judgement that would *cognise* the object and provide us with actual knowledge. These judgements remain merely *transcendental* necessities, which is to say that they ultimately concern not knowledge itself, but its conditions of possibility:

> when judgement is used teleologically, it indicates determinately the conditions under which something (e.g., an organised body) is to be judged in terms

of the idea of a purpose of nature; but judgement *cannot* adduce a principle derived from the concept of nature, taken as object of experience, *authorising it to assert* a priori *that nature [makes products] by reference to purposes*. (CJ, 34/194, emphases added)

So, we remain at the level of the transcendental conditions of knowledge which apply in the case of the animal. The teleological judgement does not provide us with any knowledge about the object but merely clarifies what must be involved in the judgement that something is an 'animal'.

In any case, it is by means of the notion of purposiveness, attributed both to the subject in the freedom of its imagination's play and to nature itself in the guise of the animal, that the third Critique proposes to bridge the gap between nature and reason, the breach which defines the earlier Kantian philosophy and which later German idealism set itself to heal.

j) The irrepressible biologist in us

It should by now have become clear what the judgement of the beautiful and the judgement of the animal have in common, but we should also have some sense of the distance that separates them. Perhaps this will help us to explain why it is difficult for Kant to speak of beauty and the animal in a single breath.

We saw earlier that the reason for this difficulty is that, in order to experience an animal, we must have a concept of it and judge the animal according to the perfection with which it embodies that concept. We test the degree to which the sensible matches up to the intelligible, the real to the ideal. Even the scientist could find the object of their knowledge beautiful, but only by resorting to a bracketing of this knowledge and wading upstream towards a pre-conceptual purposiveness in the faculties' free play.

We wondered how far this abstraction might be taken: should we strip away all concepts, including the concept of the 'living thing'? After our detour through the *Critique of Teleological Judgement*, it seems that this will prove more challenging than the abstraction of the more specific properties which particular animals might possess. Adjudging something to be an *organism* requires a specific kind of judgement, one which, while akin to the judgement of taste, is nevertheless distinct from it: the teleological judgement cannot withdraw all the way to the level of a sheer *purposiveness without a purpose*, conceptuality without any concept at all, for it must understand the organised whole to be *itself* a determinate concept — the self-actualising potential which Kant calls 'purpose'. The biologist we are can never conclusively suspend *this* judgement. Perhaps this explains why Kant, when he speaks of a scientist who *can* make this abstraction, refers not to *zoology* but to *botany*? With plants it is possible, with animals, not.

Thus if we want to hold to the judgement that what stands before us is an *animal* and nothing else, we shall be unable simultaneously to consider it *beautiful*. To assert the beauty of *anything* we need to withhold any concepts which might determine what it is, but this is impossible when we are faced with a subjective necessity of the experience itself: in taking the entity for an animal, we make a teleological judgement, not an aesthetic one, and this judgement involves a *concept* which cannot be parenthesised.

In the judgement of taste, what is revealed is the *possibility* of collapsing the division between freedom and nature, while in the teleological judgement of the animal, we see the *actuality* of this collapse: an actual instance of autonomous freedom posited as belonging to nature or as 'emerging' within it. But what happens when these two instances fall together? For surely we do encounter things which we deem both beautiful and animal. It seems that Kant's conceptual framework prevents him from articulating this. Nevertheless, he will have supplied us with a great many of the concepts that we need in order to understand this encounter.

In the experience of the animal, the potential for nature's comprehensibility becomes actual; the suspicion of a freedom in nature, intimated in the exhilaration of the free play of the imagination, is confirmed in the autonomy of the animal's self-organisation. Or, *vice versa*, the effect of the beautiful allows us to hope that the purely local intelligibility of nature found in the animal may be universalised. Animals give us cause to hope that all is not lost for us in nature, that we might not be so alien as we first feared.

If this comes somewhere near the truth, then Kant's work may be said to demonstrate why the experience of a beautiful animal is so significant for human beings, and in particular why an intimate encounter with a favoured (perhaps domestic) animal is so enchanting. In that impossible meeting with a beautiful animal, the experience of nature's rationality and freedom is redoubled — nature seems particularly hospitable to our intellect, since here the potential for intelligibility becomes actual.

Perhaps there is nothing surprising in all this, for what part of nature is more closely akin to us than the animals and, most of all, those tame animals which do not flee us or repel our understanding with their sublimity?

Perhaps in the end, Kant remains unable to articulate this explicitly because he begins from the still metaphysical presupposition that animal and man exist not on a continuum, as we are more liable to suppose today, but are separated by a rigorous border of opposition. The contrary theoretical position, whether born of an inherited belief in evolutionary biology or derived from some other source, may also be *felt*, and animals are the entities which give us a particularly acute pre-theoretical sense that mind and nature are not distinct. This would explain the great joy with which we are favoured on those rare occasions when we are allowed to share something of their world.

Perhaps Kant's encumbrance when it comes to thinking animality and beauty together will explain why in the end he felt compelled to deploy the notion of the 'charming' in place of the 'beautiful' and refused to consider a coincidence of beauty and charm without equivocation. For our part we consider them integrally connected precisely in the experience of the animal that we love, because our non-alienated belonging to the plane of nature is revealed to us here, and joyfully at that. We might recall the episode of the animal's song, where Kant wavered between finding it beautiful and affirming within it a quite other kind of 'cheerfulness'.

Is the animal's sincerity so touching because the charming animal presents us with a region in which man and nature overlap? If man is actually involved with nature in his very being then his own actual existence and that of the animals at an empirical level cannot fail to be a significant part of this experience; thus in the case of the animal, supposedly *dis*interested beauty would be inseparable from the charm that is beauty's *interested* form.

As in our hearing of a superior freedom in the animal's melodious voice, the experience of a charming beautiful animal might lead us to change places with the animal, becoming their inferior on precisely the terms by which we have long measured our sovereignty, on a territory no longer quite our own, in which the cautious interactions of the living creature, wary but curious, allow us to feel once more a part of nature.[20]

k) Beyond Kant. Hegel.

We have perhaps already gone far enough to provide some confirmation of our hypothesis that Kant, for all the epiphanies of his text, is not quite able to tell us what happens when two distinct instances of a fusion between nature and freedom meet, what is revealed in the flickering light of the sparks generated by such a short-circuit between beauty and animality.

So, if Kant remains unable to speak freely of the beautiful animal, we must go on to ask whether the encounter we are trying to understand is indeed best captured by adopting the Kantian point of view. Kant's way of posing the question begins from the assumption of a gulf between nature and freedom and the only subsequently discovered need to bridge it. This bridging takes the form of a search for those *infrequent* moments within nature which suggest that it might be possible for man to overpower nature with his rationality and to seize it conceptually. Now, as the sudden turn of our phrase suggests, this might not in the end amount to so innocent a relation as the encounter with a tame and friendly animal, but rather comprise an unjustifiable domestication of the 'outside'.

Would we therefore have better luck if we began from the presupposition of a certain naturality that man and beast initially share in common, or if not that then some third thing which might unite freedom and nature by preceding their division? In other words, rather than attempting to reduce nature to the measure of our concepts, might we not entertain the possibility that in a certain sense *we* are 'reduced' to the level of animality, or perhaps that man and animal are both situated on some plane which is absolutely not the unique province of either. For in truth, although he will not quite have been able to speak of or conceive it, it is precisely this kind of experience that Kant has allowed us to describe.

But what might precede both nature and freedom, what might allow man and animal to stand on the same ground? Let us consult Hegel. He poses the question: what if nature in itself were rational? This allows us to consider the possibility that the terrain upon which we might walk with the animals as equals is not a sub-representational, non-conceptual domain, and hence hardly a reduction even for those who balk at man's post-metaphysical demotion. In light of this, we might imagine that Hegel will have fewer problems than Kant in speaking about the beautiful animal because, for him, it is not *as if* the world were made for us, moulded to our understanding; up to a point, nature really *is* intelligible — the split between the inconceivable 'in-itself' and the conceivable 'for-us' is overcome, just as the bad infinite necessarily makes way for the good or the true.

This other beginning is something that Hegel allows us to think. The Hegelian philosophy begins at a point prior to the positing of oppositions, including the rigorous separation between nature and freedom. It puts to work a dialectical machine that posits and then overcomes such oppositions, precisely by making it apparent that they are its own invention and thus belong to the concept. This gives us reason to hope that Hegel will help us take another step towards the experience of the beautiful animal.

Chapter Three

Hegel and Nature

HEGEL'S PHILOSOPHY OF NATURE

Let us spend some time reading Hegel's *Philosophy of Nature*, not least because of its inherent interest, but also because of its reputed difficulty, as well as the common opinion that it is an endeavour which was either misguided at the time or has since been superseded by more materialist approaches to nature, including the natural sciences themselves — these are illusions which must be dispelled, and the text's reputation for difficulty demands of us a clear account.[1]

This reading might initially seem a rather circuitous way of making another pass at our object, but the journey will not be without profit in its own right, and we shall reach our goal in the end, better equipped, having illuminated Hegel's starting point and its relation to Kant's, as well as the 'dialectical' method with which it stands in such intimate relation.

We must learn to see nature with Hegelian eyes, and in particular the relation between nature and spirit, the terms in which Hegel rethinks Kant's opposition between nature and freedom. Spirit (*Geist*) constitutes, broadly speaking, the realm of humanity, its experience and thought, and the way these are reflected in objective form in its 'culture'. In fact, we shall first encounter 'spirit' in Hegel's 'philosophy of *nature*' and the way in which this philosophy conceptualises the natural world as an increasingly distinct *anticipation* of spirit in its rationality and freedom. This will demonstrate the possibilities that a Hegelian dialectic might afford for our conception of the relation between man and animal, and in particular the form that this relation takes when we experience a beautiful animal.

The discipline of the philosophy of nature as such might be said to confront the aftermath of the Kantian attempt to reconcile nature and freedom. We know that the problematic relation between the two was the starting point for German idealism (Fichte, Schelling, Hegel) just as it was for Kant's own twilight work.[2] We might say, then, that the question of whether we can make sense of the beautiful animal is *the* question of post-Kantian philosophy, which is also the question of whether there can be such a 'posterity'. Our hypothesis is that Hegel is in a better position than Kant to accommodate the beautiful animal within his philosophy, and it is for this reason that our first resort will be Hegel — even if this entails bypassing Schelling, who is perhaps by now the most renowned exponent of the philosophy of nature.[3]

In Hegel's Philosophy of Nature, we shall be concerned in part with the attempt to describe — and to describe the necessity of describing — the dialectical emergence of spirit from nature. We shall be particularly interested in the question of whether dialectics can offer us a *pro*spective account of the genesis of man from animal, and if it cannot, the extent to which this relation can only be understood by philosophy in a *retro*spective way, as the *presupposition* of an event which will, as far as philosophy is concerned, always already have taken place. We shall attempt to determine whether, despite everything Hegel gives us in the way of an account of the emergence of spirit from nature, he does not in the end view nature exclusively from the standpoint of spirit and the concept, as would befit the idealism he (not unambiguously) espouses.[4]

SCIENCE AND PHILOSOPHY

So what is the philosophy of nature? The philosophy of nature is not a *science* of nature: that is to say, it is not empirical (or experimental) physics. Nevertheless, it is not indifferent to physics. Hegel defines the philosophy of nature as *'rational physics'*, 'the cognition of nature by means of thought [*Naturerkenntnis aus dem Gedanken*]' (PNI, 193/11 §Introduction). Thus it investigates the *meaning* of the question, 'What is nature?' (PNI, 194/12 §Introduction), an ontological question which philosophy has often assumed to be the very precondition for the empirical sciences, and which these sciences themselves remain unable to address. Philosophy would thus lay out the transcendental conditions for empirical science, as if a sovereign philosophy could dictate a priori the possible manifestations of material nature.

But Hegel does not oppose philosophy and science in this way. For Hegel, on the contrary, *science also thinks*, it just keeps quiet about it, refusing even to whisper to itself this apparently unpalatable truth: 'empirical physics contains much more thought than it will either realise or admit [*in ihr viel mehr Gedanke ist, als sie zugibt und weiß*]' (PNI, 193/11 §Introduction).[5] Thus, in fact, '[b]oth [philosophy of nature and physics] are a thinking cognition of nature [*denkende Erkenntnis der Natur*]' (PNI, 193/11 §Introduction). But it is in each case a different kind of thought, perhaps akin to the two faculties which Kant identified as Reason and Understanding, with Hegelian philosophy firmly on the side of reason, rethought in a very particular way — as 'dialectical' in Hegel's own sense.

The thinking of nature discovers *thinking* itself *within* nature. The very motor of spiritual development — the growing self-consciousness of rationality — is found foreshadowed in nature. Thus, the philosophy of nature, in combination with the physical sciences, demonstrates that nature and spirit are by no means simply in opposition, but that 'spirit has a presentiment of itself [*ahnt sich*] in nature' (PNI, 194/12 §Introduction).

That said, the two are nevertheless distinct, and to that extent, 'nature is an alienation [*einem Fremden*] in which spirit does not find itself' (ibid.).

This is how Hegel answers the question of what nature is: it is the anticipation of spirit, the form assumed by the concept when it first sees the light of day, becoming 'external' or 'outward' in Hegel's terms. In this way, thought estranges itself in a foreign medium and appears only in the distorted grimace of a hotchpotch of contingent formations, which seem to the natural scientist, correctly in one respect, to have been thrown together at random: 'In the sphere of nature, contingency and determinability from without come into their own' (PNI, 215/34 §250).

I. Nature's necessity

Nature as teleological: Purpose and concepts in nature

Nature is rational: it is logically ordered and there is a reason why things happen there in the way that they do — thus natural events are characterised by necessity. But, on the other hand, they are also imbued with contingency, chaos, and irrationality. Nature is the manifestation of thought and spirit, but in an obscure form. This dual character we must now clarify.

To understand nature's rational necessity, first of all, we must return to Kant's animal.

Kant's theory of the organism as a natural self-actualising concept was formative for Hegel's philosophy of nature. Nature, for Hegel, is teleological and this is why it can be grasped in a way that is 'Notional' or 'conceptual' (*begrifflich*): it 'opens the way for the Notional point of view' (PNI, 195/13 §245). For Kant, nature resembled our reason insofar as it contained purpose.[6] In the animal, one can posit a certain freedom in nature and hence, in Hegel's terms, a certain spirit. In the organism, nature manifestly begins to spiritualise itself, and it does so by embodying the concept, however imperfectly:

> To see purpose [*Zweckbegriff*] as inherent within natural objects [*Dingen*], is to grasp nature in its simple determinateness, e.g. the seed of a plant, which contains the real potential of everything pertaining to the tree, and which as purposeful activity [*zweckmäßige Tätigkeit*] is therefore orientated solely towards self-preservation. (PNI, 196/14 §245A)

By positing and pursuing its own goal the natural entity determines itself in its development and functioning — it is autonomous and hence free, for it abides solely by its own necessity and is not determined by anything else. Thus, the organism is a 'presentiment' of spirit — that spirit which alone is truly free since it is *aware* of its freedom *as* freedom: its rationality is ultimately manifest to it without any distortion at all. Spirit will thus be the consummation of the freedom to be found inchoate within nature.

Hegel takes the insight gleaned from Kant's theory of the organism and generalises it to the whole of nature: nature at all of its levels contains hints of the rationality that will blossom when spirit emerges with the arising of man from the animal kingdom; the organism is merely the most manifestly rational and free part of nature, but this spirituality can be glimpsed almost everywhere, if one looks hard enough.

Glimpsing concepts in hindsight

The perception of concepts in all parts of nature can take place only in *hindsight*, by one who has risen to the level of the fully self-conscious deployment of thought: the human being.[7] The philosophy of nature is in this sense, like almost all of Hegel's philosophy, a retrospective account. This can help us to understand more clearly the relation between philosophy and physics:

> The material [*Stoff*] prepared out of experience by physics [*aus der Erfahrung bereitet*], is taken by the philosophy of nature at the point to which physics has brought it, and reconstituted [*bildet ihn wieder um*[8]] without any further reference to experience as the basis of verification [*Bewährung*]. (PNI, 201/20 §246A)

What this reconstruction brings to light are those parts of nature which can be seen to resemble concepts, to abide by their 'deductive' (or rather, 'dialectical') order, and to approximate their relations of implication. The natural material which thus anticipates the concept is then gathered together before being laid out in a systematic way, and this system will comprise the Philosophy of Nature.

Thus Hegel will demonstrate the truly extraordinary extent to which rationality may be found amidst the apparent *ir*rationality of nature: 'Physics must therefore work together with philosophy so that the universalised understanding which it provides may be translated into the Notion [*in den Begriff übersetze*] by showing how this universal, as an intrinsically *necessary* whole, proceeds out of the *Notion*' (PNI, 201/20 §246A, emphases added). The philosophy of nature makes nature, which in its arbitrariness might have resisted rational understanding, intelligible, or rather it wrings every last drop of intelligibility from its fabric:

> The philosophy of nature distinguishes itself from physics on account of the metaphysical procedure it employs, for metaphysics is nothing but the range of universal thought-determinations [*allgemeinen Denkbestimmungen*], and is as it were the diamond-net [*diamantene Netz*] into which we bring everything [*allen Stoff*] in order to make it intelligible [*verständlich*]. (PNI, 202/20 §246A)

Philosophy takes the deliverances of physics, which are based on the givens of sensory experience (already somewhat idealised in the form of universal laws and species), and renders them as intelligible as it is possible to do, which involves presenting them in a form as closely akin to the concept as their nature allows.

Realist and idealist interpretations of the Philosophy of Nature

Here we reach a crossroads, for there are two readings of this insinuation of conceptuality within nature: a realist and an idealist. For the realist, reason is objectively present within nature, and the philosophy of nature merely brings it to light; for the idealist, reason is not objectively present in nature but is projected upon its surface by philosophy. In the passages we are about to read, the idealist interpretation, although it would seem today the most appropriate, given the prevalence of a materialist approach to nature, in truth becomes very difficult to sustain.

Hegel's notion of a conceptuality within nature and hence the very idea of a philosophy of nature compel us rather to rethink the opposition between realism and idealism in this context. This necessity becomes glaring when we witness Hegel speaking of the idea itself *as* a reality, and this in the context of the *organism*.

This troubling of the distinction between idealism and realism is reminiscent of the wellsprings of idealism in Plato, where Ideas (*eidē*, *ideai*, the plurals of *eidos* and *idea*) were asserted to be the highest form of *reality*. The only significant difference here is that, unlike Plato, Hegel makes an explicit connection between real ideas and the animal organism: '*This idealism*, which recognises [*erkennen*] the Idea [*die Idee*] throughout the whole of nature, is at the same time *realism*, for the Notion of living existence [*Lebendigen*] is *the Idea as reality* [*Realität*]' (PNIII, 111/438 §353A, emphases added).

The animal sublates the opposition between realism and idealism.

One might say that the distinction between realism and idealism cannot in the end apply to a dialectical approach because what we find in the reality of nature is an incipient form of the idea — the concept[9] — which is not yet an idea in the fullest sense. Hence the idea can be said *neither* to dwell within nature inherently (for only in spirit can entities become fully adequate to their own concept) *nor* to be merely projected there (for there really are purposes in nature); or it may be said to be both.[10]

The organism is the pinnacle of nature in the precise sense that it is the high water mark of real ideality — the animal most fully and explicitly embodies the concept. But in doing so, it is merely a 'microcosm' of the *whole* of nature, each part of which evinces a rudimentary rationality just as far as its particular character allows.[11] In the animal, the idea stands before us, materialised, and indeed before *itself* in a certain way, since material nature here becomes aware of itself for the first time — it is now self-related or 'subjective'. The animal encapsulates the rationality of the whole of nature and thus supplies a privileged way in to the very idea of the rationality of nature. If the philosophy of nature can be written only retrospectively, from the standpoint of spirit and the human being, then perhaps, in order to understand just what the philosophy of nature *is*, we should begin with the animal, the most perfect, because the most spiritual, part of nature.

In this context, let us read what is perhaps the final word on the procedure and task of the philosophy of nature:

> The determination and the purpose of the philosophy of nature is therefore that spirit should find its own essence, its counterpart [*Gegenbild*], i.e. the Notion, within nature. The study of nature is therefore the liberation of what belongs to spirit within nature [. . .]. This is likewise the liberation of *nature*, which in itself is reason; it is only through spirit however, that reason as such comes forth from nature into existence [*Existenz*]. (PNI, 204/23 §246A, emphasis added)

By revealing the rationality incipient within nature, we can demonstrate the way in which this reason comes into its own in the realm of spirit, as here it can acquire self-consciousness, and thus in the end one demonstrates the superiority of spirit over nature. Nature in itself is rational; indeed, it *is* reason itself, and yet in such a way that reason does not yet (fully) 'exist'.

The philosophy of nature demonstrates just how far nature can be seen to be rational. The extent to which Hegel is able to find precursors of spirit and the necessity of its rationality within the apparently contingent manifestations of nature is quite breath-taking. It is one of the ironies of the *Philosophy of Nature*'s reception that it is precisely this extent which has generated the long history of dismissal and ridicule to which it has been subjected — that one might derive (correctly as it turns out) the number of planets there are in our solar system. . . .

Indeed, perhaps it is only in an age so thoroughly imbued with a materialism wont to think that nature is entirely devoid of thought, conscious design, and the creative intention which motivates it, that we can discern the magnitude of Hegel's achievement, in light of which our strongest feeling might well be awe at the extent to which conceptual structures may be evinced in nature.

From the collapse of the opposition to the restoration of distinctness

That said, it is precisely the extremity of this 'rationalisation' that gives rise to Hegel's *own* criticism of a certain totalitarianism of the concept, the 'pan-logicism' or 'hyper-rationalisation' that sees in *every* phenomenon (*pan*) the expression of rationality (*logos*), and henceforth assumes the hyper-rationalist position according to which one can deduce a priori *everything* that occurs and everything that exists within nature (not to say, culture) and hence affirm that everything happens of necessity. The extreme heights to which rationalisation is taken in Hegel's philosophy of nature imposes the necessity of a critique inasmuch as here rationality is applied to that realm which even *Hegel* will admit is somewhat alien to reason.

So far we have seen how nature and spirit, the natural and the rational, are not as rigorously opposed to one another as Kant had supposed; now we must demonstrate the sense in which they nevertheless remain distinct, that spirit is alienated by nature, and the reflection which it discerns in the mirror of nature remains distorted. This distortion may be placed under the heading of the *contingency* of nature, which Hegel goes so far as to call nature's 'weakness' and 'impotence'.

II. Nature's contingency

The odyssey of the concept: Alienation in nature and its supersession

What of nature is contingent? To answer this question, we must first explain *why* nature is contingent, and that will involve us in the question of what nature is, and what place it occupies within Hegel's system.

Let us therefore recall the structure of Hegel's 'Encyclopædia'. The Encyclopædia is composed of three volumes and its divisions give expression to the structure of Hegel's philosophical system: the *Logic*, the *Philosophy of Nature*, and the *Philosophy of Spirit*. Most significant to us here is the fact that Hegel's encyclopædia opens with *logic*, the science of rational thought: it addresses the question of what it means to think and what Reason is. This immediately opens onto the question of the 'object' of thought: what is it that thought can think?

Thought cannot be the thought of nothing, since thinking is taking place and this act of thought is not nothing — it exists; therefore thinking and being are in some way correlated with one another, as Parmenides will have stated at the very beginning of Philosophy. So, if thought is not simply, and unjustifiably, to presuppose the existence of anything beyond itself, it must begin by thinking this 'being', and nothing more (SL, 69/67–68).

Thought thinking itself, in its own being, reason producing an inventory of its own contents: this is logic. But logic can only go so far without *also* deducing the necessity of something *beyond* thought — and this other of thought, which thought itself generates, is not confined to being, understood simply as the 'correlate' of thought; eventually, the dialectical unfolding of the notion of being must result in the postulation of *nature* as that which stands *outside* of thought, opposed to it. Subsequently, from the existence of nature may be derived the existence of spirit.

Nature is understood to be what arises when the development of pure logic, thought's internal consistency and exhaustive unfolding of itself, reaches its limit. Thinking and being cannot become 'objectively true', fully themselves, unless thought posits something that stands apart from it. The meaning of speculative dialectics, Hegel's 'method', is that in order to *be* one's self, one must first *know* what one is, and in order to know what one is, one must place before one's self a mirror, in which to acquire this knowledge. This means that the *subject* must take on an *objective* form — and such is the role of nature with respect to thought. Thus, rational thought must split itself in two, externalise itself, become an object, and in this passage beyond itself, in this bifurcation, nature is born.[12]

Broadly speaking, thought is 'inward', 'subjective', related only to itself and not to anything beyond itself, as it meditates upon its own essence. It does not share itself with anything else by deigning to *appear*. Nature would be the first form in which the idea — logic — *shows* itself: 'nature is [. . .] one of the modes [alongside spirit, one may presume] in which the Idea manifests itself' (PNI, 206/25 §247A). 'Nature has yielded [*ergeben*] itself as the Idea in the form of *otherness* [Andersseins]' (PNI, 205/24 §247). Hegel always speaks of manifestation as an 'externalisation', turning to face outwards, becoming explicit, just as the rose concealed in the interior of a bud is urged towards its blossoming. Nature *is* this externality (*Äußerlichkeit*) or blossoming of thought: the idea is here *'external to itself'* or 'the negative' (PNI, 205/24 §247). Nature is the first form, the least self-conscious and least rational, in which thought appears, opening itself to the outside and becoming effective in this exterior.

Nature is the mirror of thought, the objective form of its subjectivity. But the idea and its specular image contradict one another, and the way this contradiction manifests itself is in the *contingency* of nature, a contingency which thought lacks. 'In so far as the *contradiction* of the Idea is external to itself as nature, one side of it is formed by the Notionally generated *necessity* of its formations [*Gebilde*] and their rational determination within the organic totality [*organischen Totalität*], and the other by their indifferent contingency and indeterminable irregularity' (PNI, 215/34 §250).

In the end it will not be possible to resolve this contradiction within the realm of nature and therefore a transition to a qualitatively different realm will become necessary, a realm which nevertheless emerges from nature and from its contradiction with its own idea: *spirit*. The idea is driven to manifest itself externally. The initial 'naïve' form of manifestation is always inadequate to that which it attempts to reveal, for it remains opposed to and outside of that which it manifests, as an object stands opposed to its subject, or the finite to the bad infinite. But it is also a necessary step along the way to an adequate manifestation, to *being* in the fullest sense, or 'objective truth'. The plant must eventually bear fruit, but without the blossom, there is no fruition.

The way to overcome the opposition between the subjective and objective forms of one's self is for the subject to *recognise* itself in its creation. One must learn to treat the object *as* one's very own, one must return home from this alienation. The mirror image reflects only a distorted version of one's self, and the struggle is to recognise that behind those distortions it is one's own face that is staring back. One must learn to discern which of its features are in fact distortions and therefore not truly a part of one's self. In nature, this distortion is contingency, and the task of the philosophy of nature is precisely to indicate this and to show us not so much how to disregard it, but how nature itself, in its self-determination, its progressive unfolding towards the animal — and ultimately towards man — *itself* gradually strips away these imperfections: 'The thinking view of nature must note the implicit process by which nature sublates its otherness [*ihr Anderssein aufzuheben*] to become spirit, and the way in which the Idea is present [*vorhanden*] in each stage of nature [*Stufe der Natur*] itself' (PNI, 206/25 §247A).

To make things intuitively clearer, Hegel employs the religious image of God's creation, the becoming real of his ideas by *fiat* (cf. PNI, 204/23 §246A). In these terms, Hegel describes the position of the Philosophy of Nature in the following way: 'The divine Idea is just this self-release [*entschließen*], the expulsion [*herauszusetzen*] of this other out of itself, and the acceptance of it again [*in sich zurückzunehmen*], in order to constitute subjectivity and spirit' (PNI, 205/24 §247A). So the return to self out of otherness is the moment at which spirit arises: indeed, spirit *is* this very returning — and it is here, in the return to paradise rather than the expulsion from it, that the philosophy of nature is to be situated: 'The philosophy of nature itself belongs to this pathway of return [*Wege der Rückkehr*], for it is the philosophy of nature which overcomes [*aufhebt*] the division [*Trennung*] of nature and spirit, and renders [*gewährt*] to spirit the recognition [*Erkenntnis*] of its essence in nature' (PNI, 205/24 §247A).

Nature is created as an expulsion from the realm of thought, but the *philosophy* of nature is a way of returning *from* nature *to* thought, precisely by teaching reason how to recognise itself among the distortions of nature. In the very last lines of the *Philosophy of Nature*, Hegel confirms that, '[t]he aim of these lectures is [. . .] to find in this externality only the mirror of ourselves, to see in nature a free reflection of spirit' (PNIII, 213/539 §376A). But in this reflexive gesture, one does not simply return to the beginning, since the place at which one arrives is no longer the same as it once was: it is spirit. Spirit is the self-consciousness of reason, reason's recognition of its own essence achieved by way of the other (nature) and a return to the self (spirit).

The name for this self-relation is 'subjectivity' or 'self-consciousness'. The Philosophy of Nature is the dawning awareness that these strange creatures gazing inscrutably back at us may have something to teach us, that in the book of Nature one can discern the cipher of Reason. The animal scrutinises the human being from the pages of the *Philosophy of Nature* and offers to tell us what we are — for Hegel, this in fact is the *only* function of the animal and its look.

The philosophy of nature is clearly not concerned primarily with 'nature' in the sense current today and perhaps for a long time, the radically materialist vision in which nature is not just lacking in reason but infinitely recalcitrant to thought. The task of the philosophy of nature is precisely to view nature from the *later* standpoint of spirit, in order to achieve something *for* spirit, and that is to begin the task of *freeing* it from the alienation it experiences when faced with its natural counterpart. Thanks to this philosophical reworking of nature — this rendering-philosophical of the natural, this philosophising *of* nature — reason comes to see that it is not in a foreign land when it finds itself in nature, but somewhere it can learn to call home.

Here the contrast between Hegel and Kant is at its most stark. Hegel cannot be said to begin with reason and nature opposed to one another, since nature *originates* in thought, on his account. Later they *become* opposed, when thought posits nature as its own other, the object to its subject, but even this is not the last word, for this division will subsequently be overcome. Kant could heal the dichotomy of nature and reason only *analogically* with the transcendental necessity of the 'as if', the mere assumption that nature and freedom are not entirely and always alien to one another. The pervasive character of rationality in the Hegelian system forestalls the existence of any insurmountable opposition, not least because the only genuine oppositions which can exist are of its own creation.

Contingency and the remnant alienation

And yet nature *is* other to thought: materialism and idealism are not opposed on this point. What we need to determine is the peculiar nature of Hegel's idealism, and why this standpoint allows him to think of nature and, most importantly, of the animal and even of beauty in the way that he does.

Now that we have explained *why* nature is contingent and what consequences this has for the Philosophy of Nature, let us examine in more detail how these irremediable contingencies manifest themselves: what *is* nature's 'otherness', and how does this affect Hegel's understanding of beauty and animals?

For reason to recognise itself in nature's mirror, it must learn to differentiate between those features of the image which are its own and those which are not, the latter belonging exclusively to nature, not thought. Certain of these distortions are not to be overcome: when reason gazes at its reflection in nature, the pool over which it stands is never untroubled by ripples, the looking-glass bleared or cracked. The philosophy of nature does not simply teach us to recognise the concealed rationality of nature, it also reveals that aspect of its otherness which is quite insurmountable, and this is its contingency: 'Nature is the Son of God, not as the son however, but as abiding in otherness, in which the divine Idea is alienated from love [*als außerhalb der Liebe*] and held fast for a moment [*für einen Augenblick festgehalten*]. Nature is self-alienated spirit [*Die Natur ist der sich entfremdete Geist*]; spirit, a bacchantic god innocent of restraint and reflection has merely been *let loose* [ausgelassen] into it' (PNI, 206/25 §247A). If the pond were quite calm, there would be no need to surpass nature and look to spirit and its products for a full sense of our humanity, a humanity in which reason finally reaches the apogee of self-knowledge.

If nature is rational in its general structures, reason cannot account for the particularities of its individual forms. Here contingency nourishes itself. 'This contingency is particularly prevalent in the realm of concrete individual formations [*konkreten Gebilde*]' (PNI, 215/34 §250). Hegel speaks of these 'concrete formations' as 'an ensemble of juxtaposed properties, external and more or less indifferent to one another, [. . .] [which are subject to] external contingent determination' (PNI, 215/34 §250).

And yet, at times Hegel seems to risk suggesting that, given time, *nothing* in nature will escape the light of reason's illumination:

> One must start from the Notion, and even if it should as yet be unable to exhaust what is called the 'abundant variety' ['*reichen Mannigfaltigkeit*', perhaps a

reference to Kant] of nature, and there is still a great deal of particularity [*Besondere*] to be explained, it must be trusted nevertheless. [. . .] The Notion holds good of its own accord [*gilt für sich*] [. . .], and singularity [*das Einzelne*] will therefore yield [*geben*] itself in due course. (PNIII, 111/438 §353A)[13]

Hegel will later clarify things by suggesting that it is possible to achieve *both* a complete 'notional comprehension' of nature *and* to acknowledge that a remnant irrationality will always be abroad in the world. This would mean that philosophy could rationalise *all* of nature *without* thereby depriving it of its ultimate resistance to conceptuality. To explain how this could be possible, Hegel deploys the notion of the 'trace': 'Traces [*Spuren*] of Notional determination will certainly survive in the most particularised product [*das Partikulärste*], although they will not exhaust its nature' (PNI, 215/35 §250R). Despite nature's failure to be *completely* objectively truthful — commensurate with the concept — nothing in nature lacks rationality altogether; it shows through everywhere, but cannot bloom without inhibition.

This ineradicable unreason distinguishes nature from spirit and the history of the world, which constitutes the progressive achievement of spiritual self-consciousness (PNI, 216/35 §251). Nature is endowed with a residue of contingency which the rational unfolding of spirit will eventually cast off.

In the externality and indifference of its various parts, which lack the systematic interconnections of a fully rational system, nature reveals its discrepancy from reason and the freedom it brings: 'In this externality, the determinations of the Notion [*Begriffsbestimmungen*] have the appearance [*Schein*] of an *indifferent subsistence* [gleichgültigen Bestehens] and *isolation* [Vereinzelung] with regard to one another; the Notion is therefore internal [*als Innerliches*], and nature in its determinate being [*Dasein*] displays *necessity* and *contingency*, not freedom' (PNI, 208/27 §248). Even the organism, the most rational and 'free' part of nature, suffers in this regard:

> it is not only that in nature the play of forms has unbounded and unbridled contingency, but that each shape [*Gestalt*] by itself is devoid of its Notion. *Life* is the highest to which nature drives [*treibt*] in its determinate being [*Dasein*], but as merely natural Idea, life is submerged in the irrationality [*Unvernunft*] of externality, and the living individual is bound with another individuality in every moment of its existence [*Existenz*], while spiritual manifestation [*geistigen Äußerung*, externalisation] contains the moment of a free and universal relation of spirit to itself. (PNI, 209/28 §248R)

Nature's impotence — idealism — nature's shortfall

Thanks to its accidental particularities sullying the preponderance of its generally rational order, nature may be said to oppose the concept. Or, if one adopts the standpoint not of material nature but of ideal spirit — if, in other words, one is ultimately an idealist — here nature reveals not its strength but its 'weakness', its failure to live up to the notion. Natural things remain inadequate to their concept, they lack a certain truth: '[n]ature is *implicitly* [*an sich*] divine in that it is in the Idea; but in *reality* [*wie sie* ist] its being does not correspond [*entspricht*] to its Notion, and it is rather the unresolved contradiction [*unaufgelöste Widerspruch*]' (PNI, 209/27–28 §248R). This is what Hegel calls nature's 'powerlessness' or 'impotence': 'The *impotence* of nature [*die* Ohnmacht *der Natur*] is to be attributed to its only being able to maintain the determinations of the Notion in an abstract manner, and to its exposing the foundation of the particular to determination from without' (PNI, 215/34 §250).[14]

From the standpoint of idealism, nature is *fallen*: 'nature has also been regarded as the Idea's *falling short* [Abfall] of itself, for in this external shape [*Gestalt der Äußerlichkeit*] the Idea is inadequate [*Unangemessenheit*] to itself' (PNI, 209/28 §248R). Although Hegel does not explicitly ascribe this view to himself, neither does he disavow it.

The richness of nature and a divergence on the subject of beauty

We are approaching an important difference between Kant and Hegel. It concerns the very source of beauty in nature.

The weakness of nature, for Hegel, is also a strength inasmuch as it bestows upon nature something unique: to this very impotence Hegel attributes nature's *richness*, the manifold diversity that we have already encountered in Kant. Not being entirely fettered by logic and conceptuality, nature is free to bloom in all its variegated extrusions. In the following passage, this diversity is explicitly juxtaposed with nature's 'irrational contingency', as Hegel speaks in one breath of '[t]he infinite wealth and variety [*Mannigfaltigkeit*] of forms, and the utterly irrational contingency which mixes with the external order of natural formations' (PNI, 215/34–35 §250R). Its failure to be exhaustively conceptual enables the irreducible particularity of nature, and this explodes in the profusion we love so well.

We should not forget that, on Kant's account, it is just this unconceptualisable profusion that makes nature beautiful. At such moments, nature displays a multiplicity so rich it eludes the application of a determinate concept.

For Hegel, it is the other way around: nature *first of all* eludes the concept and *only thereby* becomes profuse.

For Kant, the role played by beauty and the beast was to demonstrate within nature a recognisably conceptual element, that even in the impenetrable immensity of the forest there was a song we could recognise and love. The beautiful animal revealed to us a shoreline upon which man and animal could lay down together. It will steadily become apparent that this is also true for Hegel, but the beauty of nature does not lie in its profuse multiplicity; for Hegel, this profusion testifies to the fact that, in certain of its aspects, nature eludes the concept altogether and thus becomes *ugly*.

For Hegel, nature's contingent wealth on occasion runs so wild as to escape the grip of the concept, failing even to encourage the free play of conceptualisation in which Kant discerned the basis of our experience of beauty.

Thus unlike Kant, for Hegel the diversity of natural things here indicates an essential difference between reason and nature, but this in no way impugns the power of the *concept*; it rather impugns the power of *nature*. Kant would never have said such a thing, nor would he have agreed with Hegel that it is precisely *because* nature is inadequate to its own concept that its profusion blossoms forth.

But this is Hegel's novel way of avoiding a panlogicisation of nature — affirming nature to approximate the concept down to its minutest parts — while at the same time preserving an idealistic standpoint and hence a philosophy of nature worthy of the name. Nature does not match up to the majesty of the concept, and hence there are parts of it which philosophy must simply give up on: '[t]his impotence on the part of nature sets limits [*Grenzen*] to philosophy, and it is the height of pointlessness to demand of the Notion that it should explain [*begreifen*], and as it is said, construe or deduce these contingent products of nature' (PNI, 215/35 §250R). But in that case, so much the worse for nature![15]

A monstrous failure to fall under the concept

Nature's failure to live up to the concept results in profusion, but so far from agreeing with Kant's estimation that this profusion is beautiful, Hegel thinks that nature's excess with respect to the concept can result in ugliness. The richness of nature can become so hypertrophic that it spills over into the production of monstrosity, precisely *because* nature here resists the regime of the concept. If nature is untrammelled by rationality, then it may be that it generates, alongside charming creatures, also depressing grotesques. It is factually the case that this wave of profusion carries the development of certain creatures beyond the boundaries which a conceptual articulation might have set for them, and it engenders monsters.

In nature, one will never find a perfect horse or indeed any entity that is entirely adequate to its concept, any moment in which universal and particular coincide absolutely. But it seems that this flaw in nature — the discrepancy between nature and concept — is more *patently* manifested by those creatures which fail to fit under any concept whatsoever, or which slip a little further than is normal over the borders of any one concept, those organisms which we might define as 'abortions': 'The difficulty, and in many cases the impossibility of finding clear distinctions for classes and orders on the basis of empirical observation, has its root in the inability [*Ohnmacht*] of nature to hold fast [*festzuhalten*] to the realisation [*Ausführung*] of the Notion' (PNI, 216/35–36 §250R). The 'intermediate and defective formations' which fail to fall within classes defined by the conceptual order are described by Hegel as 'monsters', 'abortive' creatures that have 'miscarried' (*Mißgeburten*):

> Nature never fails to blur essential limits [*Grenzen*] with intermediate and defective formations [*mittlere und schlechte Gebilde*], and so to provide instances which qualify every firm distinction [*Unterscheidung*]. Even within a specific genus such as mankind, monsters [*Mißgeburten*] occur, which have to be included within the genus, although they lack some of the characteristic determinations which would have been regarded as essential to it. (PNI, 216/36 §250R)

To such intermediate formations one might add such half-breeds as the virus, and, miscegenated in another way, the *fossil*, stone-animal. But all of these examples can be treated as mere grist to the mill, bolstering Hegel's claim for the precedence of the concept: borders need to be drawn before they can be transgressed, and in order to 'classify such formations as defective [*mangelhaft*], imperfect [*schlecht*], or deformed [*mißförmig*]', we must presume a prototype of the species, and this delineation of the prototype cannot be carried out empirically, for it is precisely according to its measure that empirical species are identified in the first place: 'This prototype cannot be drawn from experience, but has as its presupposition the independence and worth of Notional determination' (PNI, 216/36 §250R). To identify a deviant, one must first have a concept *from* which it deviates.[16]

The beautiful animal in nature. Two lives: Nature to spirit, on the line.

So if the profusion of nature can result in ugliness, where does *beauty* reside?
  Why, in the animal, of course!
  Nature is imperfect, a shortfall of spirit with respect to itself (from the philosophy of nature's retrospective standpoint), an inchoate but gradually developing form of spirit, and the highest point of this development is the animal. The organism is that part of nature which runs right up against the threshold of spirit, and the resemblance it bears to spirit makes the animal beautiful.
  If we are in general concerned with the beautiful animal, we are speaking of an encounter between animal and *man*, in which man finds the animal charming. In terms of the dialectical process of the encyclopaedic system, these two

bump up against one another at the very end of the *Philosophy of Nature*, in the transition from the Philosophy of Nature to the Philosophy of Spirit.

Let us attempt to understand the precise way in which the animal may be said to occupy this position, as the most uncanny precursor of spirit.

Referring to the mutual externality of the parts of matter, *partes extra partes,* and the lack of necessity in their juxtaposition, Hegel tells us that, '[t]houghts are not co-ordinated in nature, for Notionlessness [*Begrifflosigkeit*] holds sway [*Herrschaft*] here, and each material point appears to be entirely independent of all the others' (PNI, 210/29 §248A). This should be set alongside the following remark on Life as the highest form of nature, closer to spirit (in the form of 'subjectivity') than any other: 'Subjectivity is first encountered in life, which is the opposite of extrinsicality [*Gegenteil des Außereinander*]' (PNI, 210/29 §248A).

Here the importance of Kant's theory of the organism for Hegel becomes most apparent. Hegel accepts Kant's vision of the animal as a conceptual totality and yet approaches it from an altogether different point of departure and with another destination in mind: 'The organic body is still a whole composed of a multiplicity of mutually external members [*Außereinanderseiende*, and hence still part of the material world of nature], but each individual organ subsists only in the subject, and the Notion exists [*existiert*] as the power [*Macht*] which unites them. In this way the Notion, which is something merely inward in Notionlessness, first comes into existence [*Existenz*] in life, as soul' (PNI, 210/29 §248A).

The parts of an organism are teleologically subordinated to the whole, organs and organism united in a way that intimately foreshadows the relation between a (universal) concept and its (particular) moments.[17] The concept first exists in and as the animating soul of the living thing. The animal has one foot in nature, one, tentatively, in spirit.

Hegel describes the transition from nature to spirit as a move from 'mere life' to 'living' in some fuller sense: a resurrection — to *immortal* life. 'It [the Idea] does this ['*positing* itself as what it is *implicitly*'] primarily in order to take on *living* being [*als* Lebendiges *zu sein*], but also in order to transcend [*aufhebe*] this determinateness, in which it is *merely life* [*nur Leben*], and to bring itself forth into the existence of spirit' (PNI, 216/36 §251, emphasis added).

The notion of life therefore occupies two positions in Hegel's system:

a) on the one hand we have a life lived exclusively within spirit, the life of the resurrection beyond finite individual life, the survival and transmission of cultural memory, the accumulation of self-consciousness that is passed on from one generation to the next and even between cultures, in the procession of world-history that stands under the sway of the 'world-spirit', a life for which death is not the end, but the beginning of a freedom that surpasses nature.

b) On the other hand we have the natural life of the organism which touches the threshold between nature and spirit, as an elementary self-relation, soul or 'subjectivity', which, simply by virtue of *living*, is touched by death even if it never draws its full consequences, and hence opens up a space within nature where the *spiritual* relation to death might form, since natural life must be *made* to die in order for free spirit to rise from its ashes:[18] 'the life of Spirit is not the life that shrinks from death and keeps itself untouched by devastation, but rather the life that endures it and maintains itself in it' (PhG, 19/36 §32). Thus the passage to supernatural freedom begins.

In an Addition to §251, Hegel describes life — in a way that seems to ambiguate between the life of nature and the life of spirit — as 'that being-within-itself' (*Insichsein*) which is achieved when the Notion returns to itself, attaining a 'subjective unity' that constitutes the germ of subjectivity proper, which is to say, 'spirit' (PNI, 217/37 §251A). As if to clarify why 'life' would be used to describe both the state of nature and the state in which the Idea returns to itself, Hegel insists that the externalised 'immediate' existence of the idea in the form of nature is not simply left behind 'as an empty shell' or 'rind' (*Rinde*) in the transfiguration of nature into spirit:

> Beginning with the externality in which it is first contained, the progress of the Notion is therefore a turning into itself in the centre [*Insichgehen ins Zentrum*], i.e. the assimilation into subjective unity or being-within-self [*Insichsein*] of what is, to the Notion, the inadequate existence of immediacy or externality; not so that the Notion withdraws from this existence and leaves it as an empty shell [*eine tote Schale*], but so that existence as such is immanent within itself, or adequate to the Notion, and so that being-within-self [*Insichsein*], which is life, itself exists. The Notion wants to break the rind [*Rinde*] of externality in order to become itself. Life is the Notion which has reached its manifestation and stands displayed in its clarity. (Ibid.)

'Life' is precisely the point reached at the *end* of the Philosophy of Nature, although in a sense the analogical character of which we would need to consider, it seems to extend everywhere in nature — Hegel speaks of '[t]he eternal life of nature [*Das ewige Leben der Natur*]' (PNI, 220/39 §252A) and in the third Part (*Abteilung*) of the *Philosophy of Nature*, on 'Organics', he suggests that even the dead earth in its geology may be considered an organism. Is this life natural or spiritual? Do *fossil rocks* live in the same sense that a bird lives or artworks live on? Are these entities seen as dynamic only because they are approached from the standpoint of spirit and hence touched by the finger of the dialectician and his 'organic' mode of thinking?

> Life is the Notion which has reached its manifestation [*Das Leben ist der zu seiner Manifestation gekommene Begriff*] and stands displayed in its clarity; at the same time however it is the most difficult for the understanding [*Verstande*, as opposed to Reason, *Vernunft*] to come to terms with, because the understanding finds it's easiest to grasp whatever is simplest, abstract, and dead [*Tote*]. (PNI, 217/37 §251A)

Reason is organic and alive; the understanding deals only with the dead.

The passage from the merely living to the life of spirit describes the transition from (the philosophy of) nature to (the philosophy of) spirit. Since each stage in a dialectic is always the determinate negation of what preceded it, we might say that the life of the *spirit* is precisely a sublation of the life of the *organism* and that it can arise only on that basis. This would not simply be another transition *within* spirit, but rather the transition from non-spirituality to spirit as such.[19]

Something like the spiritual procedure of sublation is indeed to be found in nature in the life of the organism and the processes which characterise it. This leads Hegel to make the following remarkable statement: '[a]s this supreme point of nature [*dieser höchste Punkt der Natur*], animal life is therefore absolute idealism [*Das Leben des Tiers ist so . . . der absolute Idealismus*]' (PNIII, 102/430 §350A).[20]

The organism's plural members maintain an 'ideal' unity thanks to the teleological governance of the animating soul, while the animal's metabolic relation with its environment, digesting the outside, somehow uses the *material* to fuel the *ideal* — food ultimately for the *mind*, 'food for thought'. By all these means, the animal is the natural analogue and forerunner of spirit and the dialectical gesture.[21]

The animal in its very animation foreshadows the process of idealisation, and one might, from a materialist point of view, even go so far as to say that the very fact of idealisation first emerges here, albeit in an inchoate form, and that here we uncover the transition from a non-dialectical form of transition to dialectical transition itself — the beginning of sublation proper. If Hegelian man can make sense of nature, if he finds it intelligible, it is because the logic of his own reason is obscurely manifest in its structures; but if this is so then the animal is most intelligible of all, foreshadowing as it does the very highest form of rationality, the dialectic.

For Kant, the organism was to be treated *as if* it embodied the concept, but here there is no analogy: the animal really is intelligible, it really is a concept.

But does this make it beautiful? Will something in Hegel's reworking of the animal's conceptual character allow him to speak freely where Kant could merely stutter, and affirm that the most intelligible and free moment in nature occurs when beauty and the animal *coincide*? Can Hegel allow us to make better sense of the beautiful animal?

To press on with our question, we shall turn briefly to Hegel's account of the organism from Part III of the *Philosophy of Nature*, which is recapitulated in an exceptionally clear way in his lectures on *Aesthetics*, where we also find an account of beauty and, most importantly, a contrast between artificial beauty and natural beauty.

To read about the animal, or at least the organic, we could have turned almost anywhere in Hegel's *œuvre*, since the organism, for essential reasons, crops up everywhere: at the end of the *Logic*, in the final part of the *Philosophy of Nature*, in the *Aesthetics*, even in the *Phenomenology*, where animals are spoken of as digestive machines of sublation, superseding the particularity of the givens of sense and anticipating human reason.[22] Animals leave their tracks all over Hegel's corpus: they are augurs of the dialectic and often its very figure — rational thought is the phoenix that takes flight in the guise of Minerva's wise old bird. Reason itself is organic — thought is a kind of animal.[23]

Chapter Four

Beauty in Nature — Hegel's *Aesthetics*

HEGEL'S *AESTHETICS*: BEAUTY IN NATURE

Hegel recapitulates his account of the organism from the *Philosophy of Nature* in a place we might not initially have expected: his lectures on *Aesthetics*. The *Aesthetics* gives an account of the beauty of the work of art, the work of man, which Hegel attempts to set off against another kind of beauty, and that is natural beauty. Within this realm, the beauty of the animal occupies a crucial place.

By reading the *Aesthetics* on the animal organism we shall clarify what remained obscure of the previous chapter, and that is the question of precisely what in nature is the source of beauty, and what is its relation to the animal? This will also have the effect of elucidating the relationship between Hegel and Kant on the topic with regard to which we have already witnessed their divergence — beauty. But there is an important structural analogy between the works of the two thinkers here, since both Kant's *Critique of Judgement* and Hegel's *Aesthetics* encompass within the span of a single book beauty and the animal, but the manner of their treatment is tellingly different in each case.

THE ORGANISM AND BEAUTY

Nature for Hegel is the manifestation of the concept, and the most adequate among these manifestations is the animal organism. It enjoys this status due to the way in which its members are united, ideally, by the soul of the animal, which mimics the manner in which the universal concept relates to its particular contents, its particularisations to which it spontaneously gives rise. This is why, in the *Aesthetics*, Hegel will repeat the trope we identified in the *Philosophy of Nature* and speak of the 'idealism of life' (*Idealismus der Lebendigkeit*) (A, 120/163), just as he describes the living creature's existence as 'objective idealism' (A, 123/166). 'For philosophy is not at all the only example of idealism; nature, as life, already makes a matter of fact what idealist philosophy brings to completion in its own spiritual field' (A, 120/163). The organism is a walking, purring concept.

What Hegel adds to his account from the *Philosophy of Nature* is that nature, and in particular life, constitutes the very first appearance of *beauty*. Life in nature is beautiful: since animals *are* concepts that breathe and amble around, the reality of the organism bears a sufficient resemblance to the concept which it embodies for it to be considered 'true' and certainly the most 'objectively true' part of nature. The shining forth of truth simply *is* beauty for Hegel: the manifestation of the supersensible ideal in the sensible real.

For the same reason, we might even say that nature as a whole, nature as such, is beautiful, for *all* of nature displays the concept to sense, just as far as it can: 'nature in general, as displaying to sense [*sinnliche Darstellung*] the concrete Concept and the Idea, is to be called beautiful' (A, 129/174). Nature is beautiful because, 'when we look [*Anschauung*] at natural forms that accord with the Concept [*begriffsmäßigen Naturgestalten*], such a correspondence [*Entsprechen*] with the Concept is foreshadowed [*geahnt*]' (A, 129/174).[1] The *Philosophy of Nature* devoted itself to identifying just such a natural adumbration of the conceptual: secretly it was always a treatise on beauty. Beauty is the sensible manifestation of truth. All of nature manifests this truth to different degrees, and the most truthful thing in nature is the animal — therefore it is the most beautiful.[2]

THE DISTINCTION BETWEEN BEAUTIFUL AND UGLY ANIMALS: ANIMATION

Not only are there distinctions between the degrees of truth and beauty on display in the natural world, there are degrees even within the animal kingdom, and indeed, not every animal appears beautiful to Hegel for they do not all embody the concept in the same way or with equal success. On this basis, one can distinguish between beautiful creatures and ugly ones, the more beautiful and the less, according to how perfectly each approximates the essence of animality, the concept.

Activity and mobility are crucial to an animal's beauty. Hegel avers that ugly animals, such as the sloth, are ugly because of their 'drowsy inactivity'

(A, 130/175), and that 'natural beauty is inner animation', which is to say the immanent activity of the soul as it unifies and animates the plurality of bodily members and organs. Since we know that this teleological process mimics the dialectical particularisation of the universal as it occurs at the level of thought, natural beauty is hereby identified with the most explicitly *dialectical* part of nature. Reason is mobile and the concept is alive, it determines its own development autonomously through determinate negation, the movement of the dialectic, and insofar as the animal soul does likewise, it manifests truth and is therefore beautiful.

That said, it is not only inactivity which makes an animal ugly: here we find, once again, monsters skulking in Hegel's text. The philosopher insists that, 'we cannot find beautiful' those forms which are amphibious, those animals which fail to fall within the conceptual divisions that reason would ideally wish to find in nature (A, 131/176). Hegel goes on to list, without classifying them all together under any obvious type, although many of them may be said to be amphibious in their elements: fish, crocodiles, toads, and a small swarm of insects. Even beyond amphibians in the narrow sense, the animals which seem assured of a place within the category of the ugly are the 'hybrids' (*Zwitterwesen*), interminglings (*Vermischungen*, the products of *vermischen*), monsters such as the duck-billed platypus in which bird and quadruped disturbingly commingle (A, 131/176).

In the following statement, Hegel seems to conjoin these two sets of ugly animals — the inactive and the monstrous, the unmoving and those which have gone too far or taken a wrong turning — and decisively excludes them from the realm of the beautiful:

> to the sphere of living natural beauty there belong neither the one-sided restrictedness [*einseitige Beschränktheit*] of organisation, which appears deficient and meaningless and points only to limited [*begrenzte*] needs in the external world, or such mixtures and transitions [*Vermischungen und Übergänge*], which, though not so one-sided in themselves, yet cannot hold fast to [*festzuhalten*] the specific characteristics of different species. (A, 131/176)

The inactive animal is already monstrous due to its lack of animation: the absence of free self-determination causes it to lag behind the march of the concept. Ugly animals are those furthest from spiritual life and seem to have only a tenuous commitment to *natural* life, either because of their sluggish torpor or because they have in other respects fallen between the cracks of a conceptual articulation, where there is no future. In either case, nothing will become of them. Ugly animals approximate the static comprehension of the Understanding, just as the most active and mobile creatures stand closest to Reason and to the concept.

Birds occupy a special place in this respect: their song is more akin to the speech of man than any other animal sound and their souls closer to the dynamism of reason. They are the most alive of living things in both senses of the term 'life', natural and spiritual. They are the most animal of animals, the most animated, and yet also the most spiritual, save man.

BREATH, SPIRIT, AND BIRDSONG

The animal comes closest to the human, closest to perfection, when it approximates human speech.

According to Aristotle, animal *phōnē* gives voice to feeling, specifically the sensations of pleasure and pain, while its superior, human form, *logos*, the more articulate and articulated voice, can also enunciate what is good and evil, just and unjust, it can speak the law and that which is right (*Politics*, 1253a). But making this distinction hold fast proves to be less than straightforward.

Hegel follows Aristotle in alerting us to the importance and uniqueness of '[t]he animal's vocal faculty [*Stimme*]' as an expression of sentience (PNIII, 105/433 §351A). His first example is a form of vocalisation upon which he bestows an especial status: birdsong. 'The theoretical emanation [*Das theoretische Sich-Ergehen*] of the singing bird is a higher kind of vocal faculty [*eine höhere Art der Stimme*] [. . .] and is so advanced that it has already to be distinguished from the general vocal power possessed by animals' (PNIII, 105–106/433 §351A).[3] Birdsong seems to stand apart from all other animal sounds. The tweeting of birds seems to hold a peculiar fascination for philosophers, as if it came to perplex the oppositions they would like to assert, so bewilderingly close does it come to the human voice — it can seduce us into thinking that it surpasses our own in freedom and beauty.

It has been the task of Derrida's deconstruction to point out that, for Hegel, as for most philosophers after Aristotle, the voice (*phōnē*) is the nearest the sensible material world draws to the ideal realm of thought (*logos*).[4] It is the reality most akin to ideality. Thus the spontaneous cries of the animal, while expressing feelings rather than rational thoughts, nevertheless emanate from that faculty of the animal which most closely approximates the transcendence of conceptual thinking: 'The vocal faculty comes closest to thought [*Die Stimme ist das Nächste zum Denken*], for in the voice pure subjectivity becomes objective, not as the particular actuality of a condition or sensation, but in the abstract element of space and time' (PNIII, 106/434 §351A).

Again following an Aristotelian tradition, Hegel posits an intimate relation between *pneuma* and *psychē*, 'spirit' and 'soul', respectively. The Greek *pneuma* is the Latin *spiritus*, 'breath', the breath of life within the animating soul (*psychē;* in Latin, *anima*). In Hegel, spirituality is the preserve of the human, and its life is not the life of animals but the concept that lives and breathes.

Breath may be shown to instantiate the dialectical gesture of positing one's self beyond one's self, before overcoming this separation and restoring unity to the self: spirit as *spiritus*. For Hegel, breath is the interior air which externalises itself in various ways, either visibly in the form of condensed gas on a cold day, tobacco smoke, or audibly by means of a particular kind of vibration — sound or speech (*phōnē*). When this vibration is articulated in a certain way it becomes language (*logos*). This externalisation is similar to and yet exceeds the animal's externalisation of its soul in the multiplicity of members and organs which work together to comprise a single unified organism. No animal will ever breathe on a mirror only to draw its own picture therein, or to smoke. But will it speak?

The voice embodies the particularising of a universal, a *flatus vocis*[5] which is then broken up by the human being's infinite powers of articulation to form a multiple yet coherent body of sound, a *logos*. Breath's vibration travels from the animal's interior to its exterior and thus expresses its subjectivity in objective form: 'The resonance [*klingt*] of animal being is autonomous [*aus sich selbst*] however. Subjective being reveals its psychic nature [*Seelenhafte*] by vibrating inwardly [*in sich erzittert*], and by merely making the air vibrate' (PNIII, 106/434 §351A). Soul is an inward vibration, and this soul is objectively manifested by an internal breath becoming voice as it sets the outer air aquiver. The more vocal the animal, the greater the interiority — or 'soul' — it seems to express in the exterior.

But why is the *bird*'s vocal capacity privileged above those other animals which squeak, chitter, and miaow? The especial character of the bird's song seems to be related to its capacity for *flight*, which may be taken to be the ultimate form of the animal's progressive uprooting from the gravity and immobility to which stone and plant remain entirely given over.[6] 'The animal's singularity of place is exempt from gravity however, for gravity is not rigidly binding upon the animal' (PNIII, 105/432 §351A). Thus in the bird's free flight, spirit comes as close as it can get to unbinding itself from matter and its oppressive gravitation, thus truly coming into its own. On the road to the liberation of thought and spirit from external matter, the taking flight of the animal brings to its highest point the uprooting of the plant that constitutes the animal's inherent motility. Clearly it is for essential reasons that the most apt metaphor for the gesture of spirit is an owl at dusk.[7]

In this regard, again, not all animals are equal. Hegel contrasts the bird's relation to its element (air) with the fish's relation to its milieu (water): 'The fish live in water and are mute, but the element of the birds is the air, and they soar freely through it; separated from the objective gravity of the earth, they emanate into the air, and express their sentience [*Selbstgefühl*, auto-affection] in their own element' (PNIII, 106/433 §351A).

In the air they 'soar *freely*' (*schweben die Vögel frei*) and are *liberated* from that earthly matter which does not autonomously produce sound but makes a noise only when struck. Thus the bird, inhabiting the ideal element of air, most opposed to the earth, stands furthest from the mute solidity of matter and closest to the human voice. It is as if one's vocal capacity were progressively liberated from the dumbness of metal and stone as one raised one's self higher and higher above it.

Hegel's exposition soon moves onto the internal vibration of the mechanism which produces the voice and its transmission into the outer air: that the bird's element is precisely the æther in which voice can resonate most freely, without the hindrance of solid earth, combined with the winged creature's ability to move at will in all directions, allowing it to disseminate its message still further, endows the song with a range and liberty which no other animal sound can possess. Birdsong would thus stand closest to the human Gospel, and we should not wonder that it was these creatures above all who seemed to understand St. Francis when he preached.

THE PERFECT ANIMAL

The animal becomes more perfect the more closely its sounds come to resemble the human voice. But unlike Kant's birds, the Hegelian fowl does seem to be put firmly in its place. The freedom of its soaring is a borrowed freedom, a reflected glory, even if the animal might be said to embody an incipient concept.

The more human an animal becomes, the more perfect an animal it is, the more accurately do its movements conform to the proto-dialectical essence of the animal soul. But this means that the most perfect animal will no longer be simply an animal; for Hegel, the perfect animal, strictly speaking, is the *human being*.

'These processes [of the living entity] are developed in the fullest and clearest way [*vollständigsten und deutlichsten ausgebildet*] in the human organism, which is the perfect animal [*vollkommenen Tier*]' (PNIII, 108–109/436 §352A). If there is a perfect animal, it is no longer (just) an animal: 'Man is an animal, but [. . .] precisely because he *knows* that he is an animal, he ceases to be an animal' (A, 80/112). Knowledge itself has a material effect. It is a characteristically Hegelian gesture to assert that *epistemology* has a direct impact upon *ontology*.

Man is perfect, and the animal, alas, falls short. As nature attains its highest point, the animal bespeaks a beginning of spirit, but an aborted beginning, unable to progress beyond the level of the animate soul and the ability to form habits. It is as if a line of development had been abruptly halted and the animal left forever unhappy, dimly sensing that it belongs to a lower level of creation. Hegel does indeed assert that the animal is condemned to a life of suffering, but he seems to attribute it more precisely to the fact that, '[t]he milieu of external contingency contains very little that is not alien, and as it is continually subjecting animal sensibility to violence and the threat of dangers, the animal cannot escape a feeling of *insecurity, anxiety, and misery* [unsicheres, angstvolles, unglückliches]' (PNIII, 179/502 §370R).[8]

In this context, Hegel reaffirms most explicitly that his way of reading the animal kingdom is suffused with hindsight: we have all along been interpreting *non*-human animals from the standpoint of the human: 'a *universal type* [Typus] is present in this supreme organism [*höchsten Organismus*, the human], and it is in and from this type that the significance of the undeveloped [*unentwickelten*] organism may first be ascertained and assessed [*erst erkennbar ist und an ihm entwickelt werden kann*]' (PNIII, 109/436 §352A). In Hegel, that which arrives at the end posits everything that came before as its predecessor, stripping away those only momentarily troubling aberrations which do not fit into its genealogy, and most of all those which constitute dead ends, lines of filiation which led nowhere. We shall meet one of these abortive species later on, in the form of the fossil.

In any case, the notion of the perfect animal as one which has left behind its animality leads Hegel to suggest that the ultimate reason for finding animals beautiful, and hence the only justification for so denominating them, is that they resemble human beings. At least in some cases, when one is speaking of the emotions which nature stirs within us, animals appear beautiful because they demonstrate the grace of spirituality. Beauty in nature is always an anthropomorphism:

> we call animals beautiful if they betray an expression of soul [*Seelenausdruck*] which chimes with human qualities such as courage, strength, cunning, good nature, etc. This is an expression which, on the one hand, does of course belong to the animals as we see them and displays [*darstellt*] one aspect of their life, but, on the other hand, it belongs to our ideas [*Vorstellung*] and our own emotions [*Gemüte*]. (A, 131–32/177, translation modified)

This notion serves to anticipate the later development of the *Aesthetics*, since ultimately the truest beauty for Hegel is not the animal's, but the human's.

HEGEL'S SUBLATION OF THE BEAUTIFUL ANIMAL

All in all, Hegel does overcome many of Kant's inhibitions when it comes to enunciating the syntagm 'beautiful animal', and he devises a theory of nature which allows him not only to make sense of the notion but even to assert that animal beauty is the highest nature can offer. And yet, an apogee is always the beginning of a descent, and at this moment of triumph, a discrepancy opens up. To be truly beautiful, an animal would need to renounce its animality and become human. Up to this point, Hegel had experienced no difficulty in invoking beauty and the beast in the same breath, but just here the fragility of their connection becomes apparent. The beauty we found in the animal world was merely an anticipation of humanity. Animals are not beautiful in themselves, but only insofar as they serve as mirrors to our narcissism.

In the end, the beauty of nature, even nature's highest manifestation, is not *true* beauty, for Hegel. First, it is an unself-conscious, sensuous beauty — not beautiful *for itself*, but only 'for *us*' (*für uns*) (A, 123/167). Animals do not *know* how charming they are, and for Hegel this impairs their beauty rather than — as we would be inclined to say — enhancing it:

> If therefore within this natural sphere we were to bring the inner total unity of life to our ken, this could be achieved only by thinking and comprehending; for in nature the soul *as such* [*die Seele* als solche] cannot make itself recognisable, because subjective unity in its ideality has not yet become explicit to itself [*für sich selbst*]. (A, 128/173)

Thus the beauty of animals is, for Hegel, not complete in itself, and nor is the idea. It is as if the incipient self-relation, which in the animal takes the form of auto-affection, here reveals its inadequacy: it falls short of self-*consciousness*. Ultimately, the soul of the animal is not '*present to itself*' (für sich selbst) as an 'ideal unity' (A, 132/177). Animal is to man — the perfection of the animal — as 'implicit' (*an sich*) is to 'explicit' (*für sich*) (A, 132/178).

Hegel suggests, here as elsewhere, that beauty in its highest form has an intrinsic connection with *individuality*, and individuality is precisely what members of the animal kingdom lack. The animal has 'only the beginning of a particular character' (A, 132/178). Man, modern Western man in particular, achieves this individuality in a consummate form.[9]

NATURAL AND SPIRITUAL BEAUTY

Apart from the irruption of birdsong from the pages of the *Philosophy of Nature*, we have been reading Hegel's *Aesthetics*. Why would natural beauty or the beauty of animals have been broached in such a text? Solely in order to set it off against artificial or, more precisely, spiritual beauty. Ultimately, the work of art, wrought by human hands, is, like man himself, more truly beautiful than the animal. The reason for this, broadly speaking, is that the artwork is produced deliberately, with the intention of being beautiful, by a being not of nature but of spirit, and hence with a certain self-consciousness on the part of the concept. The artwork is the product *of* spirit. Spirit objectifies itself in the artwork, and the subject recognises itself therein.[10] Hegel puts it quite frankly: 'everything spiritual is better than any product of nature [*alles Geistige ist besser als jedes Naturerzeugnis*]' (A, 29/49), or, in the more beautiful rendering by Bosanquet: 'everything spiritual is better than anything natural' (ILA, 34).

The artist creates an artwork. An artwork is a sensuous manifestation of spirituality, and in this sense its beauty is a reflection of man's rational spirit presented in concrete form to one's self and others. The artist inspires, animates, or ensouls nature by deliberately injecting a spiritual content into a material form. This elevates the artefact above the 'mere' work of nature and frees the natural material of that arbitrariness and irrationality, that particularity and contingency which taint nature and detain it just short of the concept.

This subordination is easier to sustain in the case of *non*-living nature, however, since the *living* thing is ensouled already and does not need man's help. But as we indicated in our opening remarks around the true and the bad infinite, it is clear why animals might be refused the beauty that human figures embody and that artworks are capable of displaying: insofar as they cannot *wholly* approximate the human beings whose traits they to an anthropomorphising gaze on occasion display, animals remain sunk in nature where the bad infinite is the rule. Life is merely life and not yet truly spirit.

But the inadequacy of natural beauty even affects the work of man. Hegel ultimately finds the beautiful *as such*, even in its very highest expression — art — to be inadequate to the truth of spirit. This is because it remains overly attached to its *material*, still too sensuous, insufficiently ideal (A, 79/111): the mirror in which beauty is reflected from creator to receiver has its tain. What is problematic about material is that, always and necessarily, it is a *particular* material, whether wood, stone, clay, paint, or sound. This renders the artwork excessively dependent upon the unpredictability and unevenness of *nature*: the grain of the wood, the lines of fracture in the stone — even when the beauty of man is in question. This is why the very highest form of art is the *poem*, for here the material taken up and moulded into a certain form has the least impact on the finished work. According to Hegel's idiosyncratic reading, the particular words chosen for the poem, along with their sounds, are an *arbitrary* means of conveying the intelligible content, that ideal spiritual meaning which is the true 'message' of the work of art and the ultimate source of its beauty.

This is as far as the artwork can go, and even here there is a certain dependence — today we are more likely to say an *infinite* dependence — of content upon form, in the materiality of the words' sound, their rhythm and rhyme, and even in their written form with its characters and marks. The poem is singular, untranslatable, and without the possibility of paraphrase. So it turns out that the zenith of artistic creativity shares something with the pinnacle of natural creation, the transition from animal to man: art, upon achieving its perfection, immediately ceases to be — caesura. Just as the artwork comes into its own, it has already begun ceasing to be. Just like the animal.

From art then, we are compelled to move on to the other two forms of 'absolute spirit' — religion, and finally philosophy, where spirit returns to itself and assumes its highest form, pure thought thinking itself, the full self-transparency of thought, a reversion to the beginning, the *Logic*, where God's mind contemplated itself for want of anything better, in temporary isolation from everything real.

TRANSITION: LEAVING BEHIND

The *Philosophy of Nature*, and the *Aesthetics*, perhaps the whole of Hegel at least until the very end, is a philosophy of departure, a thought of farewell. Everything is left — which is not to say erased without a trace but raised to an ideal level and so 'left' also in the sense of 'left alone', as in the demand to 'leave it be', to allow something to be what and where it is. For Hegel, each entity is *truly* what it is only when it has run its course.[11]

The same might be said of the beautiful animal. Natural beauty is a step on the way to artistic beauty, and the animal in its manifestation of soul is a rung on the ladder by which nature ascends towards the human embodiment of spirit. The animal is what it *will have* become.

But this means that the Hegelian dialectic is never able to say that there is such a thing as a perfect and perfectly beautiful animal *in* itself, an animal which is not precisely thereby a human being. The fully functioning dialectic would gather up such an 'imperfect' instance (the non-human animal) into its machine and transform it into a mere moment, to be surpassed by the ensuing procession. Dialectic is able to view the animal only in hindsight, as a precursor to the human being, beautiful only inasmuch as he is. But this does not allow us to understand an animal which would be beautiful in itself. With the animal, taken sincerely *in* its sincerity and charm, we find a bad infinite which is not only indifferent to the good but heedless of the very opposition between bad and good. The animal is that moment which remains content in its indifference to the dialectical machine, outside of history, undeveloping, like a coelacanth. The animal has been left behind by any sort of progress and merely lives without lacking anything, insisting in the circularity of its habitual paths with absolute sincerity.

It is as if the dialectic, after its initial experience with sense-certainty, is too canny to recognise sincerity. Hegel's refusal of perfection to an animal that does not know itself to be perfect is precisely what we are attempting to resist: for Hegel, one cannot be a perfect animal, or indeed a perfect anything, without immediately thereby becoming something else. It will take a renewed modesty on the part of man to gaze upon the beautiful animal and not see in it merely a mirror of his own perfection. Truly to capture such an animal in its beauty, sincerity and charm, we would need to *freeze* the dialectic just before the animal slips away from itself and becomes fully human, as nature finds itself entirely overcome by spirit. Hegel might have considered such a voluntary ossification of reason a kind of madness, or even a bestiality on the part of the philosopher. All the same, we shall attempt it, with and beyond Hegel himself: to treat a process which should be alive with a non-natural life surpassing the 'mere life' of animals as if it were dead — as if that spiritual life had become a *fossil*.

What of those animals of which nothing became?

Illustration 4.1.

Chapter Five

Fossils and the Fossilisation of the Dialectic

There is another kind of animal we should like to consider, and that is the fossil, the stone-animal. Fossilisation operates in precisely the opposite direction to dialectical sublation and thus drags it back to a threshold at which dialectical rationality itself ceases to be organic and turns to stone — becoming fossilised. Only in such a state can the dialectic properly train its attention upon the animal without constantly straying ahead to the human being it would like to think of as its perfection.

THE FOSSIL OF THE DIALECTIC

What are fossils? Has philosophy ever truly spoken of them?[1]

Let us consider the fossils of those animals which no longer exist or have exactly the same form as of old, as if in the intervening æons no time at all had elapsed for the coelacanth or nautilus — or more precisely, perhaps, no history. They constitute a dead end in evolution. They became nothing and saw no need to: these animals were not sublated, but simply ossified. Dialectic has two options when it comes to such entities: it can either discard them as not assimilable to a dialectical sequence; or dialectic can learn from the fossil to understand *itself* differently and, so far from disregarding the fossil, to fossilise itself.

We shall consider the process of fossilisation as a precise counter-movement to the dialectical motion of spiritualisation. Fossils would be elements within nature which are just as indifferent to the opposition between good and bad infinity as are living animals in their habits, and to understand them we must become as indifferent as they are, allowing our dialectic to dawdle for a while.

We shall see that this gesture is necessary if the dialectic is to encompass the perfect and beautiful animal.

FOSSIL-WRITING

First, we need to build up a properly philosophical concept of the fossil.

One crucial aspect of this, pointed out by Quentin Meillassoux, is that the fossil constitutes a trace of the past, the record of a time before man and in some cases — if we think of fossilised wood and leaves — prior to the age of the animal. We already have some resources for conceptualising this trace, and first among them is Derrida's generalisation of the notion of *writing* beyond the literal sense in which it refers primarily to the human use of a stylus to preserve thought or speech and thus to keep records which will outlive the fragility and finitude of the memory they supplement and supplant — the conscious activity of transcribing concepts (in ideogrammatic writing) and sounds (in phonetic or alphabetic writing). Writing in its generalised sense would include every form of trace, any mark left in a medium that is *present* by something which is *no longer* present (or not yet) — the presence of absence — with the marks constituting a 'written' record of that absent entity. This expansion beyond the 'strict sense' is marked by the prefix 'archi-' in Derrida's word, 'archi-writing'.

In light of this, it is no stretch at all to describe the fossil as a kind of writing — indeed, we already speak of the 'fossil-record'.

The fossil as writing will cause some trouble for the Hegelian dialectic and specifically for the distinctions it wishes to uphold between nature and history, or nature and spirit.[2]

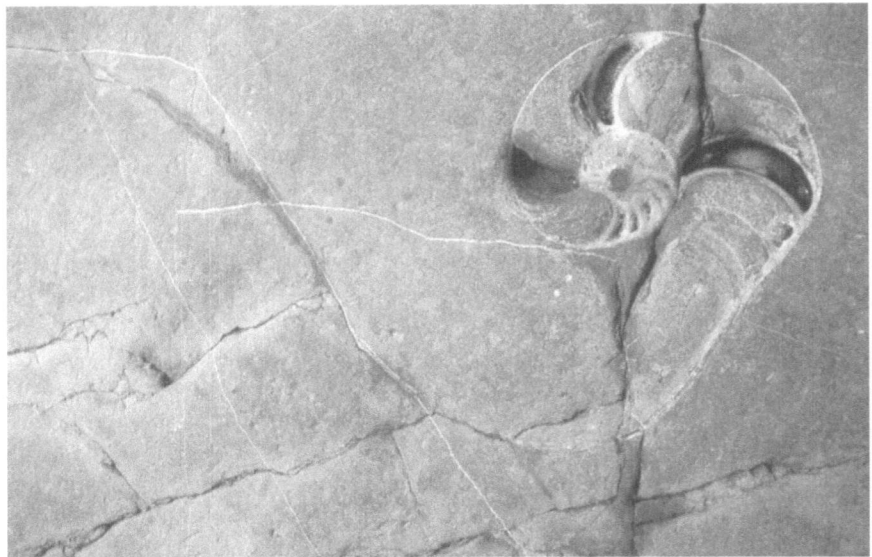

Illustration 5.1. Fossil writing, near Lyme Regis.

Illustration 5.2. Fossil scribbles.

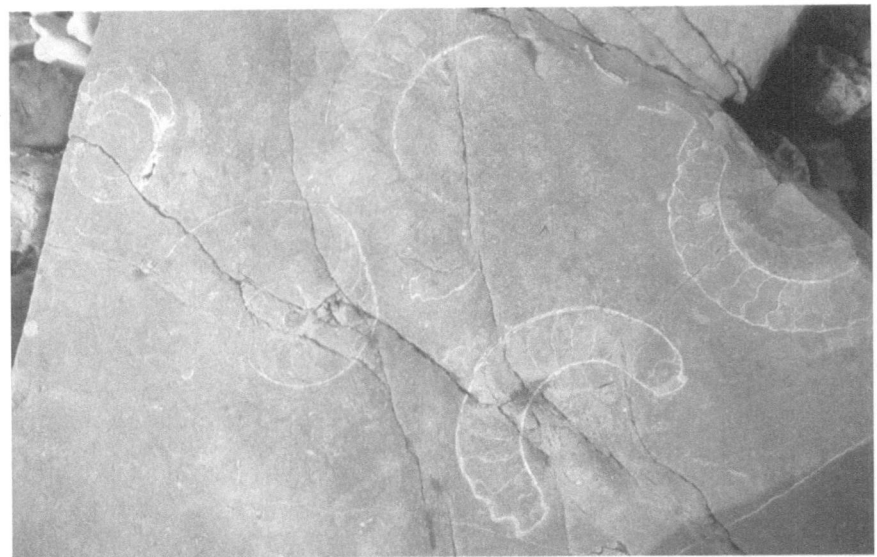

Illustration 5.3. Fossil graffiti.

Illustration 5.4. Fossil graffiti.

Illustration 5.5. Fossil graffiti.

Fossil writing, however, is unlike any writing we have yet seen in philosophy, even in deconstruction. So let us begin to construct a concept of its formation; we shall then go on to compare it more closely with the deconstructive notion of the trace; and finally, we shall determine the extent to which it departs from Hegel's own theory of writing. This will help us shed some light on the effects of fossilisation within the dialectic itself.

THE FORMATION OF FOSSILS

How is fossil writing formed?

First, the animal must die, and it must decay, and with these two gestures in conjunction a space will have been carved out in the material real. This void is a necessary precondition for the fossil-writing that is to fill it.[3] What first enters the breach is water, and this will play a crucial role in the fossil's development. Most of the fossils that remain to us — which is to say those which have survived in a legible form — lived and died in water. Their sarcophagi are to be found in the sedimentary rock laid down on the beds of ancient rivers and oceans. Water seeps into the hollow left behind by the decay of the once-living body of the animal, and minerals are deposited there. Over an extremely long period of geological time, the matter which has entered these spaces becomes compressed and condensed to the point of eventually constituting a stone replica of the living animal, which perfectly fits the mould that its absence has left.

Fossil-writing is an inscription the setting down of which is followed by an almost unfathomably extended period of latency; eras pass before a legible record comes to appear, and even beyond that, another remarkably protracted hiatus must elapse as the fossil-record awaits the arrival of a reader capable of even noticing it, let alone recognising it as a script — to say nothing of being able to decipher its inscription.[4]

The animal to be fossilised writes itself without the intention to write and without any intention of being read.[5] Indeed it writes during an epoch in which there are no readers capable of experiencing it *as* writing — perhaps it will not even become 'writing' until such a reader makes its appearance.

While it seems likely that these fossils were from the start and throughout the process of their formation at least in principle visible, tangible, and odorous to some forms of sentient life — perhaps even in their deepest and most obscure burial, to microscopic life — in order to be read in their full significance they must await an extremely advanced form of *homo sapiens*. If, in order to understand our encounter with this petrified creature *as* an act of reading, the nature of reading and writing themselves must have been rendered thoroughly transparent then perhaps we could say that the eternally patient fossil was waiting for the arrival of both G. W. F. Hegel and Jacques Derrida, among others still later. It has, in other words, taken an inordinately long time to generate the elements of a human being and a philosophy which might be capable of rendering the fossil intelligible and of understanding what it might mean to describe fossils as a kind of writing.

The fossil, then, is a trace of the most curious kind, so curious that one might well wonder if either the Hegelian or the Derridean discourse will ultimately be able to contain it.

FOSSIL-WRITING, METAPHYSICAL WRITING, AND ARCHI-WRITING

That said, we remain infinitely indebted to Derrida for the very idea that fossils might be construed as a kind of written trace. Let us determine the extent to which deconstruction can accommodate the fossil in its literality.

On the metaphysical, which is to say pre-deconstructive, account of writing, the trace is an external record of a concept that is internal to the soul, or of a word that remains proximate to the soul in being spoken with the living breath of the speaker. Speaking remains under the control of the author of that speech, whereas a leaf of paper always risks being blown away, or the author's forgetfulness and absence, right up to the point of death. As Derrida pointed out, writing is for this reason described by Plato as an orphan (Derrida 1981 [1972], 77/86–87). It constitutes a record or 'memory' external to the living memory of the soul. This has advantages and disadvantages: it is possible for the note to endure as a reminder of something that our finite recollection is always capable of forgetting; but at the same time, its physical separation engenders the possibility of a loss of meaning without any hope of restoration. With the separation from the living and breathing speech that could have spoken up for this writing, now bereft of support, the text is confronted with the eventuality that its meaning will never be deciphered, for its 'father' is no longer there to explain it.

Derrida does not disagree with this account of writing, but merely disputes the idea that such a written trace must always be *derived* from and hence secondary to a fully present living speech and the absolutely transparent intention which governs it. If metaphysics, which includes all of philosophy, if not all of Western thought and language, posits a hierarchy between speech and language, *phōnē* and *logos*, and if this, like all oppositions, privileges just *one* of its opponents, implicitly or explicitly considering that half to be the *origin* of the other, then Derrida will put this relation and this privileging in question. He will do so in the name of a certain writing that conditions the very *possibility* of that speech which will always have been presented as standing at writing's very foundation.

At the very least we can say that a distinguishing mark — in other words, a written trace — is needed to distinguish between two sounds or 'phonemes', and these sounds are precisely what constitute articulated human speech. According to the structural linguistics of Ferdinand de Saussure, speech can only be the enunciation of a pre-existing system of language comprised of 'signifiers' that have no essence or presence of their own but acquire their individual identity only by being differentiated from all of the other signifiers in the language. The very *absence* of these other signifiers is thus *present* within each signifier, in the form of a trace, and indeed these traces constitute the very body of the signifier itself, for signifiers have no other more substantial presence. Derrida's name for such traces is archi-writing, an inscription which conditions speech and puts in question both its priority and the idea of a full and original presence upon which it would depend. The hierarchical opposition between life and death, speech and writing, is thus placed in doubt.

But where do fossils stand in relation to both the metaphysical and the deconstructive conception of writing?

The fossil seems to occupy a curious position between the two.

With metaphysics, the fossil implies a precedence of the living with respect to the dead: the fossil is — or once was — an animal: it was living, and now is dead. The living spirit has become a dead letter, and events needed to proceed in that order for the fossil-writing to appear.

But the comparison with metaphysical writing may be taken a step further: fossils correspond up to a certain point not just with the genesis of writing but with its very nature.

Writing always introduces the possibility of a certain dissemination of meaning, its infinite equivocation and even its loss. This risk is a consequence of the gap that separates the writer's intention-to-say-and-to-mean something (*vouloir-dire,* 'meaning') from the written marks themselves, which are inscribed in an external medium. Thus, first of all, a *spatial* distance is introduced between meaning and its record. This spatially distinct mark is then able to endure long after the author has moved away, even infinitely far, into the obscurity of death — and thus a *temporal* discrepancy is also opened up, heightening the danger of dissemination.

How do things stand here with respect to the fossil? In this case, spatial difference does not come into it, for the living body and the dead trace must occupy the same space; but the temporal difference is greatly magnified, and over the ages in which the fossil rises to legibility there is the most acute possibility of degradation in the recording, a lapse not in living memory but in the earth and its strata, unfolding with the glacial languor of geological motion.

So if for a moment we discount the absence of spatial distinction between the living body and its dead inscription, fossils might plausibly be taken to count as a form of writing which would by and large be recognised as such by the metaphysical tradition.

But then things become less clear.

In the formation of fossils, the animal body is bequeathed to posterity, but involuntarily: the animal writes without any *intention* of doing so. Let us therefore investigate the possibility that one of the sharpest distinctions between fossil-writing and the metaphysical form lies in the absence of deliberation that would govern its setting-down.

We should give this point its full weight since we might well have thought the fossil strongly reminiscent of one of the most metaphysical ideas of nature and writing that we possess — the 'book of nature'.[6] According to a conception common among Christian thinkers of the Middle Ages, if not always and everywhere, the whole of creation was saturated with signifiers of god's intention, the book demonstrating on its every page the infinite knowledge, power, and benevolence with which He set about creating it. Nature thus constitutes a volume whose words merely await an enlightened or credulous human being to come along and decipher in it the signs of an intelligent designer.

The difference between this religious hermeneutics and a secular interpretation of nature would be that on the latter account the fossil inscribes itself in nature without *meaning to*. But this difference is everything.

Illustration 5.6.   Shale pages in the Book of Nature, Lyme Regis.

We know that metaphysics asserted a certain distance between writing and authorial intention, and yet here, in the case of the fossil, the *possible* absence of paternal support that characterises all writing becomes an ineluctable *necessity*. The living body of the fossil structurally cannot be alive at the same time as the dead writing that its body eventually constitutes. This is precisely a result of the lack in *spatial* distance between the body of the animal and its written record — which we temporarily allowed ourselves to place in parentheses. It must now gradually be restored to its full significance.

Such a complete absence of intention would hardly be allowed on the traditional account of writing — this unwitting inscription seems to exceed by too great a margin the narrow sense of writing to which metaphysical theories tended to restrict themselves. Thus, when it comes to the question of intention, the fossil record would seem to trespass the borders of metaphysics, if only by a hairsbreadth, and edge a little closer to deconstruction.

Even a relatively cursory glance reveals that the fossil shares some of the positive traits that Derrida attributes to archi-writing. From the beginning, in *Of Grammatology* (the first version of which was composed in 1964), Derrida will speak of writing in the form of certain *biological* inscriptions: these include genetic codes and the retention of (memory-) traces, which are essential to the progressive formation of habits (Derrida 1997 [1967b], 84/125–26).[7] The idea that a living being can receive traces, and indeed that its life depends upon these written marks, is clearly present in Derrida's work. Is it but a short step from here to thinking of the animal's entire body becoming trace?[8]

THE FOSSIL BEYOND DECONSTRUCTION AND METAPHYSICS

In truth, one is given cause to wonder whether in fact the deconstructive theory of a generalised writing at the basis of sense, even alongside the theory of biological traces, can fully capture what is peculiar to the writing of the fossil. Curiously enough, the fossil seems to represent in at least one of its facets a reversion to a *pre*-deconstructive, metaphysical form of writing. We have already seen which: fossils, by their very nature, cannot but imply the precedence of the living animal over the dead writing that it is to become. At the same time, we have yet to draw the full consequences of the fact that the dissemination which takes place in fossil-writing is *temporal* rather than spatial. This is distinctly unlike Derrida's vision of writing. So let us now develop both of these points in order to illuminate the ways in which fossil-writing may not altogether adequately be captured by the Derridean account.

In fossilisation, the living body becomes absent and yet leaves behind an enduring trace that is akin to an epitaph or sarcophagus. The fossil is a living body turned to stone, become hieroglyphic, a living word transformed into an inflexible dead letter that retains its outline. There is a life, akin to speech, which is recorded by a writing that would be posterior to it — the living body of the animal is immortalised in these stony traces. The animal cannot live at the same time as its fossilised form, and so there must be a chronological disparity between its living and dead state, and they must follow one another in that order. To that extent, the fossil is *writing* but not *archi*-writing, writing in its metaphysical guise.

This is the first respect in which the fossil eludes Derrida's notion of writing. But there is another difference, which does not amount to such a 'regression', for there is one aspect of the fossil which seems to elude *both* the metaphysical theory of writing *and* the deconstructive. Here we return to the idea of dissemination and the protracted period of development from latency to manifestation that the fossil undergoes. The writing of the fossil, unlike that of the human is, despite the temporal delay, not *spatially* separable from its living precedent. Fossil-writing is spatially identical with the disposition of the living body itself: it has merely turned to stone — the fossil animal will have written its own record with its very body. Thus the difference between life and its written fossilic trace is a temporal but not a spatial one.

The possibility of dissemination does indeed arise with the fossil but only thanks to the dimension of time, not space. The lack of spatial distance *limits* dissemination, while the temporal discrepancy between the construction and appearance of the written record reintroduces the possibility of scattering and loss. In the end it is not certain that this distinction between time and space when it comes to dissemination is something that deconstruction could allow: '*différance*' is explicitly both temporal ('deferral') and spatial. And even for metaphysics, the written mark must be separable from the spoken word and its guiding intention: this is even part of its definition, and it seems that this separability is not merely temporal. Indeed, deconstruction derives its definition of writing *from* the metaphysical concept, which it then merely generalises and re-positions with respect to the traditional hierarchies.

How far, then, have we progressed in our attempt to engineer a concept of fossil-writing, by means of this comparative study of fossils, metaphysical writing, and archi-writing? We have learned to generalise the notion of writing from a narrow metaphysical sense in which, for all the potential risks to the preservation of meaning inherent in the exteriority of the medium, an intention to write preceded the act of inscription. And yet, the fossil seems to resist capture by deconstruction and stray back towards the metaphysical in the precedence it gives to the living over the dead. But we have taken a step further: the fossil seems to elude *both* metaphysics and deconstruction insofar as it involves no spatial distinction between the living animal and the dead fossil record.

In general, the fossil is a kind of photograph of the living being at the moment of its termination, a death mask or effigy.[9] To make more headway in our attempt to conceptualise the fossil in this sense, let us seek assistance from Hegel. This will lead us back to the relation between fossils and the dialectic.

FOSSIL WRITING AND HEGELIAN WRITING

A fossil is a record of a certain period of (pre-)history created unintentionally by the very living body of the animal, a cast which came to fill the exact void that its living body left behind. This casting took place in an era populated by nothing that was capable of reading this record or of recognising the face that was so gradually being inscribed in this stone. After an almost inconceivable period of geological time, the ossified animal became legible, and later still a reader arose who was capable of deciphering these marks.

Thanks to the deconstructive theory of the trace, we are able to read the fossil as a kind of writing, but the discrepancies we have identified between Derrida's theory of writing, the metaphysical concept, and the writing of the fossil have given us some insight into the peculiarity of the petroglyphic trace. We shall now contrast our concept of the fossil-trace with the theory of writing that one finds in Hegel, and examine the way in which Hegel himself tries and ultimately fails to incorporate fossils into his own philosophy. We shall then determine how this failure, along with the discrepancy between the two kinds of writing, renders our concept of the fossil more precise and in turn allows us to modify our understanding of the dialectic.

There is writing in Hegel — indeed it lies at the very heart of his thought, for it is a writing that makes possible a certain kind of survival, an outliving of the natural life of the body: this writing thus enacts the idealising motion of dialectical sublation. For this reason, a further investigation of Hegel's thought will do more than just teach us about the fossil for its own sake. Since Hegel himself employs writing as a metaphor or metonym for the dialectical process itself, the contrast between this writing and that of the fossil will enlighten us as to what must be done to the dialectic in order to clear a space within it for the fossilised animal. It is in just such a space that the living, breathing, beautiful animal might thrive, for in order to make sense of this beloved creature, the dialectic itself may have to undergo a procedure of fossilisation.

Medusa turned the living being to stone — perhaps the intransigence of the mute rock will have a similar effect on the organic thought of the dialectic.

THE TWO PLACES OF WRITING IN HEGEL'S DIALECTIC: DIALECTIC AND HISTORY

Writing has at least two functions in Hegel's system: First, as a metaphor for dialectical production.

At the beginning of the *Phenomenology of Spirit*, Hegel subjects the assumptions of vulgar, pre-philosophical consciousness to an immanent examination. First among these assumptions is that consciousness stands in direct relation with a singular space and time ('here' and 'now') which really subsist independently of it. This amounts to an implicit construal of the nature of consciousness and knowledge which Hegel names 'sense-certainty' (*sinnliche Gewißheit*) (PhG, 58/82 §90).

Hegel's task here is to demonstrate the presence of an implicit dialectic within this position, an inherent contradiction that will reveal it to be unstable, necessitating movement and initiating a self-overcoming. This 'shape (or formation) of consciousness' must be shown to pass over into some other form as it attempts to resolve the contradiction. Hegel sets about his work by demonstrating that any attempt on the part of consciousness to refer to a singularity must fail, and this failure is a result of the nature of *language*.

But why does language come into it?

We must use language in order to draw attention to the indexed entity, or simply to explicate what we take ourselves to 'mean'. The way in which language refers to singular entities is by means of 'indexicals' or demonstrative terms such as 'here', 'now', and 'this'.

For reasons that will become clear only later, Hegel proceeds to imagine what would happen to a statement containing such indexical terms if it were *written down*. He considers an attempt to refer to the present moment with the sentence, 'Now is night' (*das Jetzt ist die Nacht*) (PhG, 60/84 §§95–96). It turns out that when these spoken words are transcribed in written form, they can no longer claim a singular referent but rather reveal themselves to have a *universal* extension. This is because, unlike the spoken form, the written text can be detached from its context, and it was only this context that determined the *referent* of the indexical terms and hence the conditions for the statement's truth or falsity.

The written sentence can be extracted from the occasion and site of its inscription because, unlike the speech it transcribes, the inscription endures, it remains in existence for a timespan sufficiently protracted for its context to change. Night turns to day, and the sentence, 'now is night', once true, becomes false. The statement changes from truth to falsehood and is thus transformed into its very *opposite* by the mere passage of the sun and time.

If the statement had not been written down, it would never have had the chance of 'becoming stale', of transmuting into falsity (PhG, 60/84 §95). The written character is essential if the word 'now' is to remain self-same over time and thus end up referring to the very opposite of its original intent — when 'now' it is *day*.

That the word 'now' can index two moments which are diametrically opposed — day and night — establishes the fact that this indexical may indifferently pick out *any* moment in time. This leads Hegel to the notion that the 'now' and indeed all the indexicals (here, now, this, I . . .) do not pick out any particular thing; since they can refer to anything and everything, they are in fact *universals*.

In this context, writing functions as a precondition for the entity's dialectical transition into its opposite, and thus for the transition from singular to universal.

'Speculative sentences', which express a dialectical movement from one state to another, the latter being the explicated truth of the former, must be read *twice* if one is to grasp the truth of the statement. This truth, this result, includes the path that it was necessary to take in order to get there, and for anything to be read twice (or even once) it must be *written down*. Without being written down, the statement could not be read in a dialectical fashion as incorporating both the initial reading and the opposite of that reading. It is as if the determinate negation of the initial reading could be represented by exactly the same sentence but struck through so as to remain nevertheless legible.[10]

Given the position of the Sense-Certainty dialectic at the very outset of the *Phenomenology of Spirit*, itself the prelude to Hegel's encyclopaedic system as a whole, we might say that the dialectic could not begin without writing; writing is a precondition for the System.[11]

The second role of writing in Hegel's system shows it to be a precondition not merely of the dialectic but of the self-consciousness of spirit. Writing makes not only the beginning of the dialectic possible but also its end.

Spirit's march towards self-consciousness takes the form of *history*. Hegel's philosophy of history, and indeed the very idea of history as such, emerges at the end of the Philosophy of Objective Spirit, before subjective and objective spirit are raised to the level of *absolute* spirit, in which the one, subjective mind (*Geist*), recognises itself in the other, its objective cultural products — tangible and intersubjectively shared manifestations of the presence of spirit. Only by learning what it is to be rational and free can spirit *become* so, and history is the edifying educational process whereby spirit becomes aware of what it can do. Spirit achieves this by viewing the progressive development of its own rationality and freedom as it is reflected in objective form in the 'theatre of history', each epoch played out before it. Writing makes this history possible (cf. WH, 135/83f).

By means of its enduring, separable and hence transmissible character, writing makes it possible for the past to survive, in the accumulated layers of the historical record. The written archive allows what has gone by to outlive its own passing and the extinction of all those who were alive to witness it and recall it in living speech and memory. Writing is recording — it enables the production of cultural memory, an objective form of recollection which exceeds the longevity and subjectivity of living memory, and hence it allows an intergenerational continuity to develop — in short, a history.

History is the 'tradition' or transmission of the traces of the past. What distinguishes the *Philosophy* of History from 'historiography' in the empirical sense is that, in the former, the historical remains are selected and arranged in a certain way: a properly philosophical history will make sense of the mass of contingent and often irrational events that took place by organising a single narrative recounting of what occurred, rewriting events in such a way as to discover *sense* within them. This single sense — also a sense of direction (*Sinn* or *sens*) which is shown to characterise world history — is the gradual increase in rationality and freedom that may be discerned if we cast a philosophical eye over the passing millennia. The Philosophy of History thus elevates its subject to the level of rational necessity and hence to the plane of meaning and the ideal. The writing of history is an idealisation, and therefore a sublation. The phoenix rises from the ashes in the form of a pencil sketch of itself, or rather, a written account of its appearance.

In both the *Phenomenology* and the *Lectures on World-History*, writing embodies the survival of a singular thing beyond its natural life, and the entrance of that singularity into the ideal universality which is its truth: 'Julius Caesar' becomes '*the* Caesar'. My singular thoughts and memories become the possession of the whole culture through their inscription, preservation, and publication. My immediate, mystical intuitions, which seem absolutely profound and peculiar to me, are shown up in their generality and often their banality when I am compelled to articulate them before others. Language's truth is revealed most acutely in writing: as soon as being is expressed in language, it is transmuted from singularity into generality, or in Aristotle's terms, from primary substance to secondary essence (*ousia*).[12]

A perfect metonym for the way writing functions in Hegelian dialectic is the memorial inscription, the epitaph, on a gravestone or monument, indeed the writing of an obituary or death notice, the penning of an entry in the 'book of remembrance'. The most revealing of all these testamentary inscriptions is the most simple: the mere *naming* of the Dead.[13] The engraving of the nomination which replaces and survives the living person is an exceptional example of Hegelian sublation, the transformation of a singular concrete entity into a particular moment of an ideal universal concept, the transition from mere natural life to eternal spiritual life. Writing allows us to pass between the two notions of life that we have already identified in Hegel — natural life, the particular life of the individual, and the spiritual life which endures the death of the particular and accedes to the supernatural life animated by the dialectical movement of the concept. Writing allows spiritual survival by freeing the spirit from its natural carapace and bringing out the dialectical tracery implicit in the living being, its conceptual skeleton.

PETRIFIED LIFE

In light of the intimate connection between writing and sublation, the timeless survival of the past in a perfect idealised form, one might have thought that fossils would play a prominent role in Hegel's thought.

The fossil certainly seems to be a Hegelian animal, on the face of it. This remarkable beast is an organism become stone, and Hegel refers, apparently approvingly, to the description of nature given by his keenest rival, F. W. J. Schelling, 'a petrified intelligence' (*eine versteinerte... Intelligenz*) or 'frozen intelligence' (PNI, 206/25 §247A).[14] Nature is thought turned rock, yet viewed by the philosophy of nature in its flight towards spirit. Hegel thus indicates the implicit spirituality locked away at the core of the stone, awaiting liberation by philosophy.

Is the notion of fossilisation intimated in this characterisation of nature as 'spirit turned to stone'? With the fossilised animal but also with the endless petrified teeth, shells, leaves, and stumps of wood scattered across the surface of the globe, might we have something close to a literal rendering of Hegel's 'petrified intelligence', albeit one which we might be more reticent to describe as 'intelligence'?

It seems not, for the petrification if not of intelligence then at least of life is rather the *reversal* of sublation, a stout refusal on the part of natural life to become spiritual, and in its place a return to earth and stone. The fossil would thus amount to something like a retrospectively perceived *regression* from spirit.

All writing involves something like a dead letter, but for Hegel this dead letter is the support of living spirit. The fossil-inscription, on the other hand, leaves behind an exclusively *material* remnant, and one which does *not* have the function of making possible the idealising transition from singularity to universality that the dialectic involves. Hegelian writing cannot incorporate the bodily inscription of a calcified animal, only its spiritual transfiguration.

The history attested by the fossil seems to fall outside the Hegelian conception of history as a progressive rationalisation. The fossil is a writing which cannot be conceived as a presupposition made by history, for it is rather a writing that exists within *nature*, and it records in a way that does not lead to sublation. It need not be considered a precondition of spirit.

This is the case even if one thinks of the survival of its remnant as among the preconditions of the somewhat non-Hegelian category of '*natural* history'. This putative form of history — or at least the chapter which concerns fossils — would not interest Hegel, since it does not necessarily write solely about the survival of those entities which evince a steadily more rational structure. One would simply have to invoke again the abortive lines of descent and the arrested coelacanth as counter-examples: that of which a record is hereby left is a species isolated from the march of (natural) history, like an ox-bow lake abandoned by its river, where a placid golden fish glides without ever mutating — a cul-de-sac or dead-end, chronicled in a 'history' which is merely a scattered and fragmentary set of memories without logical order.

Not that such a natural history had been thoroughly developed in Hegel's day, and given the dependence of the Philosophy of Nature on the contemporary state of the natural sciences, Hegel himself cannot be expected fully to have understood the fossil. And sure enough he did not. In which case we might say that history can begin and end without fossils and their writing.

If fossils constitute a crime against the dialectic, it will be revealing to see what Hegel himself makes of them. For in truth, if one looks hard enough, one can unearth fossils even in Hegel's own text. Their presence, and the particular manner of their presentation, demonstrate that we are not moving altogether beyond Hegel and the dialectic here, since, as it turns out, Hegel tries and up to a certain point fails to find an appropriate place for them. This failure will help us to demonstrate that the Hegelian dialectic can and must be somewhat modified if it is to capture the fossil — and therefore the beautiful animal — or rather if we are to allow the fossil and the animal to capture and captivate the *dialectic*. The ultimate inadequacies of Hegel's account when it attempts to deal with something so close to 'petrified intelligence' and yet at the same time so alien to it, will point us in the direction of a rethinking of the dialectical gesture that we have entitled a 'fossilised dialectic'. The Hegelian theorisation of the fossil deconstructs the *Philosophy of Nature* from within and acts as a *symptom* of the text's failure to encompass what we wish to conceive, revealing as it does the ultimate reasons for this failure. It will finally bring to light what needs to be done with our dialectic if we are to make sense of the beautiful animal.

HEGEL'S FOSSILS I — THE INORGANIC EARTH 'ORGANISM' AND 'NATURAL HISTORY'

Hegel, in fact, says very little of fossils.[15] Even in the *Philosophy of Nature*, there are but three pages referred to in the index of both English translations.[16]

The fossil first emerges in the context of the history of the earth, which Hegel addresses in the third of the three main sections of the *Philosophy of Nature*: Mechanics, Physics, and Organics. It is, broadly speaking, a fossil relic not of the animal but of the vegetable.

But even before the emergence of plants and animals, Hegel is willing to speak of the earth itself as an animal: 'the geological *organism*' (PNIII, 21/347 §339A, emphasis added). In itself, the earth bears the seeds of an organism in the narrow sense, the living animal which Hegel describes as a fully unfolded or *ex-plicit* organism. The earth itself is the *im*plicitness of such a literally living thing: 'this organism has being [*seienden*] merely as an implicitness [*an sich*]' (PNIII, 16/343 §339), or as Miller has it more directly, a 'merely implicit organism'.

Taken literally, this employment of the word 'organism' would testify to a certain blurring of the boundary between geology and biology, stone and animal.[17] But this is not the only distinction that begins to grow fuzzy here — the idea of a geological *history*, a history of *nature*, also arises to fracture the fault line between nature and *spirit*. That Hegel would like to restrict this effacement is evident in his insistence on the analogical character of the invocation: the earth must be '*regarded* as having had an origin and as passing away'. In this sense at least (and probably only in this sense), 'the Earth [. . .] has had a *history* [Geschichte]' (PNIII, 18/345 §339A). The evidence for this history is to be found in the stratified constitution of the earth itself, and in fossils: 'At the surface of the earth lie buried the flora and fauna of a past world' (Miller) (PNIII, 18/345 §339A). Or as Petry's translation has it: 'The surface of the Earth bears evidence of its having supported a vegetation and an animal world which are now extinct [*vergangene*]'. Before naming fossils explicitly, Hegel speaks more specifically of 'petrified wood' (*versteinertes Holz*) (ibid.) and goes on to describe an entire 'fossilised forest' (*ein fossiler Wald*) or a 'petrified forest' as we would now have it (PNIII, 19/345–46 §339A).

And yet to warn us against reading anything of philosophical importance into the evocation of fossils, Hegel makes a point of saying, '[a]ll of this is a matter of history, and has to be accepted as a fact; it is not the concern of philosophy [*es gehört nicht der Philosophie an*]' (PNIII, 21/347 §339A). The deep past should not concern philosophy: 'The point of interest is not to determine the conditions prevailing millions of years ago [. . .]; but to con-

Illustration 5.7. Spatialised time.

centrate upon that which is present in the system of these various formations [*System der unterschiedenen Gebilde*]' (PNIII, 22/348–49 §339A).

Geology (or as Hegel puts it, 'geognosy' [*Geognosie*] — knowledge of the earth) is concerned largely with time, and the order of the laying down of strata, the chronological sequence of layers and folds which constitute the mantle of the earth: Hegel dismisses this as 'only an external explanation [*äußerliches Erklären*]' (PNIII, 21/347 §339A). 'These are mere occurrences [*bloße Geschehen*] however, and display nothing but a temporal difference. Nothing whatever is made comprehensible by the succession of stratifications, which is in fact completely devoid of the necessity which characterises comprehension [*Begreifen*]' (PNIII, 21/348 §339A).

Hegel's account of geology bears many similarities to his much earlier and strikingly dismissive account of evolutionary theory, which charges it with failing to think the logically necessary production of the qualitatively and not merely quantitatively distinct 'stages of nature' (PNI, 212ff/31ff §249). The reason why the history of the earth is without serious interest for philosophy is akin to the reason for evolutionism's falling short of a philosophical account of nature's development.[18] The *admission* of the fossil into the realms of the dialectic, together with a written natural archive that would make 'natural history' possible, would *also* put in question Hegel's denigration of evolution.

Evolutionary explanations in geology, rather like those in biology, are non-explanatory, sub-conceptual, and hence pre-dialectical. They are concerned with time and chance, and not with an order of necessity. For Hegel, geological explanations take a spatial ordering (of strata) and simply derive from it a temporal order of generation. The geological explanation of development is merely 'a transformation of collaterality [*Nebeneinander*: Miller gives 'spatial juxtaposition'] into temporal succession [*Nacheinander*]' (PNIII, 21/348 §339A), as if the order in which entities happened to emerge could tell us anything about their systematic (conceptual) relations with one another. In other words, geology imagines that it has truly *explained* the earth when it has merely laid out the factual matter of its contingent 'history'.

That said, despite the irrelevance of geology for philosophy, Hegel is compelled to admit that, '[i]nteresting conjectures may be made about the wide intervals separating revolutions of this kind' — including perhaps the fossilisation process — but, Hegel repeats, as if to reassure himself, and us, that '[i]n the historical field these are hypotheses however, and this explanation of events by mere succession has nothing whatever to contribute to philosophic consideration' (PNIII, 21/348 §339A).[19]

While our hopes might briefly flare up once again as Hegel appears to concede that '[t]here is something profounder in this sequence however' (PNIII, 22/348 §339A), it turns out that he is simply preparing to reiterate the philosophy of nature's most characteristic gesture — extracting a necessary rational sequence from a contingent irrational one, which means to select from among the products of nature those which can be seen to lead nature beyond itself towards the realm of spirit. Thus the 'deeper meaning' of geological strata and the 'organismic' development of the earth have nothing to do with time or even 'natural history': 'The significance and spirit [*Der Sinn und Geist*] of the process is the intrinsic connection or necessary relation of these formations [*Gebilde*], and here succession in time [*Nacheinander*] plays no part' (PNIII, 22/348 §339A).

In other words, all philosophy can learn from fossils is how to do the philosophy of nature as it is already understood: 'It is only rationality which is of interest to the Notion, and at this juncture this consists of understanding the dispositions of the Notion within the law ['of this sequence of formations', 'the essence of the sequence']' (PNIII, 22/348 §339A).

As if finally to drive a nail into the coffin that encloses the 'corpse' of the ageing earth-organism, and to avert the risk of its coming back to life with its own curious kind of immortality, Hegel concludes:

> One is unable to grasp [*begreifen*] everything in this corpse [*Leichnam*, viz. the history of the earth, the ancient earth itself] by means of the Notion, for it is riddled with accidence [*Zufälligkeit*, contingency]. Philosophy has a similarly minimal interest in acquainting itself with rational and systematic legislation in the dismal condition of chaos, or in getting to know the temporal sequence [*Zeitfolge*] and external causes [*äußerlichen Veranlassungen*] by which this legislation has come into being [*Erscheinung*]. (PNIII, 22/349 §339A)

It is worth noting that here the evolutionist argument concerning randomness can be turned against evolution itself: indeed it *is* possible to discern a random emergence in nature when it is envisioned chronologically, but this teaches us less than the notional relation between moments that becomes evident in the fully formed entity and will likely bear only a passing resemblance to the actual order in which these moments emerged in time.

To add insult to injury, Hegel proposes an analogy between the philosophy of nature and myth (that of Jupiter and Minerva) due to the latter's counter-evolutionary presentation of an abrupt revolutionary emergence: 'even *if* the Earth was once devoid of living being, and limited to the chemical process etc., as soon as the flash of living being strikes into matter, a determinate and complete formation is present, and emerges fully armed, like Minerva from the brow of Jupiter' (PNIII, 22/349 §339A). Hegel then goes so far as to say that, in truth, *religion* is more instructive than science when it comes to grasping nature philosophically: this for the reason that the biblical story of creation describes an entity being brought into existence fully formed and *ex nihilo*, without affirming its (evolutionary) derivation from any prior positivity:

> The account of the creation given in Genesis [*Mosaische Schöpfungsgeschichte*] is still the best, in so far as it says quite simply [*ganz naiv*] that the plants, the animals, and man were brought forth on separate days. Man has not formed himself [*sich . . . herausgebildet*] out of the animal, nor the animal out of the plant, for each is instantly the whole of what it is. (PNIII, 22–23/349 §339A)[20]

This is to speak at the level of *phylogeny*, but whatever the case may be there, Hegel is fully prepared to admit that we do find gradual change, of the kind that geology and evolutionary biology describe, at the level of *ontogeny*. Yet even here, the entity is always already what it will later become, but *in potential*, like the Aristotelian acorn (*Metaphysics*, 1049b): 'Such an individual certainly evolves [*Evolutionen*] in various ways, but although it is not yet complete at birth, it is already the real possibility of everything it will become' (PNIII, 23/349 §339A). Thus, at the level of the individual, the adult is already present in the child and perhaps even in the embryo. In this respect, Hegel compares the living thing to a crystal, with the entirety of its ultimate shape present in a single point (ibid.).

All of the foregoing indicates that fossils might have some significance for the philosophy of nature, and yet also introduce some turbulence into its procedure — this is why it is perhaps to Hegel's advantage that the science of palæontology was not so advanced in his day. Had the philosophy of nature afforded fossils the place they merited, serious consequences might have followed, including the rejection of the analogical character of the collapse into indistinction of nature and spirit. A literal collapse would take place in the name of a writing that should by rights be confined to the level of spirit and its self-conscious dialectic, a script which would in fact break down the boundary between the living and the dead, animal and rock. How could this not be a 'concern of philosophy'? The fact that Hegel found himself unable to admit this literality, along with the fossil that urges us to accept it, is symptomatic of a deficiency in his account.

It seems that fossils, those corpses and abortions of the evolutionary process, in their random non-dialectical character, their irreducible reference to a past of no interest to philosophy, their falling without the boundaries of the concept in both their species and their strange transgression of inorganic and organic nature, if not the natural and the spiritual, have no more than an illustrative function within Hegel's system.

Thus the geological account of the analogical earth-organism remains no more philosophical than the biological account of the literal organism. But, for us, this is precisely what the notion of the fossil allows philosophy — and even forces it — to put in question.[21]

HEGEL'S FOSSILS II

Hegel broaches the fossil for a second time in the section of the Organics that follows the 'History of the Earth': it is titled the 'Structure of the Earth' or as Petry has it, 'The Earth's structural composition (Geology and Oryctognosy)', the latter being the science of minerals and fossils, a knowledge of the excavated.

Hegel is speaking of minerals which become vegetable: so perhaps now we are entitled to anticipate that Hegel will provide a proper place for fossils. Even if his thought is running in the opposite direction to that of petrifaction, at least it is addressing the same confusion of living matter and rock, and one is thereby given some cause for hope that he might attempt to think the contrary motion: 'The primitive rock develops [*Das Urgebirge bildet sich heraus*] until it loses its mineralogical constitution, and joins up with a vegetable being [*es seine mineralische Beschaffenheit verliert, und da schließt es sich an ein Vegetabilisches an*: Miller gives 'a vegetable state', making it more clear that the two states belong to one and the same entity]' (PNIII, 31/358 §340A).

What is Hegel speaking of, here? The following sentence suggests it is a kind of phylogenesis, and that he has in mind certain moments of indecision or undecidability in the dialectic, where one stage of nature is in transition to another or is otherwise indiscernible from it. These would be akin to the amphibians we met earlier, with one foot on land and one in the water.

Hegel is grappling with two examples here: peat, 'in which there is no distinction between mineral and vegetable', and 'limestone formations which, in their ultimate formations, tend towards [*sich . . . hin bildet*] the osseous nature of the animal [*Knochenwesen des Tieres*]' (Miller) (PNIII, 31/358 §340A). But are either of these strictly fossils? It is as if Hegel is conceiving of the latter at least not as petrified life but as almost revivified stone, with the hard rock mutating into the animal's skeleton.

Nevertheless, lending some support to the idea that Hegel might here be approaching something like a theory of fossils, it is at this point that we find the first explicit reference to fossils in the *Philosophy of Nature*, if we can exclude the petrified forests already explored. Hegel speaks of fossils and — beyond the vegetables of peat and the more primitive forms found in limestone — specifically of fossilised *animals*.

But even here the fossil is adduced only as something with which the matter under consideration is to be *contrasted*, and Hegel immediately interdicts the explanation which we would today be inclined to give, and that is precisely fossilisation or petrifaction itself:

> The further productions of limestone [. . .] pass over into *shell formations* however, and it is difficult to say [*man nicht sagen kann*] whether these are mineral or animal. These petrified animal formations [*die Versteinerungen von animalischen Gebilden*] are to be found in abundance in limestone quarries, but although they occur in the form of shells, *they are not to be regarded as the residua of an extinct animal world* [*Residuen einer untergegangenen Tierwelt*]. There are also limestone formations which are not the residua, but merely the rudiments of the animal forms [*Anfänge animalischer Gestaltung*] in which limestone formation terminates. This is therefore an intermediate stage [*Zwischenstufe*] falling between limestone and true petrifications [*eigentlichen Petrifikationen*]. (PNIII, 31–32/358–59 §340A, emphasis added)[22]

Fossilisation is invoked, and then instantly revoked in favour of a process diametrically opposed to it.

The philosophy of nature takes its material from the physical sciences at the level to which these sciences have been able to develop it, and it seems clear that to Hegel's mind the science of palæontology had not attained sufficient rigor for him to be *certain* of an explanation which unequivocally deploys fossilisation: 'They are not yet shells which could be regarded as the remains of an extinct animal world; although, of course, that is *one* explanation [*das ist freilich die eine Weise, wie* . . .] of the petrified animal forms which are found in abundance in limestone-pits' (Miller)[23] (PNIII, 31–32/358 §340A, emphasis added). And in this connection we should stress the word 'also' in the passage just excerpted: '[t]here are *also* limestone formations which are not the residua [. . .] of the animal forms' (PNIII, 32/358 §340A, emphasis added), the implication being that some *are* the products of fossilisation.

Hegel's reticence in thinking of these formations as the posthumous remains of a more ancient world — as writing, in our sense — may be explained partly by the fact that the deep past is not central to Hegel's concern here; rather, the philosopher is attempting to make sense of the undecidability between animal, vegetable, and mineral (in the form of peat and limestone, for example) which is approaching us from the *future*: 'There are also limestone formations which are not the residua, but merely the *rudiments* of the animal forms' [Miller is more striking here: 'not the remains, but only the *beginnings* {*Anfänge*}, of animal form'] (PNIII, 32/358 §340A, emphases added). Again, Hegel cannot but return to the spiritualising movement of the Philosophy of Nature and its avowed ambition of freeing spirit from the immobile stone sarcophagus to which nature has confined it. The dialectic turns the fossilisation process around and thinks rather the becoming vegetable and animal of the mineral, in peat, limestone, and beyond.

From both a scientific and a philosophical point of view, there is nothing so strange in the idea of the generation of animals from rocks. On the level of science, one has merely to think of the evolutionary account of the emergence of the organic from the inorganic, the beginnings of life as such.[24] And philosophically, it supplies an exemplary instance of that which the philosophy of nature is attempting to identify — the foreshadowings of spirit in matter, the higher forms of life in the lower and ultimately in that which, in itself, lacks life altogether, even if in hindsight one might describe Geo — or Gaia — as an 'organism' in its implicit state. For the dialectic, in which nature is esteemed primarily for its premonitions of spirit, everything tends towards the living, from vegetal to animal life to the ever-living life of the spirit.

But to do full justice to Hegel, and as if once again to stress that fossilisation *is* considered a possibility, we should note that Hegel seems to think that limestone is involved in a *bipolar* process of vivification *and* petrifaction. The rock is not stable and substantial but rather constitutes a temporary and volatile stage within a longer and broader process. First, Hegel identifies a midpoint between mineral and animal:

> This is therefore an intermediate stage falling between limestone and true petrifications. It has to be regarded merely as a further development of conchyliaceousness [Miller: 'the nature of mollusca'], *and* as something purely mineral, for the formations [*Gebilde*] of this kind have not yet reached the consummate form of the animal [*animalischen Rundung*]. (PNIII, 32/358–59 §340A, emphasis added)

He goes on to speak of, '[t]he organic formations which begin in the geological organism [*die organischen Gebilde . . . die im geologischen Organismus anfangen*]':[25] animal and plant forms on occasion, but mainly, 'huge integral masses, thoroughly formed organically [*ungeheuren Massen, durch und durch organisch gebildet*]' (PNIII, 32/359 §340A). Thus far, we remain on the side of vivification; Hegel may be speaking here of anything that resembles organic life, although it seems most likely that he is referring to the arborescent structures invoked in the following sentence: 'They may also be found in coal-measures, where a distinct arborescence [*Baumform*] is often recognisable [*erkennt*]' — the forms of trees and perhaps the palm leaves often found in coal and other sedimentary rock (PNIII, 32/359 §340A).

And yet Hegel moves on to speak much more favourably of the hypothesis of *fossilisation*, largely, it seems, because of the sheer extent of the apparently organic material that is present here. There is 'as much organic formation in the geological organism, as there is inorganic' and '[t]his certainly disposes one to admit that there was once an organic world there which has since been destroyed by water [*im Wasser untergegangen*]' (PNIII, 32/359 §340A).[26]

Thus, in its finest moments, Hegel's text invokes both the transfiguration of animals and vegetables into stone and the opposite process of revival and spiritualisation, which breaks the spell of petrifaction. In general, however, it seems that the philosophical consequences of the idea of fossilisation are *not* drawn in Hegel's *Philosophy of Nature* or anywhere else in the Encyclopædia. The fossil, in the end, runs counter to the general thrust of the dialectic and is simply too recalcitrant to be afforded a place.

As we have already indicated, Hegel is aided in fossilisation's ultimate overshadowing by the still doubtful state of palæontology at the time, and our own text might be understood as attempting, after Hegel, to lay down the elements of a philosophy of nature which would take into account the fact that the science of ancient entities has in the intervening years achieved a much higher degree of certainty, while at the same time philosophy has learned to find a place for the accidental and contingent in a way that Hegel's philosophy had not. This would be a philosophy of nature which truly embraced the direction contrary to spiritualisation and reserved pride of place for the fossil, wilfully turning its back on the highest and most ethereal products of human spirit in favour of the geological.

The fossil in its literality seems to imply a troubling of distinctions that the dialectic as it stands is resistant to incorporating, between nature and history, the mineral and the living. On the three or four occasions where the fossil broke the surface of Hegel's text, his acuity did not fail to intimate something of its ultimate meaning, but a combination of the uncertain state of palæontology at the time, together with the stone-animal's resistance to dialecticisation, prevented these moments from constituting anything more than isolated outbreaks, temporary flickerings soon to be snuffed out. Or perhaps the scientific consensus was indeed sufficiently strong, but the overwhelming impetus of the dialectic towards idealisation swayed Hegel in the end, at the expense of a scientific explanation of fossils which a different kind of philosophy of nature might have considered more than merely 'one possibility' among others.

Perhaps we, today, might be allowed to wonder whether the fossil could in the end exert such pressure on the seams of the Hegelian system that the structure begins to come apart. In that case, the fossil would reveal in a particularly striking way the Hegelian schema along a number of its most fragile fault lines, and indeed in such a way as to point towards the modifications it would need to undergo if it were to become plastic enough to conceive the charming animal that we have been sincerely pursuing all along.

THE IMMORTALITY OF STONE
AFTER THE SECOND DEATH

To approach this point, let us consider the difference between two kinds of survival: sublation and the fossil, the latter being the survival of a purely natural non-spiritual life, an extreme representative of what, from the point of view of the dialectic, the animal does in its sincere fascination with its natural life and its indifference to the spiritual.

We should think of this survival in connection with the endurance of writing. What are we to glean from the encounter between these two kinds of writing, the Hegelian and the fossilic? What can we learn from the failure of the fossil to do more than temporarily break the surface of the Hegelian text before sinking back into its submarine, subterranean depths?

The gravestone, metonym for Hegelian writing, is not identical with the dead body of the human being it commemorates, nor need it stand in the same location. The corpse could lie elsewhere, or be scattered to the four winds, or indeed it might never have been found. This is not the only immortality of man, however, for casts were sometimes made of princes and princesses, noblemen and women, just as the death mask was common even among the socially less elevated, and one finds a number of curious saints preserved in Catholic churches around the world (I am thinking, in particular, of a church on a hill in Lucca), albeit in less immaculate states of preservation than the aristocracy and the ammonite. This suggests that the type of immortality provided by the cast is in some way superior.

Unlike the fossil, which is an *un*free donation of the animal's body to another region of nature, the return of the habit-forming plastic organism to the mechanical realm of the inorganic, the funerary inscription is *freely* raised by another or carried out (again voluntarily) at the behest of the deceased, but in any case freely, and artificially — it is a product of spirit, not nature.

If fossils are the trace of a time before spirit and before sublation, then to begin to think them it may help to imagine the eradication of the spiritual order itself. If we survey the world from the standpoint of the extinction of the human race, the juddering halt of dialectical spiritualisation, might we not even stand closer to seeing the world as *animals* do?

In any case, this apocalyptic vision is not unheard of in the history of philosophy and literature, nor is the strategy of envisioning a time *after* the death of man and the destruction of his chattels in order to envisage a time *before* man.[27]

So let us linger a while longer with the posterity and outliving of man. If fossils can survive human extinction then this thought experiment might allow us to gain a better insight into their particular kind of immortality, if such it be.

In this direction, we might go even further than the death of man and imagine the destruction of the entirety of *living nature*. Even after the destruction of both nature *and* culture, after the death of natural life and the extinguishing of spiritual life — the termination of the phoenix's regenerative cycle — the fossil lives on. The fossil's immortality exceeds the death of the 'death of death', the termination of sublation, the absolute negation of determinate negation.

In the end, our 'immortal' death drive will pass away, our own species become extinct, and all our works fall to ruin. Thus will spirit fall prey to decay or the cremation that the sun will visit upon the earth and all of its creatures.

Such a thought of extinction is not idle. We know that the symbolic order of language (bound together by 'writing') in which spiritual preservation and transmission take place is vulnerable today more than ever to catastrophes both natural and artificial (from comets to warfare and the Anthropocene). Neither the animal (for the most part) nor the fossil depend upon the order of spirit or culture in order to survive. The fossil and the animal could survive humanity, happily playing, heedless of the absence of (the first generation of) those capable of deciphering their inscription and finding them beautiful. Without (people to read the) books, shelves afford an undisturbed sleeping place for cats.

But the fossil can survive the extinction even of nature and the other animals.

So let us imagine a human being, perhaps speaking on behalf of the entire race, who wishes not to be remembered by means of a written inscription on his tomb but to be erased altogether from the book of life. Man alone can choose to have his or another's life recorded in historical memory or to have it forgotten, every last trace eradicated, if such a thing is possible.[28] The desire for an absolute forgetting, erasure of all traces and of every last trace of this erasure, is for Lacan a possibility only within the symbolic order, since this entire realm can be wiped out or become entirely illegible with the extinction of the species. Such would be a 'second death', succeeding that of natural life.

For the Marquis de Sade, 'second death' means rather the cessation of the entire natural cycle. Crimes, including murder, are not crimes *against* nature but precisely participate in its circuit of corruption and generation. For Sade, a second death would seem to be a second *order* of death, in which what would come to an end is the very cycle of birth and death itself: the death of natural nativity.

If both the Lacanian and Sadean senses of second death were to occur, as seems more and more likely with each passing year, in ecological cataclysm or some more abrupt and terminal war, biological or nuclear, what would remain? The fossil, immortal in its stone effigy, would lie untouched, waiting, without hope or expectation of future readers who might come across it and marvel at its tracery?[29]

In contrast to the perhaps finite immortality of man and nature, is the fossil not immortal in a more absolute sense? Petrified life, an ossified moment in the process of living matter becoming rock, ceasing to develop any further and yet in a certain way not ceasing to live — if we are able to speak of 'immortality' here, it might be taken to be an immortality of *natural* life, in that life has here taken on a form in which it cannot die, but survives its own extinction and even the second death of both nature and culture. This is a survival stronger than the immortality of spiritual life. Is the survival of the fossil, therefore, the absolute exacerbation of the bad infinite of the living animal in the sense that its undialectical indifference to development is here set in stone?

In the difference between these two forms of survival, the resurrection of the phoenix and the immortality of the ammonite, our guiding questions might ultimately begin to find an answer.

But to call the stone animal 'immortal'? The animal cannot die, says Heidegger, and nor can the stone, but for different reasons — unlike the animal, it has never lived. But what of the stone *animal*? It has certainly lived, and it has died, but it cannot die again, a second time. It has survived its death in another form, just not in the way of the Hegelian resurrection, a survival of the real in an *ideal* conceptual form. Rather, the fossil lives on in a *real* petrific form. The non-human animal, individually speaking, has no ideal survival, but it does have a real one as it passes into the form — supposedly 'lower' yet — of the stone. In this case, the negation contained in the word 'im-mortal' should be heard differently to the Hegelian negation of negation, the death of death.[30]

THREE FORMS OF UNDEATH: HORROR, COMEDY, AND FOSSIL

Under the weight of Žižek's corpus, and our own willing exposure to its repetitions — itself a kind of bad habit and bad infinite on the part of author and reader — we have become accustomed to employing the notion of the 'un-dead' to describe the human (death-)drive identified by Sigmund Freud, and it will not be without profit if we compare it to the immortality which we find in the animal enshrined in stone.

The fossilised animal does not live or die, it neither grows nor decays. Is it then a form of im-mortality as defined by the 'infinite judgement' upon which Žižek has insisted, indicating as it does a third zone between the living and the dead? The petrified animal spans the two, just as the undead death-drive does, but it does not live in quite the same sense as that which is death-driven. If the drive is a moment of petrification or death at the heart of the living, the fossil is perhaps a living at the heart of death, a death which retains a memory of life and thus cannot be altogether dead.

The undead of the Lacanian death-drive is often taken to be the topic of horror or comedy,[31] and yet there is a third type of undeath, suited to neither: the non-death of the fossil. The animal becomes immortal in the form of the fossil, and its particular immortality is one which can, with its sublimity, inspire awe[32] — but if we imagine certain trilobites congregating and playing together on an ocean bed, in a way that has taken four hundred million years to be appreciated, it is also not without a certain *charm*.

The fossil will teach the dialectic how to modify itself in order to understand the animal in its charming sincerity. To treat the death drive and its madness as a rite of passage to be undergone is to view it dialectically in the orthodox sense; the fossil is something that remains frozen on the threshold between animal and stone, organics and mechanics, a regression from the former to the latter, a *counter*-dialectical movement. Its dogged resistance is what will ultimately allow the dialectic to encompass the animal, which stands on another threshold, between nature and spirit, in such a way that it need not be understood as an imperfection to be overcome in the direction of the 'perfect animal'.

The fossil eludes dialectical thought and thus demands either a non-dialectical thinking or a new way of operating the dialectic. We have adopted the latter approach, to modify Hegel's understanding of animals and their beauty. The fossilised dialectic is thus the final stage of our journey through sincerity with Wittgenstein, Levinas, and Lacan, towards the philosophy of nature and aesthetics of Kant and Hegel, in pursuit of the beautiful animal.

THE BEAUTIFUL FOSSIL: CONTINGENT ENCOUNTER OF MAN AND ANIMAL

It is not only animals: fossils are also beautiful — and what is beautiful, and awesome, about them is the sheer number of contingencies that went into our ever encountering them at all. Fossils constitute an encounter between man and animal that is all the more beautiful for its improbability. This beauty and its contingency will finally let us understand the beauty to be found in the encounter with a naturally living animal, and allow us to conceive of the animal as beautiful *in itself*, not as a mere forerunner of the human being, from the standpoint of a dialectic in fossilisation.

Fossils amount to the record of a time before there was anything *for* which the record could be made, a legibility and intelligibility of nature which were not created by or for any intelligence, and for which such an intellect was to be lacking for many millions of years to come. The ability to read fossils, which is to say to envisage them as a form of written record and to understand the signification of that trace, renders nature conceivable, sealing off the abyss between nature and reason. We should recall here that for both Kant and Hegel, the appearance of a certain rationality within nature gave rise to the radiance of beauty, and this rationality in its highest form was to be found in the animal, the concept which moved and breathed.

But in the case of the fossil, something is different. Could either Kant or Hegel have envisaged it? That the fossil, as opposed to the animal, should have become intelligible as a form of writing — an immortal trace of life — is not something that is transcendentally necessary for the experience of the fossil as an 'object': after all, nothing need experience this piece of rock as a once-living thing and hence as an organism that embodies a certain concept understood as a purpose (as with the other sentient beings who might frequently have padded across it over the millennia). Indeed, the organism is dead and no longer functions either in part or in whole with any purpose in mind, and if we need not see the fossil as once having been alive then there is no necessity for experiencing it as a trace.

This fossilisation *necessarily* takes time, but there was no necessity for fossilisation as such to occur, nor for any fossils to survive. The traces of an extinct world could just as easily have been eradicated once and for all, or never even have been left, and nature might never have worked out how to develop a creature capable of reading the signs that these prehistoric animals accidentally left behind.

There is no necessity at all to the survival of any fossil, nor is there any necessity to the arising of an entity capable of seeing them as anything other than a rock to bask upon in between hunts and matings. That the fossil trace survives, and that one fine day a human being should have come along who could both understand it as a trace *and* conceive the meaning of that trace (that it signifies the existence of extinct life), is wholly contingent. This, Hegel at least would not have allowed. The subsequent legibility of the fossil institutes a continuity between man and nature which need not have happened.

The experience of the fossil that we have been attempting to describe is an entirely contingent encounter between (extinct) animal and (living) man. It is a beautiful experience. No fossil, however grotesque or fearsome, is not beautiful if one appreciates all of the contingencies which went to make up this encounter.

What our experience since Hegel has taught us is that the *necessity* of such a beauty does not exist — and let us note that this experience is what has been implicitly recapitulated over the course of the present work. So in the beginning it was equally possible that nature would *not* be beautiful (or true), and that no creature would ever have felt the emotion of the charming and the always surprising joy of an encounter with a beautiful animal. Indeed, it was perfectly possible that once man had arisen he might have remained alienated from nature for all eternity. One can only imagine the kind of devastation he would have wrought had this been so, in light of just how far this destruction is being taken by one actually blessed with the faculty of appreciating beauty in nature. One might even wonder if the appearance of an archaic or Romantic aspect to our own discourse is precisely a sign that such an attitude to nature is being lost, and at the same time, when it comes to the environment (or environments), an indication of the dangers that such a loss entails. In the end there is some warning to be read in the deterioration of our preparedness to be charmed by the animal's sincerity, preferring rather to drown in irony and to allow the 'charming' to enter our vocabulary only in the degraded and patronising form of the 'cute'.

Illustration 5.8. Exposed section of an ammonite, above an inaccessible shore. Ours might be the first eyes to alight upon this creature since the day it died, two to four hundred million years ago. Had we not walked this way on that day, it might never have been seen, for the cliff of mud and shale was soon to crumble and be swallowed by the sea once more.

We were by chance lucky enough to have been given a non-alienated relation to nature, to enjoy the possibility at our most fortunate moments of seeing this, of reading the signs set in stone, in the form of beauty — and yet we are at risk of squandering this fortune.

It is after all plausible that animals might find each other beautiful, or that in the mirror relation involved in mating, a primitive form of conceivability is implicit in the recognition of one's kind and the perception of an incipient beauty in the form of the prospective mate. But no animal has ever fallen in love with a fossil. Only man can appreciate its beauty, and with an absolute and this time entirely unambiguous disinterest, without the danger of zoophilia which remains distantly possible in the case of the living animal.

Thus, the beauty of fossils allows us more distinctly to delineate two important features of our own account of beauty: beautiful animals can be experienced only by man, not by the animal itself or by other animals, and in one sense at least — to be distinguished from the favouring of our cherished little animal, whose *existence* does mean the world to us — it is characterised by an absolute disinterest, being utterly distinct from the natural reproductive need or any form of eroticism. This disinterest is rendered irrevocable by the sheer magnitude of the temporal abyss that separates man and animal in the case of the fossil. This is an abyss into which all remnants of the extinct animal could have fallen without trace, and thus it indicates the miracle of the sheer number of contingencies which had to coincide in order for the fossil to exist in the form of a meaningful writing.

The enduring of the animal in the form of writing institutes a new kind of continuity between animal and man, nature and reason, an elision of alienation, which neither Kant nor Hegel was fully able to express, and hence it gives rise to a kind of beauty which they could not altogether account for.

Fossilised belemnites and ammonites pre-date anything to which they could be *given*, at least to anything capable of reading them as a trace and thus appreciating their beauty. Fossils allow the non-given to be given to us. They allow us, four hundred million years later to appreciate the immense charm of three trilobites playing together on the floor of an ocean now lost beneath the deserts of Morocco. These sandstone effigies also constitute a trace of this immense sea and a record of the mighty sandstorm that engulfed it — a trace of this erasure.

Illustration 5.9.

Illustration 5.10.

The invisibility of a dark seabed and the depths in which these 'antediluvian' sea creatures propelled themselves from time to time is illuminated for us along with the impossibility of experiencing a past which preceded all human sight and intelligence — but in such a way as to preserve its darkness *as* darkness.[33] After all, to find something charming or beautiful falls short of an *epistemic* relation — we do not *know* the animal or the fossil, we do not approach it as a scientist, zoologist, or palæontologist might. The darkness is preserved in the case of the fossil partly by means of the transformation of material from carbon to stone; a prehistoric creature brought back to life artificially, inanimately stuffed, or reconstructed in a museum, does not have the same charm.

FOSSILISED DIALECTIC

The fossil evinces a process that runs counter to the dialectic — not towards the heaven of ideas but into the darkness of the earth. To Hegelian eyes, this would seem an unconscionable regression, even more disturbing and undialectical than the animals caught between two elements. It is as if the reality of the animal were drawing further away from its notion and from spirit, and thus not only freezing the dialectic, as in the animal's repetitive driven behaviour — which we have called, from another angle, its 'sincerity' — but positively putting it in reverse. It is the absolute rejection of spiritual life in the name of *natural* life, but a natural life immortalised in stone.

In the fossil, the dialectic has been petrified. Nothing any longer changes or develops — it remains eternally the same, as if frozen in time, awaiting an encounter with whichever human being is lucky enough to chance upon it. The good infinite thus cedes its place to the 'bad'. We have been attempting all along to reassess the bad infinite, since this was the first tool we picked up — from Hegel's work — in our attempt to make sense of the animal's sincerity, that charm which we deemed beautiful. The animal *can* be understood by dialectic, but improperly, while the fossil cannot be understood at all. We would suggest that to use philosophy in order to make sense of the beautiful animal, we must learn from the *stone*-animal how to fossilise its dialectic.

The effect that the fossil has on the dialectic allows the latter to open itself to the animal. The fossil gnarls up the dialectical machine, rendering it inoperative, but precisely thereby it allows the dialectic to respond to animality, in its bad infinity, in its sincerity, and its especial immortality, distinct from the resurrection of sublation. The dialectic would need to freeze if it was to capture this turning away from spiritual life in favour of an infinite immersion in natural life that the fossil indicates and the animal in its perfection embodies. The animal knows nothing of spirit, and cares even less.[34] This infinite immersion, indifferent to all spirituality, is precisely what the animal radiates in its charm.

Within the dialectical system as a whole, this fossilised refusal of the spiritual life of the resurrection in the name of a stony immortality, is metaphorical; but in the philosophy of nature, the fossil is *literally* present, or rather a literal lacuna, a telling sign of what needs to happen to the dialectic.

The human being has the ability to be *more* than dialectical, and to decipher the traces left by the fossil in the dialectical system. This ability is what allows it to be charmed by the animal, so much so that it becomes a little animal itself and gives up on dialectical progress for a time, captivated as the animal captivates dialectic (a revenge, of the most charming kind, on its captors).

DIALECTICS AT A STANDSTILL.
THE FOSSILISATION OF THE DIALECTIC.

Walter Benjamin has evoked the powerful notion of 'dialectics at a standstill'. Can this help us to clarify our notion of a fossilised dialectic? Certainly the two concepts are not identical, but the proximity and differences between them should allow us to make our definition more precise.

Let us read one of the canonical definitions of this standstill:

> It is not that what is past [*das Vergangene*] casts its light on what is present [*das Gegenwärtige*], or what is present its light on what is past; rather, image [*Bild*] is that wherein what has been [*das Gewesene*] comes together in a flash with the now [*Jetzt*] to form a constellation. In other words, image is dialectics at a standstill [*die Dialektik im Stillstand*]. [. . .] [T]he relation of what-has-been to the now is dialectical: not temporal in nature but figural [*bildlicher*]. Only dialectical images are genuinely historical [*geschichtliche*] — that is, not archaic images. The image that is read — which is to say, the image in the now of its recognisability [*Jetzt der Erkennbarkeit*] — bears to the highest degree the imprint of the perilous critical moment on which all reading is founded. (Benjamin 1999a, 463/578)[35]

Past and present are strung together by a jagged streak of lighting that illuminates what is before us, freezing it in the starkest of lights for a brief moment, before it vanishes once again, as if caught in the glare of a flashbulb was something from the past which has finally become 'news'. The figures on this moonlit scene stand petrified. The past is a photograph that awaits the right moment to be developed.

We might well argue that there *is* something peculiar to our time, or at least to our present and personal interests as readers, which has made it possible for us to read the Kantian and Hegelian texts on animality and beauty in the way that we have, in a certain conjuncture with the contemporary moment in continental philosophy. We have endeavoured at the same time to avoid the presumption that they hereby become intelligible — or 'recognisable' — for the very first time or that this is their only and ultimate sense. Rather, we hope to have brought to light a potentiality inherent in the texts themselves, with certain interests, practical and theoretical, in mind.

In this regard at least, Benjamin's notion stands close to ours, and yet the fossilisation of dialectic has a slightly different sense. What we wish to speak of is an unfolding process that hits a snag and gets caught at a particular moment, and, rather than forging ahead, begins to rotate around this point of tethering. As it circles, it begins to forget the goal it was originally striving for, along with the very idea of progress and the true infinite — it starts to immerse itself in the bad infinite of a circular repetition. Spirit gradually ossifies and becomes fossilised — within *history* a moment of *nature* is reconstituted. The animal that is organic dialectical reason returns to stone, and 'intelligence' is 'petrified' once again.

MAN PETRIFIED

The fossil fossilises the dialectic. But in a certain way the animal also petrifies us: bewitched and charmed we forget the necessity for dialectical progression and become as if statues — something like animals ourselves.

The freezing of the dialectic involves *us* in a moment of sincerity, the sincere and repeated fastening upon a particular moment without absorbing it into a broader whole, abandoning all concern for progress. To describe *not* making progress, *not* performing a dialectical sublation — in short, the bad infinite — in a *positive* way is ultimately what we have been attempting with the words 'sincerity' and 'charm'. Hence, in this depiction of the animal, we are performatively demonstrating the human capacity to revalorise, undialectically, the bad infinite. This revalorisation involves fossilising the dialectic at the stage of the organism and thus allowing it to think the animal as perfect, rather than locating the animal's perfection in man.

The animal, we know, is indifferent to dialectic and the impulse to supersede the bad infinite to pursue the good or the true. The animal is indifferent to us and our philosophy. But it is possible to be fascinated by a creature that displays such indifference. Indeed, this is its very charm. We agree with Hegel that the animal does not find *itself* beautiful in the way that we do, and therefore, in order for the charming to exist, there must be *another* entity which is capable of being charmed, and this is the human being. In the fascination which the animal's indifference exerts, we find ourselves inter-ested, on a terrain shared with the animal. With our participation in the animal's world, do we not become a little more animal ourselves? In our enchantment, we begin to forget the dialectic, and in this shared indifference to the true infinite, we are assimilated to the animal. To fixate upon a certain moment, to circle endlessly around particular topics and texts in the way that we have, is to become somewhat animalic ourselves, to join the animals in their wilderness — animal-philosophers.

What does it tell us that in our common indifference to dialectic, the animal comes to overlap with the human world, or, more precisely, that we are admitted onto the very margins of its remarkable territory? Might it be that there is an element of man himself which is resistant to dialectic, or that dialectical reason and spirit are *not* part of what is most proper to humankind? Man is indeed the animal of conceptual labour, the entity in which philosophy happens, but he is also the animal capable of refusing work and languishing voluntarily in a state of 'inoperativity' (*désœuvrement*).

Chapter Five

MADNESS AND THE FROZEN DIALECTIC: DERRIDA, HEGEL, AND GENET

But, for a human being, is this approach to philosophy not a trifle mad? In the case of the human, is the mode of survival belonging to the animal-fossil not a kind of madness? Is the bad infinity of repetition not embodied in the obsessional ritual which *outweighs* all concern for natural life and health, not to speak of our properly human vocation, the 'good life' beyond 'mere life'?

Indeed, the similarities between the animal and the insane are significant, as — on the other hand — are their divergences. One should compare animal sincerity with the compulsions of neurosis and its symptomatic tics. Derrida has even (implicitly) compared psychosis to this type of attitude towards the dialectic, in his mighty volume juxtaposing Hegel and Jean Genet, *Glas*. This has indeed been silently inspiring us from the beginning (cf. Derrida 1986 [1974]).

Derrida might be said to have identified moments at which the dialectic simply refuses to move on, or at which a certain subject does not feel the rational compulsion to 'do philosophy' which Ludwig Feuerbach, an avowed inspiration for Derrida early on, identified as a secret presupposition of Hegel's 'presuppositionless' dialectic: 'is it not after all a presupposition that philosophy has to begin at all?' (Feuerbach 1972 [1839], 59/28) (cf. Derrida 1978 [1962], 69n66/60n1).

The madman does not respond to contradiction in the correct, philosophical way, but lives that unresolved, counter-rational incompatibility. Derrida identifies the possible freezing of the dialectic in this sub-rational way by pitting Hegel against Genet in a schizophrenic text of two columns (and more). He demonstrates the ever-present possibility that a certain shape of consciousness will be unable or unwilling to negate itself determinately and spawn a new, more rational shape. It will remain cut off from itself, discrepant, schizoid, circling around itself as if forever chasing its tail, the snake of the bad infinity of circulation.

For Hegel, this undialectical madness is the human's slipping back to the threshold which it shares with the animal. So what, if anything, differentiates (mad)man from animal here?

In the case of the animal, one cannot describe its circularity as a pathological state since it does not even have the *potential* to determinately negate, even though the Hegelian scheme, if not the greater part of the philosophical tradition, has implied that the animal is nothing but a stunted human.

In the case of man, it is always possible for a rational mind to lose its grip on reason and with it the ability to make any more dialectical progress. This might make us wonder why we should feel obliged to make progress, to learn from our mistakes, to break out of the circle, enter history and take up the vocation of humanity. Why should a contradiction or a disparity between one's notion and one's reality be intolerable?

Does insanity beckon? And are we not welcoming it voluntarily if we go still further and attempt to make the transition in the *opposite* direction, freely descending from spirit into nature, from man to animal? Are we going mad? Is it possible even for a Hegelian to fall in love with this land it was destined to leave behind and indefinitely postpone its departure?

But the Hegelian would classify this as a 'bad habit' on the part of man. A good habit, on the other hand, would be one which allows the human being to raise itself *above* the level of the animal — to which it is nevertheless always capable of slipping back. Are we mad? Are we caught up in bad habits? To distinguish our position from Hegel's, let us go into the question of madness and habit in a little more depth.

FIXATION ON A PART, ALIENATION, AND THE NEUROTIC BODY

Becoming fixated on a certain point, without having any ultimate justification for doing so, has long been associated with the folly of a bad habit. A habitual repetition, at its most extreme, becomes an unreasonable obsession, while a good habit can gently ease us out of such an obsessive compulsion to repeat and restore us to normality — where 'normality' means 'dialectical progression'. Madness is like a bad habit, and to become good dialecticians we must work our way out of such habits and develop 'good' ones (cf. Malabou 2005 [1996], 24–27/41–44, 55–76/79–110 et al.; Malabou 2008, vii–xx).

What is a 'good habit' and how can it rescue us from automatism? Catherine Malabou has demonstrated that Hegel himself was not unaware of the possibility of the dialectic being frozen by madness. Thus the potential to get stuck at a certain stage or caught in a gap between stages is not just an invention of literature, or of Genet in his idiosyncrasy; it was recognised by Hegel himself as a hurdle to be surmounted in every instance of anthropogenesis.

In derangement, one's mind remains fixed on a single part of the whole — one thing which ought *by rights* to become a moment in a broader dialectical progression towards the total resumption of every stage of the development in a rational order, to assume the ideal form of the concept: a totality. This recalcitrant part takes on a life of its own and preoccupies our attention to the exclusion of all else. In this sense, madness and dialectical reason are utterly at odds on a Hegelian account, and this is precisely why madness must be *assimilated* by the dialectic as one of its moments, as a rite of *passage*. Madness is a trial which must be endured if we are to cross the border between nature and spirit.

Madness is thus the risk of remaining an animal or a child just short of the Age of Reason, or regressing from humanity to bestiality and being frozen on the threshold, caught eternally between the animal and the human, in that borderland of the organism, the incipience of organic reason, which we are supposed to enter only in order to bid it farewell and so enter the perfection of animality that is the human.

Reading the Anthropology with which Hegel's *Philosophy of Spirit* begins, we alight upon the idea that madness is an essential part of the anthropogenic process. The fixation of madness is a possibility that stands at the gateway to manhood. But how precisely are we to understand 'madness' here? How to raise it to the level of a concept?

We can do so in relation to the problem of how we become self-conscious, and first, how we simply become self-*related*. Selfhood amounts to the most ontologically primitive form of self-consciousness and describes the simple form of self-relation. Selfhood is the reflexive relation to that 'other in the same' which is that *to which* we relate in the process of constituting a relation to ourselves — for in self-relation there is always an *I* and a *me*, a nominative and an accusative, the one *relating* and the other being related *to*, like the start and endpoint of the same circular trajectory stretching between 'I' and 'myself'.

The madness of becoming human is the alienation inherent in the formation of selfhood. The hazard of tying this loop is that I can always fail to complete the process of recognising this other within me as fully a part of myself. The circle may not finally be closed if the point of arrival and point of departure are not perceived as identical. If this occurs, I find myself inhabited by another, alienated from myself, and insanity beckons.

Here, it is useful to refer to Slavoj Žižek's reworking of Malabou's account. One of the important elements which he adds here is that the relation between the subject and the potential alien which haunts it may be identified with the connection between spirit and *body*. The body is my potentially maddening other because, while spirit is ideal, free, and rational, the body is material, automatic, graceless, and irrational. It must somehow become imbued with spirit if it is to be properly assimilated (Žižek 2009, 101).

In the more psychoanalytic aspect of his text, 'Discipline Between Two Freedoms', Žižek suggests that there is an aspect of the body which is yet more difficult to subdue than the body as such, and that is the part in which a neurotic tic is manifest. This part of the body persistently refuses *conscious* spiritual control, for the neurotic tic is precisely the symptomatic manifestation of the *un*conscious. So difficult are these symptoms to eradicate that the help of others must be sought in the form of psychoanalytic treatment. But, for Hegel, the cure for irrational behaviour is *habituation*.

To make sense of this idea, we need to understand the specific guise that habit assumes in the case of man.

The stone does not acquire new habits. In the transition from mineral to animal the *ability* to form habits emerges. The animal surpasses the plant by learning how to escape the absence of spontaneous locomotion, the passivity of remaining rooted to the spot, and thus takes an important step towards the absolutely free flight of spirit. Habit grants the organism the possibility of moving away from the bi-univocal stimulus and response of simpler organisms which remains almost indistinguishable from the cause and effect of unfree matter.[36]

But this is to speak at the level of phylogeny; ontogenetically, an animal is unable to form new habits, at least to the same degree that humans are. There is no single habit that a human being is not free enough to break or contract. And yet, we are also infinitely free to fall from this grace: human beings can sink much lower than animals in the acquisition of bad habits.

Once the habit is contracted, the splendid plasticity of the organic can become ossified and return to stone, failing to develop any further — good infinity turns bad, the line curls up to form a circle, and nothing is produced. It is as if a fine talent had gone to waste. Bad habits remain without work, without issue — one is simply caught in a loop, endlessly repeating a gesture which leads nowhere. In this oblivious addiction, one's attention is fixed on a single point, a symptom, we might say, of a madness one does not know.

HABIT AS THE CURE FOR MADNESS

So how, in the case of man, does habit solve the problem of madness? How does it facilitate the transition from nature to spirit? Here we shall once again take Žižek as our guide (Žižek 2009, 95ff).[37]

In the process of becoming human, habit is the preventative of madness, and if one suffers its onset, habit is the cure. Habit allows the other within us, the body in its clumsy mechanism, to be inspirited with a free, graceful, and skilled motion. Through this learning of skill, the body can be taught to shed its unfree mechanical reactions and master new ones. In the grace with which habit endows the body, the freedom of spirit for the first time becomes a real possibility — a premonition within the animal of the human it is destined to become.

Habit raises the unfree body bound by externally given mechanical laws towards the autonomy of the free spirit — much as the bird which has been leading us a merry dance through the history of philosophy learns to take flight. Thus, through habituation, the body ceases to be alien to the spirit that animates it and comes gradually to acquire the potential to cross the boundary between the natural and the spiritual. The division between us and ourselves slackens and from our actual or possible alienation a certain self-sameness is restored. This is why Malabou identifies habit, the prophylactic of madness, as a notion which binds together the Philosophy of Nature and the Philosophy of Spirit (Malabou 2005 [1996], 25–26/43).

THE PSYCHOANALYTIC READING: MADNESS AND DEATH DRIVE

And yet here we must depart somewhat from Hegel's analysis of madness. We are impelled to do so by an insight gleaned from psychoanalysis: this is reflected in our decision to speak of 'symptoms', for these tics — always repeated endlessly in the same manner — are also expressions of a *desire* which we are for some reason unable to acknowledge, refusing to grant it admission to self-consciousness. The idea of being once and for all rid of an unconscious and its manifestations is a Hegelian dream we no longer share.

Žižek and the Slovenian School of Mladen Dolar, Alenka Zupančič, and others, have attempted to bring Hegel and psychoanalysis together in a fashion that will help us to locate the precise moment of our departure from Hegel. For Žižek, the insanity one finds in Hegel is a precursor to the psychoanalytic notion of the death-drive (*Todestrieb*). This drive is the 'compulsion to repeat' that lies at the heart of our desire and lends the latter its insatiability. Drive thus marks the boundary between the animal with its finite *needs*, serviced by instincts, and the human with its infinite *desire*. In drive, we witness the transition from natural need to culturally — which is to say symbolically and technically — mediated desire, from finitude and the ultimate possibility of satiation to an infinite and eternal dissatisfaction. For psychoanalysis, and to this extent it remains in agreement with Hegel, the death drive and the obsessional madness it perpetuates constitute the mediating moment of anthropogenesis.

The drive is a natural instinct gone wrong, hindered in its natural aim and ceasing (merely) to serve a natural need.[38] The instinct has been corrupted either by cultural interference or through a perturbation immanent within nature which opens up the possibility of culture. To derive a philosophy of nature or a philosophical anthropology from this notion is to see it as a *natural* animal need which is *naturally* inhibited in some way, and thus it allows us to explain *naturalistically* the emergence of a feature or set of features that characterise the human being alone among all the animals: desire and all of the various sublimations and laws which both satisfy and do not satisfy this desire, the technical prostheses which go to make up human culture.

For psychoanalysis, this drive is to be found only in the human being, at its very origin, and amounts to a natural instinct hampered in its attempts to find satisfaction in its goal. The drive can neither directly aim at its target nor disregard it altogether, and thus its linear trajectory is transformed into an endless circling of the object, which leaves it forever unable either to enter its atmosphere or to escape the tug of its gravity (Lacan 1998 [1964], 161ff/147ff, esp. 177–80/162–64, cf. Žižek 2014 [1982], 118).

The drive involves another kind of bad infinite, which will eventually allow the neurotic ritual to be born. The death drive is, despite its name, immortal, indifferent to life and death in the sense of natural life and its survival. It is 'dead' in the sense of a mechanism or machine: Lacan translates Freud's '*Wiederholungszwang*' (compulsion to repeat) as '*automatisme de répétition*' (repetition automatism — an automatic machine for producing the bad infinite) (Lacan 2006 [1966], 10/15). Instincts in animals aim ultimately at the organism's survival, while the death drive, on the other hand, imbues man with an exacerbation of survival *in articulo mortis*, an undead persistence that may even lead the human being willingly to die in pursuit of the strange obsession which haunts it. Thus the death drive can become a suicidal tendency, but it institutes self-destruction only *in the name* of something better than (natural) life.

Certainly, the suspension of natural need and the exclusive valorisation of natural life are prerequisites for the emergence of spiritual life and the dialectic, but the lesson of psychoanalysis is that this departure from nature also makes possible the madness of repetition. Desire initiates both the dialectic and its indifferent refusal.

THE LEVINASSIAN INFLECTION

We have been speaking thus far exclusively of the individual, its desires, and its habits. But psychoanalysis also teaches us that desire is intersubjective, it is a relation between two, and our desire for someone else is bound up with our own (perceived) desirability and being-desired. So, for instance, we might desire someone who demonstrates to us our own desirable character, seeing what is concealed from us about ourselves, and that is the quality or trait which makes us desirable.

To approach this point, we might inflect our account of habit by something we have learnt from Emmanuel Levinas: the necessity of taking into account the Other when we are thinking about the constitution of our 'selves', that there must always be at least two of us before we can 'be' anything at all. We must take into account not only our own habits and tics, but those of the other and our relation to them, along with their relation to us. We began this work alone: our very first example was that of shaving — *I* shaving *myself*, and the ennui provoked by this repetitious gesture, which, according to Sartre, was ultimately carried out by my 'habit'.

Perhaps these rituals are not signs of madness, but thresholds of humanisation that resist or constrict natural processes *in* a natural fashion, the animal becoming 'auto-immune' through inoculation, using nature against itself, pitting bad infinite (shaving) against bad infinite (regrowth, stubble, intolerable hirsute profusion). Certain forms of '(bad) habit' amount to an adoption of animalic behaviour that nevertheless makes humanity possible. One clears a space for the dialectic and the truly infinite, and all this at the risk of a tedium which can lead us to neglect these daily tasks and send us scuttling back towards our animality, or a level more debauched than the beast — for instance, the wearing of beards.[39]

Yet we are still alone. So let us imagine that *another* is shaving us, that we are grooming someone else, out of love — that we are being watched in the execution of our task or watching another performing their rituals as sincerely as they can. The peculiarities of the habits we need to indulge, the idiosyncrasies of the way in which we carry out our bad infinite may even go so far as to inspire love. The boundary that repression institutes between the conscious and the unconscious constitutes the individual's 'character' and renders them appealing in their singularity as it sets them apart from the generality. Thus one can imagine being attracted by these neuroses in another, to *us* the symptomal appearance of something that remains inapparent to the one who bears them.

The name which Lacan gives to the cause of the other's desirability, that which in their own eyes is merely an annoying glitch, an imperfection excluded from their ideal self-image (their ego) as an aberration, is the '*objet petit a*'. The 'object small *a*' is that part of the other (*autre* — hence the '*a*') which causes us to desire them, but which they do not recognise as part of themselves: it is the difference which distinguishes me from the image that I have of myself, which Lacan describes by analogy with the reflection that I recognise in the mirror. This is my 'other' with a small 'o', the 'little other', not qualitatively different from myself. But different nevertheless. This difference is made flesh in the *objet petit a* and may be understood along the same lines as the imperceptible inversion that takes place in the swapping of right and left that separates me from what I see of myself in the looking glass, at least in the eyes of an onlooker who can see both. To me, this distinction is not apparent, and the uncanny effect of seeing one's self in a photograph is a result of one's having become accustomed to this inversion. The singular Real which renders me subtly unlike my double is unknown to me.

This lack of self-knowledge, this erring with respect to ourselves, is what makes us desirable to others. The source of my attractiveness is that I remain a mystery to myself without being aware of it. What is most enigmatic — 'unconscious' — about me is just what the other finds desirable, but this in turn makes the experience of *being* desired an anxious one, since we cannot see what it is that the other desires in us, what they take us to be, and this can lead us to fear losing that *je ne sais quoi* without being aware of having done so.

Lacan captures this anxiety of non-knowledge in the Devil's question from Jacques Cazotte's *Le Diable amoureux*: in Italian, '*chè vuoi?*' — 'what do you want from me?' 'what am I in your eyes?' (Lacan 2006 [1966], 690/815, cf. Cazotte 1991 [1772], 34/59, 45/68, 102/119).

Thus we might ask: is (intersubjective) desire a valorisation of the bad infinite as it exists not in animals but in *humans*? Is our desire for the other in their petty madnesses akin to our being charmed by the animal's sincere repetitions?

THE DIFFERENCE BETWEEN DESIRE AND CHARM

In fact, an important difference remains between the desirous interest we take in humans and the entirely non-erotic relation that we enjoy with the animal. Desirability is not charm. While we may be led to desire the other for their quirks, these are in truth the very opposite of sincerities: symptoms are unwitting hypocrisies. The cat's devoted attention to the fish is quite distinct from the benumbed fixations of neurosis.

The animal's concentration upon its daily tasks cannot be experienced as the manifestation of something else, disavowed, to be treated and eliminated. In humans, this frozen dialectic of bad habit and the tics of neurotic madness can become unsnagged and the machine rendered once more functional and productive. In animals, dialectic is going nowhere and was never meant to leave this cul-de-sac. The possibility of restarting the dialectical machine in the case of man, of *recovering* from neurosis, is what allows the orthodox Hegelian to read the human being's obsessions as deficiencies which should ultimately be superseded. Man will never be (simply) an animal, precisely because he has the potential to escape the marches or margins in which the neurotic often feels more at home.

These patches of bad infinity represent the failure to actualise a potential which the beast does not possess: the merely living creature is not meant to get better, its habit has nowhere to go, it is not meant to break out of the circle and embark on an historic development — it has no 'fate'. But this means that what would be witless inanity in a human being can take on the charm of an infinite sincerity in the animal.

It is with regard to the exclusive valorisation of the possibility of departure and leaving behind — dialectical progress in the way of the good infinite — that we part company with Hegel, and we do so partly in the name of the *universalisation* of neurosis that psychoanalysis proclaims, the ineluctability of our childhood and animality in adulthood, nature in culture. Supersession will not supersede repression. None of us shall cease to be neurotic, unless we become something even worse. Perhaps it is in just these kinds of apparently regressive human behaviours that we find an overlap between man and the animal, a way to remain lodged in the borderland that we have invoked, the neurotic's receptivity to the animal that is one of the most exceptional and valuable features of the human being as such.

All of which is to say that one can view the animal from above or below, retrospectively or prospectively — perching higher up or lower down among the branches of the Porphyrian tree. One can see its habits from the point of view of stone and plant as a progression beyond the rootedness and graceless automaticity of the mechanical, and from this angle, habit is as yet neither good nor bad, but merely progress in comparison to what came earlier. Or one can view the animal's habitude from the standpoint of the human, whence it will appear to be a permanent instinctually programmed 'bad habit', just waiting to be surpassed when humanity proper arrives on the scene. To think of the animal as caught up in bad habits is to assess it in the terms set by human spirit, and to condemn it as an aborted dialectic or failed sublation. But this is to view the animal in terms of *what became of it*. The perspective of the end will only ever be able to envisage the animal kingdom as standing in need of redemption, and it will never be able to think of its inhabitants as beautiful and perfect in themselves.

Conclusion

LEARNING PHILOSOPHY FROM ANIMALS

Animals are lucky enough never to have been troubled by the standpoint of the true infinite. The beauty of the animal and the serenity of its fossil express to us this untroubled character. Perhaps this is what charms us so. For here we witness the possibility of a 'benumbed captivation' (*Benommenheit*) which has by no means to be viewed as occupying a lower level in comparison with the human being's openness to beings as such and as an (infinite) whole. This is ultimately man's 'theoretical' side, his ability to abstract from the *practical* vision of things in which a particular project always limits our understanding of what an entity can be. Here is a pre-philosophical finitude of 'environment' (*Umwelt*) and ambition which need not be considered from the standpoint of theory or philosophy. But what we wish to establish in closing is that an experience with animals can help to liberate us from our own egocentric and anthropocentric horizons and may teach us a new way in to this 'disinterested' theoretical vision. We would thus move beyond Heidegger's 'clearing', and towards Rilke's 'Open', in our pursuit of a new, more animalic philosophy.

Even if the human being is the animal in which 'philosophy happens' (Heidegger 1995 [1929–30], 7/10), it is also the only animal capable of undoing the damage that philosophy has done. Perhaps this gesture of unweaving is a necessary one, since we can hardly begin from anywhere except our own being-human and the philosophy to which we are prone. To then cast the gaze of Medusa at the dialectic, which is to say, to see philosophy from the standpoint of the *animal* and its bad infinite, is as close as we can get to bestowing a gaze upon the animal itself, a gift which Derrida found lacking in even the most zoophiliac of philosophies. And philosophy in turn may learn from its own envisioning.

We have not disputed philosophy's consignment of the animal to the realm of the bad infinite; rather, we have depended upon it, but we have assigned it a new value. By viewing this valorisation of the true infinite through the eyes of the animal, we human animals have put that evaluation in question, along with the *right* of philosophy to decide upon the animal's value. We have taken into account how the *animal itself* would view philosophy and its evaluation. Thus we will have allowed the animal to *look back* at philosophy, rather than simply being transpierced by its gaze.

In allowing ourselves to be charmed by the animal and attempting to understand this experience, we have allowed the animal within us to make its own essay at philosophy. Without the beautiful animal itself, we could never have attempted this. Therefore, it might be said that we have learned it from the animals themselves.[1]

ON BAD READING HABITS — DETACHING THE BAD INFINITE FROM 'BAD FAITH'

In this bewitched state we have read not only the dialectic but also the history of philosophy, in our trot through certain of its most enticing avenues. We have been a little capricious perhaps, but infinitely serious in our devotion to those things which took our fancy. We have allowed ourselves to become distracted and then fascinated by certain passages which were to have been surpassed, used for other ends, or which simply remain epiphenomenal to the overall intent of the text — like Kant's 'charm' and Hegel's 'natural beauty'. We have persisted in circling around these moments, heedless of where the philosophical process was originally meant to go. We have remained, throughout our own journey, happily fixated on such things as animals and fossils, which occupy an earlier moment in the dialectical process, and the role of which is, from a Hegelian point of view, solely to be overcome.

Rather than feeling pangs of guilt, should we not perhaps remain content in this fascination, as happy as a cat fixing its daily attention on an inaccessible fish? Perhaps it is time to resist the feelings of 'bad faith' which tell us that we should always be doing *more*, the urgings of a bad conscience to which Hegel will perhaps have conceded the most, in his attempt to do *everything*, which surely constitutes one of the most astonishing and productive attempts to enjoy a clear conscience that mankind will ever have witnessed. Perhaps philosophy itself has always been such an attempt. But then again, there is something which human beings can do that Hegel does not do, and nor indeed does anyone who tries to do everything — and that is to practise philosophy like an animal.

This is to approach philosophy as if sheltering within its branches were a number of charming animals, and in our growing indifference to dialectic we have become a little animalic ourselves, pursuing philosophy as an animal might (and as it might pursue *another* animal).

If we are reading philosophy in a madly selective way, then we are from a Hegelian point of view indulging our own bad habits; but we would rather say that we are touching upon the corpus of philosophy *animalically* and thinking from the point of view of a feline sniffing at a book of philosophy and perhaps rubbing her whiskers against it, territorialising it but also deriving pleasure from it. Only from the vantage point of Hegelian man is this to be condemned as an improper approach to the text.

Humans have the contingent privilege of being able to cease feeling that the bad infinite is always a consequence of bad faith. There is a bad infinite we must learn to detach from its opposition to the good and the true, dislodging it from its Hegelian position as a mere precursor. Human beings have the remarkable ability to experience the bad infinite in the animal as charming.

This attitude to the bad infinite is indeed a specifically *human* one, and not something that the animal itself can adopt. It involves relinquishing both the dialectical and the transcendental standpoints, since it refuses to view what precedes it as an earlier incarnation of its own self — a 'positing of its presuppositions' or a retrospective announcement of those conditions which made its own actuality possible.

In terms of Hegelianism and its posterity, perhaps this would be to adopt the perspective recommended by Georges Bataille, which he contrasted with the Hegelian position — that of the masterly sovereign and his boundless extravagance, necessitating an 'inoperative' dialectic that fails to produce anything, or refuses to, leaving such laborious activity to the slave. The master simply leans back and contemplates his ornamental goldfish while the kingdom falls into ruin, aloof to the 'restricted economy' in which everything is a means to an end and all entities have their function. Instead he chooses to envisage the world in all its purposelessness.

It seems to us that, even if the cat's sneezing, washing, and scratching are purposive for the cat *itself*, nevertheless in finding this purely functional behaviour *charming* we are viewing the world in a sovereign manner that — in another regard — we have learned from the animal itself. The cat's repurposing of our artifices will have taught us to *distinguish* these practical activities from their utility: this much we will have learned from her use of a shelf for sleeping upon, a piano for sitting upon and the windowsill as a lookout for keeping track of whatever might be going on in the garden.

The way animals ignore the functions which we bestow upon equipment can cause us to waiver in our certainty that human projects are in any way definitive. The animal attitude to human equipment is one of almost complete indifference, and pragmatically this often renders the device quite unusable. Despite the appearance of similarity, this is not identical with Heidegger's account of the 'ready-to-hand' tool *breaking* (Heidegger 1962 [1927], 102ff/72ff), for the animal's invasion does not reveal that equipment's function as if this were an inherent part of it, constitutive of the very meaning of its 'being'; rather, it draws the entity back to a state of potentiality *prior* to the function that we have contingently assigned to it.

Giorgio Agamben has given much thought to the idea of seeing a richer potential in an ossified actuality, and his account of the cat playing with a ball of yarn as if it were a mouse is intended to draw us away from the 'servile' utilitarian perspective and let us glimpse another of the world's faces. In this hitherto mysterious facet, the restricted set of possible uses that have accrued to things are 'disabled' or 'deactivated' and new possibilities opened up (Agamben 2007 [2005], 85–86/98–99).[2] The context of Agamben's remark is instructive: the sovereign vision of the world is bestowed upon us by animals. And yet we alone can recognise what is taking place here — only a human being can appreciate what it *means* that a cat may treat a piece of string as a mouse's tail. Through this encounter with a charming animal, we are endowed with something of the animal's own manner of perceiving: the cat's attitude to the keyboard and the shelf teaches us to suspend our attribution of purposiveness to the world and then to abstract from the natural purposes of the animal's own behaviour. Thus we are inclined no longer to treat this obstacle to functionality as an annoyance, but rather to find it charming, a thing of beauty.

Shaving and weeding provoked ennui in the human while the feline equivalents of washing and scratching were the source of unending delight. In this delight we come to view the animal's activities with almost the same sincerity and devotion as the animal itself displays in carrying them out.

To make sense of this charm, we have learned from this indifferent treatment of us and our chattels to see the human world and its philosophy through the eyes of the animal, fossilising the dialectic, a little madly.

In looking upon philosophy as an animal would, we can treat the animal as philosophy never has, and endow it with a gaze of its own.

Notes

These notes perform all the usual functions of a scholarly apparatus, which include a more frequent allusion to specifically contemporary work than may be found in the main text, but they also introduce extended autobiographical elements and at times even constitute a second text running in parallel to the first, but along different lines, and in particular when it comes to the relation that poetry and literature enjoy with respect to animality. Both the autobiographical and the literary-poetic are, in their own way, essential to a book on philosophy and the animal, even if here they remain largely subliminal.

INTRODUCTION

1. This text was originally given as a talk at the European University at St. Petersburg, on Friday 13th November 2015, under the title, 'Beauty and the Beast: Kant and the Animal's Charm'. I must thank Oxana Timofeeva, Artemy Magun, Olga Matskevich, and everyone else who helped organise the event, along with all of the other wonderful people I met while in Russia.

I began to reconstruct the text as an essay on Sunday 22nd November 2015, and then again, after a hiatus, on Friday 13th May 2016, after which it became a book. As seems to happen in such cases, the lapse of time made room for things to happen (and even for the meaning of such assertions to change), but this text is at least in part an indirect response to Oxana Timofeeva's work, in *History of Animals* and elsewhere. It is a gift to her in the name of our mutual love of cats, and the animal more generally, which is in no way incompatible with its first and foremost having been written for my own black cat.

A later version of the text was given under the title, 'The Animal's Sincerity and Fossilised Dialectic', at a workshop on European Philosophy at the University of Bristol, on Tuesday 30th August 2016, organised by Havi Carel, for whose continued support I am sincerely grateful.

Perhaps this book is an initial and truly modest attempt — at times, here and there — to 'do philosophy', in the sense that Alison Assiter, a great friend and remarkable academic, avowed herself to be undertaking in *Kierkegaard, Eve and Metaphors of Birth*, an ambition reminiscent of Gilles Deleuze's decision to do the same following his early apprenticeship in the history of philosophy. This simply means, in my own case, that the book engages primarily with a problem, a concept or a question, before, in a second moment, deploying certain philosophers to assist with the solution (not that things are ever that simple, since the very question and the way it is posed was shaped *by* those very philosophers, along with certain others), and even breaking free of the text (almost) altogether to risk certain conceptual gestures of my own.

A great many of the thinkers and problems addressed in the present work were opened up by a number of encounters at the University of the West of England, and I must take the opportunity to thank first and foremost Alison Assiter, Havi Carel, Tina Chanter, Patrick Crogan, Iain Grant, Darian Meacham, John Sellars, and Will Stronge, among many others who came and went, the staff on the St. Matthias campus, and the exceptional students who gave us heart while the university attempted to eviscerate us.

The book was written after I had left that institution, and it was finished in the much more hospitable surroundings of the University of Newcastle upon Tyne, which meant that it could be finished much more quickly than it would have been otherwise.

That said, the initial idea, or one initial hope — to redeem the notions of the 'charming' and the 'picturesque' from their Kantian slander — is much older, perhaps even stemming from my very first encounter with Kant's third Critique, with Rachel Jones, at Warwick, in 1998–99. In that and many other respects, in particular with regard to its general concern for the relations between nature and philosophy, it can hardly be said that having been exposed to philosophy for the first time at the University of Warwick in the 1990s and 2000s has failed to leave its mark, even if my response is often deliberately contrary.

In general, let this note stand as a preliminary indication of the fact that this book is as autobiographical as any in its topics and the path that it forges to negotiate them, to the point of constituting at times an indulgence, albeit one that is not entirely unreflective. It is fitting, therefore, that the very first book of philosophy it cites is Jean-Paul Sartre's *Nausea*, which was my introduction to philosophy, and this thanks to Warwick since it was included on a list of texts to be read in preparation for a degree in Philosophy there. (The only other text I can recall having encountered before that is Friedrich Nietzsche's *Beyond Good and Evil* which belonged to my brother, but I do not remember truly understanding or liking what I found there, and it remains for me among the least read and least favoured of all Nietzsche's works.)

2. The other terrible extreme of this repetition, evoking another emotion, may be found in animals which are caged or otherwise imprisoned, that trace the same circle or figure of eight on the floor of their enclosure, restless even in their weariness. Defeated, the animal expends its last effort retreating into a corner, in a final moment of dignity, seeking whatever cover it has been vouchsafed, in order finally to pass into absolute darkness and regain the impenetrable privacy of death.

I am thinking of Gavin Maxwell's later experiences with his otters, in a remarkable household which looms large in the background of this work.

As I write these words, my own cat is herself behind bars, for the first time, against my will and her own.

3. That said, it has recently come to our attention that a new type of coating has rendered this example merely a proverb. And yet in the move from literal to proverbial truth — from the real to the ideal — we find a good example of what Hegel calls 'sublation' (in German, *Aufhebung*: also translated on occasion as 'supersession', 'transcending', 'overcoming', 'relief' [the French, '*relève*'], and even 'suspension' and 'idealisation', for reasons that will become apparent as we go along). Sublation is the precise opposite — or at least the other — of the bad infinite, in which the same thing is repeated *identically*; *Aufhebung* expresses the *true* infinite, in which the same thing is repeated *differently*, being perfected through its very repetition.

4. For a philosophy of vegetation which resists the Hegelian diminution of plants, the work of Michael Marder on vegetative life should be consulted (cf. Marder 2013, esp. 24–27, 107ff). He even speaks of weeds as falling beneath the Hegelian scythe: 'Weeds, of course, must be devoid of Spirit, seeing that [*sic*] they stand in the way of cultivating activities that render "self-less Nature" useful' (ibid., 27). In general, perhaps something like our own attempt to redeem the bad infinite may be at work within Marder's *corpus*, but in the context of vegetables.

5. Hegel certainly posits a rigorous distinction between the laws of nature and culture, or rather, between nature and spirit, time and history:

> Historical change in the abstract sense has long been interpreted in general terms as embodying some kind of progress towards a better and more perfect condition. Changes in the natural world, no matter how great their variety, exhibit only an eternally recurring cycle [*einen Kreislauf, der sich immer wiederholt*]; for in nature there is nothing new under the sun, and in this respect its manifold play of forms produces an effect of boredom [*Langeweile*]. Only in those changes which take place in the spiritual sphere does anything new emerge. The peculiarity of spiritual phenomena has given rise to the idea that the destiny of man is quite different from that of merely natural objects. For in the latter we always encounter one and the same determination and a constantly stable character to which all change can be reduced, and from which all change follows as a secondary consequence; whereas man displays a real capacity for change, [. . .] in short, he possesses an impulse of *perfectibility*. (WH, 124–25/74)

Perfectibility and hence *progress*:

> If we compare spiritual changes with those of nature, we observe that, in the natural world, individual things are subject to change, whereas the species themselves are enduring. Thus a planet, for example, leaves each particular position it occupies, although its orbit as a whole is constant. And the same is true of animal species. For change is a cyclic process, a repetition of identical phases [*ein Kreislauf, Wiederholung des Gleichen*]. [. . .] Consequently, the survival of the species consists purely in a uniform repetition of one and the same mode of existence. But with spiritual forms, it is otherwise; for in this case, change occurs not just on the surface but within the concept, and it is the concept

itself which is modified. In the natural world, the species does not progress, but in the world of the spirit, each change is a form of progress. [. . .] [I]n the case of spiritual phenomena, higher forms are produced through the transformation of earlier and less advanced ones. (WH, 128 /Hoffmeister 1955, 153–54)

Thanks to Andrés Sáenz De Sicilia for reminding me of these passages in particular.

6. We shall sometimes take the liberty of describing the true (*wahrhaft*) infinite as the 'good infinite', to emphasise the fact that, in the end, a *valorisation* is implicit in the opposition Hegel draws. The contrast between the terms which Hegel in fact uses is revealing: the infinite of sheer repetition is 'bad' (*schlecht*), which is to say flawed at the level of *both* understanding — where 'badness' carries the sense of falsity or inadequacy — *and* morality or at least 'axiology' (the 'wicked'). And yet the infinite of spirit and history, of human reason and the dialectic it involves, is merely '*true*' (*wahrhaft*). In the latter, Hegel expunges the taint of moral evaluation, but not in the former. For our purposes, which will soon become clear, it is as well to retain a sense of the moral overtones of *both* by occasionally describing the 'true' infinite as the 'good'. (This will also have the virtue of allowing us explicitly to draw an analogy between the good and the bad *infinite* and good and bad *habits*, later on.)

7. This threshold will be our concern throughout. When considering the limit that separates and joins the wild and the tame, it is always instructive to bear in mind the question of cats and *dogs*. The first chapter of the present work fastens upon dogs as a privileged example when it comes to *philosophy*'s consideration of sincerity, but they play almost no role in the rest of the book. This is telling with respect to the terrain we are setting out to explore.

That great student of animal behaviour, lover of both cats and dogs, Konrad Lorenz, describes their respective domestications in the following passage:

Only two animals have entered the human household otherwise than as prisoners and become domesticated by other means than those of enforced servitude: the dog and the cat. Two things they have in common, namely, that both belong to the order of carnivores and both serve man in their capacity of hunters. In all other characteristics, above all in the manner of their associations with man, they are as different as the night from the day. There is no domestic animal which has so radically altered its whole way of living, indeed its whole sphere of interests, that has become domestic in so true a sense as the dog: and there is no animal that, in the course of its century-old association with man, has altered so little as the cat. There is some truth in the assertion that the cat [. . .] is no domestic animal but a completely wild being. Maintaining its full independence it has taken up its abode in the houses and outhouses of man, for the simple reason that there are more mice there than elsewhere. [. . .] [T]he appeal of the cat lies in the very fact that she has formed no close bond with [man], that she has the uncompromising independence of a tiger or a leopard while she is hunting in his stables and barns; that she still remains mysterious and remote when she is rubbing herself gently against the legs of her mistress or purring contentedly in front of the fire. (Lorenz 1964 [1950], ix–x, cf. 14 on the 'domestication' of cats)

Simply put, 'the cat is a wild animal' (Lorenz 1964 [1950], 165). For Lorenz, this wildness is the source of the animal's 'charm': 'the charm of the cat lies in the fact that she displays to me, within the confines of my own home, the unbroken wildness and the subtle grace which she shares with the panther, the jaguar, and the tiger, and possesses in no less measure than they' (Lorenz 1964 [1950], 16). That this conjunction is not accidental is suggested by its recurrence one hundred and fifty pages later, where Lorenz speaks of,

> that quality of uncurbed wildness which, to me, constitutes their chief charm. I find it a constant source of wonder that I share my home with little tigers which are sometimes in and sometimes out, and which conduct their hunting expeditions and love affairs as though they still lived in their unhandled, pristine state in the wild woods. (Lorenz 1964 [1950], 163, cf. 165, 166)

In *King Solomon's Ring*, Lorenz associates charm with beauty, and thus offers us testimony that our intuitions as to the connection between the two, in spite of Kant's attempt to keep them apart, are not altogether without foundation. He speaks of, 'the charm and beauty [*den Reiz und die Schönheit*] of a new species' (Lorenz 1964 [1963], 68, cf. xxxv).

Likewise, for Aaron Schuster, the cat's independence grants us access to an untamed wilderness:

> If the cat is the privileged animal representative of this narcissistic sufficiency [which Freud identifies in children], it is because — unlike the trainable dog, who is in this sense much closer to the dialectic of culture — its wildness and predator instinct prevent it from being fully absorbed into the human world: a cat remains an aloof and undialectical creature no matter how domesticated it may be. (Schuster 2016, 130)

Schuster provides us with a treasure-trove of references in this area. He also quotes a remarkable passage from Rainer Maria Rilke, to whose *poetic* account of animals we shall return. Rilke is attempting to restore the animal to its easily forgotten status as a *subject*, and precisely by considering the cat's *gaze*: the significance of this will have been demonstrated in an unforgettable manner by Jacques Derrida, whose thought looms large throughout the present work. As we shall see in more detail later, for Derrida, philosophy has always treated animals as *objects*. That said, in what is perhaps a departure from Derrida, Rilke wonders if the cat's eyes do not see *through* us:

> Take dogs: the admiration and trust evidenced in their approaches to us often make some of them seem to have abandoned their most primal canine traditions and turned to worship of our ways, and even of our faults. That is precisely what makes them tragic and sublime. Their determination to acknowledge us forces them to live at the very limits of their nature, constantly — through the humanness of their gaze, their nostalgic muzzlings — on the verge of passing beyond them.
> But what attitude do cats adopt? Cats are just that: cats. And their world is utterly, through and through, a cat's world. You think they look at us? Has anyone ever truly known whether or not they deign to register for one instant in the sunken surface of their retina our trifling forms? As they stare at us they might merely be eliminating us magically from their gaze, eternally replete. True, some of us indulge our susceptibility to their wheedling and electric caresses. But let such persons remember the strange, brusque, and offhand way in which their favourite animal frequently cuts short the effusions they had

fondly imagined to be reciprocal. They, too, even the privileged elected to enjoy the proximity of cats, have been rejected and denied time and time again, and even as they cherish some mysteriously apathetic creature in their arms they too have felt themselves brought up short at the threshold of a world that is a cat's world, a world inhabited exclusively by cats and in which they live in ways that no one else can fathom. (Rilke 1984 [1921], 9–10/56–57, quoted in Schuster, 'Fasting and Method: Kafka as Philosopher', 12n20)

We might supplement Schuster's citation with a passage he does not quote: 'you must agree with me that a cat does not become an integral part of our lives, not like, for example, some toy might be: even though it belongs to us now, it remains somehow apart, outside [*il reste un peu en dehors*], and thus we always have: life + a cat, which, I can assure you, adds up to an incalculable sum [*une somme énorme*]' (Rilke 1984 [1921], 12/58).

Rilke concludes his piece ironically by suggesting that the only way to shore up man's world against the annihilation promised by the cat's witheringly indifferent gaze is to deny the existence of cats altogether: '*Il n'y a pas de chats*' (ibid., 13/59).

Let us note in passing that T. S. Eliot echoes Rilke's phrase, 'a cat's a cat', in capital letters, for emphasis, in *Old Possum's Book of Practical Cats* (Eliot 1998 [1939], 46).

8. Lorenz remarks upon this connection between the utility of the cat's movements and their beauty in the following passage:

There are certain things in Nature in which beauty and utility, artistic and technical perfection, combine in some incomprehensible way: the web of a spider, the wing of a dragon-fly, the superbly streamlined body of the porpoise, and the movements of a cat. [. . .] And it is almost as though the animal were aware of the beauty of its movements, for it appears to delight in them and to perform them for the sake of their own perfection. This game, the game of movements, occupies a very special place in the life of this most elegant of all animals. (Lorenz 1964 [1950], 154)

We ourselves came to wonder, later on, if the cat was not aware of her own beauty, and even of her own death, a consciousness which has long been denied to animals.

9. Hegel conjoins Kant and the Jews under the heading of the 'sublime': 'This sort of sublimity in its first original character we find especially in the outlook of the Jews and in their sacred poetry. For visual art cannot appear here, where it is impossible to sketch any adequate picture of God; only the poetry of ideas, expressed in words, can' (A, 373/480). '[T]he negative praise of the power and glory of the one God, we encounter as sublimity in the strict sense in Hebrew poetry. It cancels the positive immanence of the Absolute in its created phenomena and puts the *one* substance explicitly apart as the Lord of the world in contrast to whom there stands the entirety of his creatures, and these, in comparison with God, are posited as the inherently powerless and perishable. [. . .] [T]he sublimity of God is brought nearer to contemplation [*Anschauung*, intuition] by reason of the fact that what exists in the world, with all its splendour, magnificence, and glory, is represented [*dargestellt*] as only a serving accident and a transient show [*Schein*] in comparison with God's being and stability' (A, 364/469).

10. Martin gives us a clear formulation of the problem afflicting the bad infinite and of the connection between the two descriptions of this infinity: 'God encounters his limit in finitude; yet to be limited is to be finite. The number series is used to illustrate the infinite, even to exemplify it, yet no matter how far one goes along it one is always left with a further finite quantity' (Martin 2007, 172).

11. Quoted in Martin 2007, 169, upon which we rely for a number of references in this section.

12. Elsewhere, Hegel speaks not of the manifestation of the Father in the Son but of his manifestation in the earlier moment of *creation* and the *fiat lux*: 'when we first have hold of the infinite we have it alone, much as God before the creation of the world is alone. Yet when we have the infinite alone it is the bad infinite — just as God is not the true God if he does not manifest himself outwardly. For God is God only in the act of creating the world' (Hegel 2008, 113, quoted in Ruda 2013). According to Martin, in the *Science of Logic* at least, this distinction between god and his creation — or perhaps, to be more precise, the *creatures* which result from it — is in fact an example of the *bad* infinite (Martin 2007, 170), an unsublated opposition between the infinite mind of god and the finite nature and spirit which he creates.

13.

> '*To sublate*' [Aufheben] has a twofold meaning [*gedoppelten Sinn*] in the language: on the one hand it means to preserve, to maintain, and equally it also means to cause to cease, to put an end to. Even 'to preserve' includes a negative element, namely, that something is removed from its immediacy and so from an existence which is open to external influences, in order to preserve it [. . .]; it has only lost its immediacy but is not on that account annihilated. [. . .] But it is certainly remarkable to find that a language has come to use one and the same word for two opposite meanings. It is a delight [*erfreulich*] to speculative thought to find in the language words which have in themselves a speculative meaning; the German language has a number of such. (SL, 107/114)

14. Hegel is at his most translucent on this point at the end of the Introduction to the *Lectures on the Philosophy of World History* (WH, 150–51/Hoffmeister 1955, 182–83).

15. The third moment in the sequence is something like a negation of the second, which was in turn a negation of the first. Hence the famous description of sublation — the overcoming of the opposition that is set up between the first two terms ('I am *not* [the same as] you') — as 'a negation of the negation, i.e. an affirmation [*Negation der Negation, Affirmation*]' (PNI, 283/107 §271A), a 'negation of the negative [*Negation des Negativen*]' (PNI, 204/22 §246A), so sublation would be, with respect to the first moment, 'to negate its negation [*seine Negation zu negieren*]' (SL, 138/150).

16. The relation between the finite and the in-finite (the *non*-finite) according to the 'true infinite', to be contrasted with the same relation in the case of the 'bad infinite', in which the negation of the finite by the infinite should be understood rather as an '*abstract* negation': 'abstract negation [is] not the negation coming from consciousness, which [sc., determinate negation] *supersedes* [aufhebt] in such a way as to *preserve* and *maintain* [aufbewahrt *und* erhält] what is superseded, and

consequently survives [*überlebt*] its own supersession [*sein Aufgehobenwerden — Aufhebung* here in the sense, primarily, of "to cancel"]' (PhG, 114–15/150 §188). In determinate negation,

> nothingness is specifically the nothingness of that *from which it results*. For it is only when it is taken as the result of that from which it emerges, that it is, in fact, the true result; in that case it is itself a *determinate* nothingness [*ein* bestimmtes], one which has a content. The scepticism that ends up with the bare abstraction of nothingness [*Abstraktion des Nichts*] or emptiness cannot get any further from there, but must wait to see whether something new comes along and what it is, in order to throw it too into the same empty abyss. But when, on the other hand, the result is conceived as it is in truth, namely, as a *determinate* negation [bestimmte *Negation*], a new form has thereby immediately arisen. (PhG, 51/74 §79)

17. Slavoj Žižek explains the redoubling as follows: 'the reflective "example of the example", the exemplification of the very principle of example (of the Christian truth that God Himself becomes Man, that *this "exemplification" of God in Man is part of the very notion of God*)' (1991, 42, emphasis added).

18. Cf. the passage quoted in note 16 *supra* (PhG, 114–15/150 §188).

19. 1 Corinthians 15:26, echoed famously by John Donne: 'And Death shall be no more; Death, thou shalt die' (*Holy Sonnet X*). Hegel himself makes this connection: '*God has died, God is dead —* this is the most frightful of all thoughts, that everything eternal and true *is not*, that negation itself is found in God. The deepest anguish, the feeling of complete irretrievability, the annulling of everything that is elevated, are bound up with this thought. However, the process does not come to a halt at this point; rather, a reversal takes place: God, that is to say, maintains himself in this process, and the latter is only the death of death [*Tod des Todes*]. God rises again to life, and thus things are reversed. The resurrection is something that belongs just as essentially to faith [as to the crucifixion]. [. . .] [T]he death of Christ is the death of this death itself, the negation of negation [*der Tod Christi ist aber der Tod dieses Todes selbst, die Negation der Negation*]' (RIII, 323–24n199/246–47n, cf. 125/60, 219/150).

20. The origin of this notion of death is to be found in the dialectic of the master and the slave: 'death is the *natural* negation of consciousness [. . .]. Death certainly shows that each staked his life and held it of no account [. . .]. They put an end to their consciousness in its alien setting [*fremden Wesenheit*] of natural existence [*Dasein*]' (PhG, 114/149 §188).

To reinforce the point, one should reread the following famous passage:

> that an accident as such, detached from what circumscribes it, what is bound and is actual only in its context with others, should attain an existence of its own and a separate freedom — this is the tremendous power of the negative [*die ungeheure Macht des Negativen*]; it is the energy of thought, of the pure 'I'. Death, if that is what we want to call this non-actuality, is of all things the most dreadful [*das Furchtbarste*], and to hold fast to what is dead requires the greatest strength [. . .]. But the life of Spirit is not the life that shrinks from death and keeps itself untouched by devastation, but rather the life that endures it and maintains itself in it [*ihn erträgt und in ihm sich erhält*]. [. . .] Spirit is this power only by looking the negative in the face, and tarrying with it. This tarrying [*Verweilen*] with

the negative is the magical power that converts it into being. This power is identical with what we earlier called the subject. (PhG, 19/36 §32)

And again: 'it is only through staking one's life that freedom is won' (PhG, 114/149 §187).

21. As Heidegger puts it, installing himself perhaps unwittingly in the Hegelian bloodline: 'To die means to be capable of death as death. Only man dies [*stirbt*]. The animal perishes [*verendet*]. It has death neither ahead of itself nor behind it' (1971b [1950], 178/180, & 1971c [1951], 150–51/152. Cf. 1962 [1927], 284/240–41). Derrida will have pointed out that Heidegger and Hegel are at their closest when it comes to the question of the animal (1989 [1987], 50–51/80).

22. This is mirrored at the level of the *names* with which we address our favourite animals: to supplement Hegel's idea of an individual animal subsumed by its species, forever hindered in the attainment of full individuality, let us note that the domestic animal, or the beloved animal, is frequently given a name as a mark of its individuality (or, in a more sinister turn, its ownership: hence man — the namer's — superiority, taught to him in the garden of Eden). But as well as proper names *stricto sensu*, the human being, granted the power of naming, can take up the universal, common noun, and allow it to function as a *proper* noun: so 'cat' or 'mog' become unique individual names: 'Cat' or 'Mog' (along with diminutives and modifications of a similar type).

It is as if the species becomes individuated here in a sort of 'concrete universal' of the animal ('concrete universal' being Hegel's name for a universal which spontaneously particularises itself, engendering its particular forms according to its own immanent logic), while at the same time the whole species resonates within this one singular individual. When I see one strange black cat, I see a unique animal but also my own cat, and *each* cat. The use made here of the distributive 'each' rather than the totalising 'every' might take us some way beyond Hegel's own vision of the animal and its relation to the species.

Is this process of naming not the strict opposite of what happens to *human* names on Hegel's account? Elsewhere we shall broach his example of the surname of Julius Caesar, transformed from a proper name into the general term for all Roman leaders: thus, for humans: singular to general; but for cats: general to singular.

23. The owl of Minerva, which Hegel takes to be a representative of Philosophy's wisdom, the self-conceptualisation of spirit in its flight, taking to the air — towards the heaven of Ideas — only when all is said and done, ripe for the understanding and susceptible of being inscribed in the Encyclopædia or Book of Life (PR, 12–13/28).

Inter alia, at the very end of the *Philosophy of Nature*, the phoenix is employed to describe the very transition from nature to spirit: 'The purpose of nature is to extinguish itself [*töten*], and to break through this rind of immediate and sensuous being, to consume itself like a Phoenix in order to emerge from this externality rejuvenated as spirit' (PNIII, 212/538 §376A, cf. WH 32/98). To hear more of this animal, along with a number of others (a Derridean spider and a plastic Malabouian salamander), one should consult Catherine Malabou's remarkable text on the subject in her *Changing Difference* (Malabou 2011 [2009], 67ff/81ff).

24. At the time of writing (September 2017), the longevity of this remarkable fish extends as far as sixteen years. It continues to flourish while all around it have slipped away. As does the cat's unflagging energy and sincere devotion to fish-watching.

I should also clarify that the cat in question is in some senses rather my parents' cat — I have taken the liberty of saying 'my own', but then again the very idea of 'owning' a cat will naturally be put in question as we proceed. What could 'ownership' mean in the case of a half-wild animal which belongs to a household only when it sees fit, and which adopts a family just as much as it is itself adopted?

According to Derrida, 'a pussycat never belongs' (2008 [2006], 7/23). And as Lorenz has it in a beautiful passage,

> [n]one of my cats died a natural death [. . .]. But it is in the nature of eagles, lions and tigers that they seldom meet with a peaceful end. And this is the essence of the cat as I love it, the inaccessible, unrestrained, wild animal. Strangely enough, this is also the very reason why the cat is so 'homely', for somebody or something can only be 'at home' whose profession lies outside; and the purring cat on the hearth betokens for me the symbol of homeliness just because he is not my prisoner but an independent being of almost equal status who happens to live in the same house that I do. (Lorenz 1964 [1950], 166)

25. Philosophy has often chosen to align animals with children, as if convinced of the fact that the animal is merely an inferior form of the human, forever immature; we shall attempt implicitly to show that they are in fact vastly disparate. One can nevertheless find testimony of this alignment in the most unexpected of places, even where philosophy is beginning, supposedly, to be 'overcome', as in one of Heidegger's very rare allusions to childhood and the child's experience of the moon, in particular, in *What Is Called Thinking?*, which he even allows might be more genuine than our adult understanding (Heidegger 1968 [1951–52], 182–86/185–90). One might read in a similar fashion his allusion to 'primitive' peoples, in *Being and Time* — those who also stand closer than we to the wolves that merely howl at the moon (1962 [1927], 468–69/415–16).

Employing the examples of animals and children, Giorgio Agamben shows how *play* is premised upon the suspension of an old use and the returning of a formerly functional item to a state of pure potentiality, a non-functional, non-instrumental state, or a 'means without an end': in other words, a potential which is not modelled upon an actuality that would be its goal and hence ontologically and logically prior to it. The utensil may then become a toy.

Agamben's notion might helpfully be understood in terms of Georges Bataille's response to Hegel: the work that is produced by the dialectical 'labour of the negative' (a negation which is *productive* or 'determinate') is, from the standpoint of a more general economy, redundant. Or even within a 'restricted' economy, one can simply refuse to allow one's activity to result in an *œuvre, opus* (plural: *opera*) or work — dialectical operations are thus rendered 'in-*opera*tive' in Agamben's terms. In the first case, the object *produced* is transformed into a plaything, while in the second, the activity of production is itself reduced to the level of play or else takes the form of a non-productive contemplation which merely 'studies' the object rather than *using* it.

In this sense, perhaps contemplation, or philosophy, is the adult equivalent of child's play. In the context which interests us, philosophical contemplation might then be akin to the sincerity and charm of an *animal*, and philosophic wisdom an ultimately animalic vision of the world.

Agamben speaks of this 'rendering inoperative' also in terms of 'profanation', the displacement of an object from a sacred realm or sacral status. The passage we are about to read is one of the very few occasions upon which he suggests that the possibility of 'deactivation' belongs not just to the human being but also to the animal. The rarity of the gesture suggests that it might be possible for us to employ this passage for our own purposes, which means to understand why the cat is so appealing when it finds new uses for those human artefacts the function of which it shows such scant regard for. Consider the cat that takes to sleeping upon a book, before bestirring itself simply in order to perch upon the shelf where the book itself was to have been replaced:

Even in nature there are profanations. The cat who plays with a ball of yarn as if it were a mouse — just as the child plays with ancient religious symbols or objects that once belonged to the economic sphere — knowingly uses the characteristic behaviours of predatory activity (or, in the case of the child, of the religious cult or the world of work) in vain. These behaviours are not effaced, but, thanks to the substitution of the yarn for the mouse (or the toy for the sacred object), deactivated and thus opened up to a new, possible use.

But what sort of use? For the cat, what is the possible use for the ball of yarn? It consists in freeing a behaviour from its genetic inscription within a given sphere (predatory activity, hunting). The freed behaviour still reproduces and mimics the forms of the activity from which it has been emancipated, but, in emptying them of their sense and of any obligatory relationship to an end, it opens them and makes them available for a new use. The game with the yarn liberates the mouse from being prey and the predatory activity from being necessarily directed towards the capture and death of the mouse. And yet, this play stages the very same behaviours that define hunting. The activity that results from this thus becomes a pure means, that is, a praxis that, while firmly maintaining its nature as a means, is emancipated from its relationship to an end; it has joyously forgotten its goal and can now show itself as such, as a means without an end. The creation of a new use is possible only by deactivating an old use, rendering it inoperative. (Agamben 2007 [2005], 85–86/98–99, emphasis added)

This goes some way towards explaining the *sincerity* shared by both seriousness and play, which Lorenz, as ever, will have described so well: 'All forms of play have the common quality that they are fundamentally different from "earnest"; at the same time, however, they show an unmistakable resemblance, indeed an imitation of a definite, earnest situation' (Lorenz 1964 [1950], 155). Indeed Lorenz addresses the precise example of the kitten, the string, and the mouse, as well as the action of snatching at a passing bird, which may well be depicted on the front cover of the present book (Lorenz 1964 [1950], 155–56).

But are the animals which so profane and play not specifically *domestic* ones, and might it not be humans who are responsible for drawing the animal away from the natural function of its instinctive behaviour? This would be the enforced infantilisation of the animal, or perhaps it would amount to another, better form of childhood, of the kind Agamben himself indicates, in which one's natural needs are met and survival is no longer at issue. This allows the serious business of hunting to be transformed into play. In this case, the animals would teach us to perceive the world in a new way, freed from the restrictions placed upon it by our own earnestly pursued projects, but in addition to this, the animals themselves, thanks (at least in part) to their cohabitation with man, would be confined to a state of infancy in which they maintain a distance with respect to the functions that their behaviours are in nature intended to fulfil.

26. Sigmund Freud saw almost all of this and also drew attention to a certain proximity between animal and child, but he seems to have been charmed as much by the human infant as by the beast, on the grounds — eminently questionable — that a self-absorbed 'narcissism' is what appeals to us in both child and animal: 'The charm [*Reiz*] of a child lies to a great extent in his narcissism, his self-contentment and inaccessibility, just as does the charm of certain animals which seem not to concern themselves about us, such as cats and the large beasts of prey' (he goes on to say the same about 'great criminals and humourists', thus making it clear that no moral value is being assigned here, either way) (Freud 2001 [1914], 89/172, quoted in Schuster 2016, 128).

Jacques Lacan comments on this passage:

> Freud points out what every human being finds fascinating and satisfying in the apprehension of a being whose perceived characteristics are those of this enclosed world, shut in on itself, satisfied, full, which the narcissistic type represents. He compares it to the supreme seduction [*seduction souveraine*] a beautiful animal [*un bel animal*] exerts. (Lacan 1988 [1953–54], 132/152).

Despite our balking at the comparison, if 'narcissism' means simply an indifference to the (adult) human's functionalisation of the world, then we would accept the term.

27. A limit perhaps marked by the line that separates the main body of the text from its subliminal notes, in which at certain moments we deal with two other genres which can and do address the animal quite differently — or let themselves be addressed by it: literature and poetry.

28. Despite Derrida's demonstration that animals may be found scuttling around his entire *œuvre*, there is little to compare with the extended treatment one finds in *The Animal That Therefore I Am* and the two volumes of *The Beast and the Sovereign* (save perhaps, indirectly, *On Touching: Jean-Luc Nancy*).

The experience around which *The Animal That Therefore I Am* may be said to revolve is one occluded by philosophy — that of being looked at by an animal, and indeed a *particular* animal, not 'the Animal' in general. Derrida finds the unified, totalising notion of '*The* Animal' already suggestive of an adherence to an oppositional understanding of the kind one finds in metaphysics, since it presupposes on the one side, 'Man', and on the other, all of the animals put together and affirmed implicitly or explicitly to share or lack some trait which would allow us to speak of an animal 'as such' or 'the Animal' in general. To this abstract universal, Derrida opposes a real singularity: the philosopher's cat, which, although unique, the author refrains from naming, as if resisting this classic Edenic stamp of ownership — although he does intimate that it *has* a name (2008 [2006], 9/26).

Whatever generosity philosophy has displayed towards the animal, a benevolent paternalism that reaches its apogee in Jeremy Bentham's assignation of the animal's equal right to ethical treatment on the grounds that, like us, the creature *suffers*, it has never stopped treating the beast as an *object* which should be approached in a certain way, either instrumentalised or not, treated well or treated badly. Philosophy has never granted it the status of a *subject*, which is to say that it has never, or almost never, considered the animal's *gaze*. As Sartre clearly puts it, unlike the eyes, the gaze may not be looked *at* — it cannot be seen; the gaze can only *look* — it enjoys the subjectivity of experience (Sartre 1989 [1943], 252ff/292ff).

At first glance, it appears that metaphysics has pitted man and animal against one another by assigning rational thought and language to the former alone (the Aristotelian *zōon logon echon* or *animal rationale*, notwithstanding Plutarch's noble attempt at a reversal [1957, 487ff]). But Derrida identifies what is in fact a more pervasive tendency, one that extends the borders of metaphysics to enclose a number of writers who consider themselves to have escaped it: and this is the refusal to understand the animal as a subject. The very ubiquity of this gesture is perhaps what allowed it to go unnoticed.

It is at the end of this long, troubling history of philosophy that Derrida evokes the memorable experience of being caught naked by his own tabby: 'along with Descartes [more or less clearly metaphysical], Kant [the first avowed critic of metaphysics], Heidegger [the most prominent representative of the *overcoming* of metaphysics in the twentieth century], Levinas [the most prominent critic of *Heidegger*], and Lacan [but what relation to metaphysics does the psychoanalyst have? and what relation does he avow himself to have?] [. . .] never evoke the possibility of being looked at by the animal that they, for their part, observed, and of which they speak' (Derrida 2008 [2006], 90/126). This amounts to philosophy (and that psychoanalysis which is all too 'at home with the philosophers' [Derrida 1998 {1996}, 56/74]) drawing a tacit line of absolute opposition between man and *all* of the other animals, whether it considers itself to stand inside metaphysics, outside, or in some other relationship altogether:

> No more than Descartes do they think to distinguish animals one from another, and, like Descartes, they speak of 'the animal' as of a single set that can be opposed to 'us', 'humans', subjects or *Da-seins,* of an 'I think', 'I am', along the line of a single common trait and on the other side of a single, indivisible limit. [. . .] No more than Descartes do they recognise any minimal right, or any aptitude to respond [a supposedly human 'response' as opposed to a machine-like 'reaction'], as such, on the part of what they call 'the animal'. (Derrida 2008 [2006], 90/126–27)

Metaphysics conceives the animal as a unified object (collectivised by any number of features, but in the end, by the inability to scrutinise and treat *man*), which the deployment of such a locution as 'the animal' prolongs and exacerbates. This treatment of animals, the elimination of subjecthood, at the level of word and concept, stands among the conditions for the possibility of today's creatural 'genocide' and mass exploitation (Derrida 2008 [2006], 26/46–47).

In this context, to speak of 'the *beautiful* animal' seems doubly risky. 'Aestheticising' animals, if that is what we are doing, would constitute a further step in the wrong direction: it is *avowedly* to treat them as objects, parading in their splendour before an enchanted human gaze. However benignly one might be led to treat them on this basis, and however charming one might find them, they remain without a gaze and without a voice, unable to look back and to speak and so to make demands.

First response: perhaps it is true that, in the first instance, we objectify animals, by contemplating them. But our account does not claim to be exhaustive — far from it. We simply wish to account for certain features of the phenomenology of our experience and in particular the 'aesthetic' experience of beauty in animals.

Second response: that said, this is an experience which *undoes* the subject-object relation and the sovereign status which the subject ordinarily arrogates for itself: the animal teaches us that the functions we assign to things are only relative, for they see things differently — they *see* (or otherwise sense). This immediately puts in question the priority of the human perspective and allows us to oscillate between the ossified actuality of our own interpretations of objects and the open possibilities which these objects manifestly present for the animal. Not only is the animal experienced as subjectal, but we ourselves, far from objectivising this subjectivity, actually come to share its point of view.

Thus, if in certain respects we objectify the animal in its beauty, nevertheless at stake in this is a transformation of the metaphysical relation between man and animal. It is as if we end up being so charmed by these remarkable creatures that we forget any longer to assert our long reiterated superiority. Thus we are led by animal beauty to reject metaphysics in such a way as to esteem the animal *more highly* than the human, while nevertheless still daring to attribute a certain uniqueness to the latter, which we locate precisely in its ability to *be* charmed and so to re-evaluate the opposition of subject and object. But the precondition of this re-evaluation is to begin with something like an animal-object, and from this starting point, we render the metaphysical structure question-worthy from within.

We should mention in this regard the inspiration we have taken from Timofeeva's response to Derrida's reading of the animal, which takes as its point of departure a brief passage in Slavoj Žižek's *Less Than Nothing* (based on a presentation we both witnessed in Berlin in December 2011). Žižek argues that Derrida's own account of the history of animals in philosophy risks enacting a totalisation analogous to that of which philosophy is indicted with respect to 'the Animal', in which *all* philosophers would be lumped together under the heading of 'the Philosopher' or 'Philosophy'.

Timofeeva demonstrates the way in which Žižek posits a new (Hegelian) opposition between Man and 'the Animal' in spite of Derrida's critique, but asks whether in the end Žižek is not taking the semblance of a totalisation of 'Philosophy' in Derrida's text too much at face value: 'Isn't it that Žižek himself naively believes that Derrida naively believed that philosophers of the past naively believed in a human-animal binary?' (Timofeeva in Hamza 2015, 107, cf. 100–109).

For Timofeeva, as perhaps for Rainer Maria Rilke, the animal conceals a secret, something that has been forgotten by metaphysics. Indeed the animal *is* the forgotten, but for just this reason (animal) life remains sheltered *within* metaphysics (as *its* forgotten) and is thereby shielded from its predations. It is as if metaphysics were keeping a secret from itself, or harboured such a secret without knowing it (Timofeeva 2012, 127). This is Timofeeva's rethinking of Martin Heidegger's notion of the forgetting of being (understood as the event in which individual entities come to appear), an event concealed and sheltered by metaphysics as it has unfolded over the last 2,500 years.

To combine Derrida with Timofeeva is to say: the animal *gaze* is the forgotten of metaphysics.

But having broached the topic of Rilke, we have, in this already lengthy note, opened the way for an excursion from philosophy into *poetry*.

Rilke constitutes a privileged point of reference among philosophers who write on animals, quite on a par with Franz Kafka, whose menagerie does not seem to include cats or many terribly charming creatures at all, and these latter are the beasts we remain in pursuit of.

Rilke's high esteem rests largely on the Eighth of his *Duino Elegies* (1912/1922), the first verse of which involves a remarkable account of the animal gaze. Overturning metaphysics, Rilke here attributes to the animal an ability to see things 'as such' (as they are in 'the Open' [*das Offene*]), rather than envisioning them merely in terms of its own finite projects. Rilke avers that the human being is *also* vouchsafed the possibility of seeing the world as an animal does, but it is a world merely glimpsed and remains the province of children, lovers, and the dying. We would add the 'lovers of wisdom' to that list:

> With all its eyes [*allen Augen*] the natural world [*die Kreatur*] looks far
>   into the Open. Only *our* eyes look back,
>   set like traps about all living things [sc. *die Kreatur/Tieren*],
>   encircled round their free, outward path.
> What *is*, in that outside, we learn only
> by looking in their faces; for we force
> even the youngest child to turn and look
> backwards into design [*Gestaltung*], not at the Open
> deep in animals' eyes [*Tiergesicht* — the animal's *face*]. Free of death
>   [*Frei von Tod*].
> That, only we can see. The free animal
> has its decline perpetually behind it
> and God before, and in its movement moves
> within eternity, like the welling springs.
>   Never, for a day, do *we* have
> pure space before us for the opening
> of endless flowers. Always there is World,
> never the negativeless Nowhere [*Nirgends ohne Nicht*]: that pure,

>   unoverlooked, breathed element we know
>   endlessly, without desire. A child,
>   if left in stillness, can be lost in it
>   till shaken out. Or we may die: may *be* it.
>   For nearing death one loses sight of death
>   and stares out, vastly perhaps, like animals [*starrt* hinaus,
>   *vielleicht mit großem Tierblick* — the animal's gaze].
>   Lovers, if the other were not standing
>   in the light, approach, marvelling . . .
>   An inadvertent view appears to open
>   behind the other . . . neither can pass
>   the other, and is in the World again.
>   Turned back to face creation's face [*Schöpfung*], we see
>   the mere reflection of the free reaches,
>   which we have darkened. Or an animal
>   mutely [*stummes*], serenely, looks us through and through
>   [*aufschaut, ruhig durch uns durch*].
>   We call this fate: always to be opposed [*gegenüber*]
>   and nothing else, opposite, for ever.
>   (Rilke, 2011 [1912/1922], 164–67. Reproduced by permission
>   of Oxford University Press.)

Here Rilke radically reverses the metaphysical positioning of the gaze while at the same time demonstrating that the animal's ability to see things as they are in themselves is *responsible* for, or at least in some way related to, certain of the determinations which *metaphysics* has assigned to it, from deathlessness to wordlessness (and later on in the same work, a lack of consciousness and a certain melancholy, 'weighed by the shadow of a sad heart [*Schwermut*]'). Such a gesture, which reverses metaphysics while retaining an oppositional account of the relationship between man and animal, we happily endorse, but from the standpoint of *philosophy* as it might be envisaged by an animal. Nevertheless, poetry and literature will have been responsible for teaching philosophy of the animal's ability to gaze.

Elsewhere, in a work closer to literature than poetry, and this time in French, Rilke speaks of the cat's gaze, in particular, in the following terms: 'You think they look at us? Has anyone ever truly known whether or not they deign to register for one instant on the sunken surface of their retina our trifling forms? As they stare at us they might merely be eliminating us magically from their gaze [*prunelles*, their pupils — Baudelaire's word — source of the uncanny luminosity of 'cat's-eyes'], eternally replete' (1984 [1921], 9/56). Perhaps this explains why the reversion of the gaze from human to animal in Rilke's work does not carry with it all of the properties traditionally assigned to man (his ability to die and to speak, for example). We are not *objects* before the cat's subjective gaze; rather we are nothing, and the renowned 'inscrutability' of the cat's look is perhaps related to the fact that, when stared at, we are being shrunk to nothing in those eyes.

Thus we have a curious form of deconstruction which is formally akin to Derrida's version in that it avoids a mere reversal, that always ends up retaining the *structure* of the opposition which it reverses and thus remains trapped in a metaphysical conceptuality, one of the most fundamental elements of which is precisely the opposition. Not that the reversal of gazes in the case of Derrida's cat seems to be anything other than the *first* stage of a deconstruction, which is indeed a reversal. But Derrida does not immediately consider the human being to be annihilated in the cat's gaze: if that is to happen, it will come later, as he unfolds the full consequences of this shaming experience of being watched by something which we previously considered to have eyes but not to see. Perhaps the deconstructive fragmentation of the unified totality of 'Man' is an annihilation of a certain kind, even if it is not what Rilke had in mind.

Nevertheless, Derrida himself draws our attention to another of Rilke's poems, 'Black Cat', where, in the animal's very gaze, the poet evokes the *fossil* which will mean so much to us. It even seems that *what* is fossilised, what withers beneath the animal's glare, is the *human* gaze. It is as if the experience of a face-to-face being-watched by the animal were enough to ossify our own perception, as if our dialectical way of thinking suddenly found itself rooted to the spot. Rilke himself does not understand it in quite this way, and we may presume that this is rather his way of speaking of the annihilation of man's subjectivity in the eyes of the cat: 'Of a sudden, as if woken, she directs [/] her face to gaze pinpointingly at yours, [/] and you meet your look within the yellow [/] amber of her round, stone-hard eyeballs [*Augensteine*], [/] caught, locked in, unexpected, [/] amber-bound like an extinct insect [*ausgestorbenes Insekt*]' (Rilke 2011 [1908], 92–93. Reproduced by permission of Oxford Univeristy Press.)

Save in the still-ambiguous case of Levinas, it is only in the subliminal space of a footnote that Derrida allows himself to mention the exceptional instance of a *philosopher* who speaks of the animal's gaze (Derrida 2008 [2006], 163–64n10–11/22–23n2). This is Martin Buber, in *I and Thou* (1923), and we shall take the liberty of quoting this text, as Derrida himself does not, since it situates the philosophical theologian somewhere *between* the poet and the philosopher (Derrida), for the cat's gaze here does not simply reduce the human being to nothing (as in Rilke) but merely puts it in *question* (such a '*mettre en question*' was always the gesture of the Levinassian Other in relation to the sovereign subject it confronts in the face-to-face, the more than likely *human* Other whose place is here being usurped by a Derridean or Buberian cat):

> [The animal's] language is the stammering of nature at the first touch of spirit, before it yields to spirit's cosmic venture that we call man. But no speech will ever repeat what that stammering knows and can proclaim.
>
> Sometimes I look into a cat's eyes [*die Augen einer Hauskatze*]. The domesticated animal has not as it were received from us [. . .] the gift of the truly 'speaking' glance, but only — at the price of its primitive disinterestedness — the capacity to turn its glance to us prodigious beings. [. . .] The beginning of this cat's glance, lighting up under the touch of my glance, indisputably questioned me: '[. . .] Do I really exist? [*Bin ich da?*]'. (Buber n.d. [1923], 96–97/92–93)

As early as the 1950s, Heidegger himself, prime advocate of the forgotten, was among the first of the philosophers to bring Rilke's thoughts on animality into contact with philosophy, as if threatening to disrupt its uninterrupted subordination of animal life. He makes reference to Rilke's animals in his lecture course on *Parmenides*, where the notion of the animal's gaze and its experience of 'the Open' are particularly important, albeit in a way that ultimately seems — despite all its promise — to return the animal to a subordinate position and to issue in the judgement that Rilke will have erred: 'The open of the unrestrained progression of beings never arrives at the free of Being, and it is precisely this free that the "creature" never sees; for the capacity to see it constitutes what is essentially distinct about man and consequently forms the unsurmountable essential boundary between animal and man' (Heidegger 1992 [1942–43], 152/226]). To confuse the two — the Open and the Clearing (*Lichtung*) — is to engage in 'an uncanny hominisation [*Vermenschung*] of the "creature", i.e., the animal [presumably by attributing to the animal an access to the Open or the 'free' which in Heidegger's sense belongs only to the human being (cf. ibid., 160–61/238–39)], and a corresponding animalisation of man' (ibid., 152/226). And such a confusion indeed eventuates in the history of metaphysics from Plato, at least, right up to Rilke himself ('it is easy to see in Rilke's poetry the last offshoot of modern metaphysics' [ibid., 158/235]). In this sense it is perhaps fortunate that 'the open meant by Rilke is not the open in the sense of the unconcealed [i.e., the free of Being]. Rilke knows and suspects nothing of *alētheia* [truth understood as clearing or "unconcealment"], no more than Nietzsche does. Accordingly, Rilke is bound within the limits of the traditional metaphysical determination of man and animal' (ibid., 155/231).

Naturally, we would disagree with this confinement of Rilke, on the basis of our reading of Derrida and the bestowal of a gaze upon the animal. But despite remaining closer to Rilke than to Heidegger, we must nevertheless acknowledge that our understanding of the animal's sincerity and contentment in relation to its finite environment is heavily influenced by, even if it is not identical with, Heidegger's earlier account of the animal in the *Fundamental Concepts of Metaphysics* from 1929–30. Here Heidegger speaks of the animal's 'captivation' (*Benommenheit*) before a finite world — its 'environment' (*Umwelt*) (Heidegger 1995 [1929–30], 239/347 et passim). He uses this word, *Benommenheit*, to refer to the animal's inability to detach itself from its own particular experience of entities, which are encountered always in relation to the animal's particular survival needs, to which its instincts remain subservient. The animal cannot experience an entity as it is in itself, in terms of what Heidegger describes as its 'as such': a blade of grass will always be seen by the beetle as a 'beetle-path'. The animal will never be an ontologist or a philosopher.

This position stands starkly opposed to Rilke's vision of the animal's unhindered gaze into the Open, and indeed this conflict might be taken ultimately to represent the strife between philosophy and poetry on the topic of the animal gaze.

Our own position might in this context be understood to sublate the approaches of Rilke and Heidegger, as would be indicated by the fact that the main body of our text (primarily philosophical) and its endnotes (in this case, poetic) are both bound within the covers of a single book — for us, the animal's world *is* finite, but it provides *us* with a vision of something like Rilke's Open, a thing in itself and as such, liberated from the particular projects which for the most part shape the non-philosophical human being's experience of the world and always shape the animal's.

It is from Rilke that Giorgio Agamben takes the title for his own book on animality, which develops Heidegger's analyses in a scintillating reading of both the 1929–30 lectures and the course on *Parmenides* (but not the other invocation of Rilke from 1927 in the *Basic Problems of Phenomenology* [Heidegger 1988 {1927}, 172–73/244–46]). Curiously enough, while subtly bringing out the *potential* implicit in every other writer he discusses, thus to carry the works in question beyond their *actual* form, Agamben does not seem to disagree with Heidegger's reading of Rilke at all (Agamben 2004 [2002], 57ff/60ff).

In a text on animal fasting in Kafka's 'Investigations of a Dog', as in his superb book, *The Trouble with Pleasure*, Aaron Schuster cites Rilke as one of the few writers (who include Baudelaire and T. S. Eliot) to have spoken at any length on the question of animals, and *cats* in particular, which is perhaps also to speak of cats and *dogs* and the respective charms of these specifically domestic creatures. Schuster agrees with our position in affirming that a certain access to non-cultural wilderness — an 'open', an 'outside' — is given to *us* in the cat's annihilating stare (Schuster 2016, 130).

The least we can say is that by now it should have become apparent that poetry can speak of the animal's gaze much more readily than philosophy can. This becomes even more glaring in the case of Charles Baudelaire, among whose many poems on the feline hardly a single one fails to mention the animal's look and the sharing of glances, the 'face-to-face' of man and cat (Derrida himself notes as much, 'Baudelaire even names the cat's gaze' (2008 [2006], 163n9/22n1):

> *Le Chat [I]*
>
> *Viens, mon beau chat, sur mon cœur amoureux;*
> *Retiens les griffes de ta patte,*
> *Et laisse-moi plonger dans tes beaux yeux,*
> *Mêlés de métal et d'agate.*
>
> *Lorsque mes doigts caressent à loisir*
> *Ta tête et ton dos élastique,*
> *Et que ma main s'enivre du plaisir*
> *De palper ton corps électrique,*
>
> *Je vois ma femme en esprit. Son regard,*
> *Comme le tien, aimable bête*
> *Profond et froid, coupe et fend comme un dard,*
>
> *Et, des pieds jusques à la tête,*
> *Un air subtil, un dangereux parfum*
> *Nagent autour de son corps brun.*
> — Charles Baudelaire
>
> Come, my fine cat, against my loving heart;
> Sheathe your sharp claws, and settle.
> And let my eyes into your pupils dart
> Where agate sparks with metal.

Now while my fingertips caress at leisure
Your head and wiry curves,
And that my hand's elated with the pleasure
Of your electric nerves,

I think about my woman — how her glances
Like yours, dear beast, deep-down
And cold, can cut and wound one as with lances;

Then, too, she has that vagrant
And subtle air of danger that makes fragrant
Her body, lithe and brown.
— trans. Roy Campbell

Le Chat [II]

[...]
Quand mes yeux, vers ce chat que j'aime
Tirés comme par un aimant,
Se retournent docilement
Et que je regarde en moi-même,

Je vois avec étonnement
Le feu de ses prunelles pâles,
Clairs fanaux, vivantes opales
Qui me contemplent fixement.

When my gaze, drawn as by a magnet,
Turns in a docile way
Toward that cat whom I love,
And when I look within myself,
I see with amazement
The fire of his pale pupils,
Clear signal-lights, living opals,
That contemplate me fixedly.
— trans. William Aggeler

When my eyes, drawn like a magnet
To this cat that I love,
Come meekly back again
And I look inside myself,
I see with amazement
The fire of its pale pupils,
Clear beacons, living opals,
Looking at me fixedly.
— trans. Geoffrey Wagner

Les Chats

Les amoureux fervents et les savants austères
Aiment également, dans leur mûre saison,
Les chats puissants et doux, orgueil de la maison,
Qui comme eux sont frileux et comme eux sédentaires.

Amis de la science et de la volupté
Ils cherchent le silence et l'horreur des ténèbres;
L'Erèbe les eût pris pour ses coursiers funèbres,
S'ils pouvaient au servage incliner leur fierté.

Ils prennent en songeant les nobles attitudes
Des grands sphinx allongés au fond des solitudes,
Qui semblent s'endormir dans un rêve sans fin;

Leurs reins féconds sont pleins d'étincelles magiques,
Et des parcelles d'or, ainsi qu'un sable fin,
Etoilent vaguement leurs prunelles mystiques.

No one but indefatigable lovers and old
Chilly philosophers can understand the true
Charm of these animals serene and potent, who
Likewise are sedentary and suffer from the cold.

They are the friends of learning and of sexual bliss;
Silence they love, and darkness, where temptation breeds.
Erebus would have made them his funereal steeds,
Save that their proud free nature would not stoop to this.

Like those great sphinxes lounging through eternity
In noble attitudes upon the desert sand,
They gaze incuriously at nothing, calm and wise.

Their fecund loins give forth electric flashes, and
Thousands of golden particles drift ceaselessly,
Like galaxies of stars, in their mysterious eyes.
— trans. George Dillon

All ardent lovers and all sages prize,
— As ripening years incline upon their brows —
The mild and mighty cats — pride of the house —
That like unto them are indolent, stern and wise.

The friends of Learning and of Ecstasy,
They search for silence and the horrors of gloom;
The devil had used them for his steeds of Doom,
Could he alone have bent their pride to slavery.

When musing, they display those outlines chaste,
Of the great sphinxes — stretched o'er the sandy waste,
That seem to slumber deep in a dream without end:

From out their loins a fountainous furnace flies,
And grains of sparkling gold, as fine as sand,
Bestar the mystic pupils of their eyes.
— trans. Cyril Scott

Sages austere and fervent lovers both,
In their ripe season, cherish cats, the pride

Of hearths, strong, mild, and to themselves allied
In chilly stealth and sedentary sloth.

Friends both to lust and learning, they frequent
Silence, and love the horror darkness breeds.
Erebus would have chosen them for steeds
To hearses, could their pride to it have bent.

Dreaming, the noble postures they assume
Of sphinxes stretching out into the gloom
That seems to swoon into an endless trance.

Their fertile flanks are full of sparks that tingle,
And particles of gold, like grains of shingle,
Vaguely be-star their pupils as they glance.
— trans. Roy Campbell

Let us close this long note and hope to make good on the promise that if 'philosophers' (those 'austere savants') spend enough time with cats, they will come to understand that they are, in truth, related, as the anonymous author of that remarkable poem, 'White Pangur', which does not fail to invoke the radiance of the cat's eyes, seems inclined to believe:

White Pangur

Pangur, white Pangur, how happy we are
Alone together, scholar and cat
Each has his own work to do daily;
For you it is hunting, for me study.
Your shining eye watches the wall;
My feeble eye is fixed on a book.
You rejoice, when your claws entrap a mouse;
I rejoice when my mind fathoms a problem.
Pleased with his own art, neither hinders the other;
Thus we live ever without tedium and envy.
— Anon. Ninth-Century. Trans. W. H. Auden

I and Pangur Bán, my cat
'Tis a like task we are at;
Hunting mice is his delight
Hunting words I sit all night.

Better far than praise of men
'Tis to sit with book and pen;
Pangur bears me no ill will,
He too plies his simple skill.

'Tis a merry thing to see
At our tasks how glad are we,
When at home we sit and find
Entertainment to our mind.

> Oftentimes a mouse will stray
> In the hero Pangur's way:
> Oftentimes my keen thought set
> Takes a meaning in its net.
>
> 'Gainst the wall he sets his eye
> Full and fierce and sharp and sly;
> 'Gainst the wall of knowledge I
> All my little wisdom try.
>
> When a mouse darts from its den,
> O how glad is Pangur then!
> O what gladness do I prove
> When I solve the doubts I love!
>
> So in peace our tasks we ply,
> Pangur Bán, my cat, and I;
> In our arts we find our bliss,
> I have mine and he has his.
>
> Practice every day has made
> Pangur perfect in his trade;
> I get wisdom day and night
> Turning darkness into light.
> — Trans. Robin Flower

29. This zoological knowledge does not necessarily involve the evolutionary account of nature given by Charles Darwin and his heirs, about which Derrida speaks very little, even though Darwinism is today perhaps the best-known and most easily assimilable of those scientific doctrines which impart a deconstructive impetus to our conception of the dichotomy between man and animal. In truth, the most significant advances for Derrida seem to have been those of primatology (cf. Derrida 2008 [2006], 59/87). Personal experience bears out the primatological insight into the proximity between man and ape: as soon as one proposes, in discussion, a feature supposed to pick man out uniquely, someone of a scientific bent will immediately adduce an intelligent or skilful ape or dolphin which has recently been found also to possess that attribute. And so one proposes another. . . . This constant redrawing of boundaries is what Agamben describes as the procedure of the 'anthropogenic machine' (2004 [2002], 26/34).

30. Albeit only from a certain point of view, with a certain 'strategy' in mind, which will have been decided upon in advance, as these taxonomies made after the slackening of the oppositional divide always are. Once the undecidability of the two formerly opposed elements has been achieved, a new decision can be made upon their differences and samenesses.

31. In attributing a uniqueness to the human being in this way I am trying to preempt a number of critiques which might otherwise have assailed this gesture: that of deconstruction, certainly, but also Agamben's, which adopts the perspective of the 'anthropological (or anthropogenic) machine' that throughout the history of the West

has continually attempted to find some trait by which to separate the human from the animal (including the animalistic part of the human being itself). The machine has now run down and should not be reignited but rather permanently disabled and contemplated in its very desuetude (Agamben 2004 [2002], 92/94). We are attempting to avoid this critique by selecting a trait which both derives from a certain *inferiority* on the part of man, and emerges only within a relation *to* animals — the ability to be charmed by a creature capable of a sincerity we are not, and the capacity to have our horizons expanded by an insight into the animal's indifference to the possibilities we attribute to things, and hence the deposing of our sovereignty.

32. 'Inter-est': a quasi-etymological connection insisted upon by Emmanuel Levinas, from the Latin, *inter*, amongst, and *esse*, to be (cf. 1998 [1974], 4/4).

33. Much of the philosophy that has attempted to revive itself after the moment of its completion has been engaged in a related project. Adorno, whom we are implicitly citing, presumably had in mind Hegel's encyclopaedic system (Adorno 1973 [1966], 3/13), but one might also think of the successive overcomings of metaphysics in Kant, Nietzsche, and Heidegger (even Derrida). The task here was not so much to redeem the bad infinite as the orthodox Hegelian account describes it, but rather to rethink its nature and place, or in some cases to give it a new role, and even to isolate a secret bad infinity in Hegel himself, generally at the very beginning, in the opening pages of the *Science of Logic*, as Søren Kierkegaard was among the first to attempt (cf. Ruda 2013).

In some of his more recent work, Žižek has raised the question of whether there is not a certain kind of repetition which Hegel's dialectic cannot encompass or control, and to our eyes, this gesture closely resembles a redemption of the bad infinite, or else it concerns a bad infinite which stands in no need of redemption at all, never having found a place in the Hegelian system:

> Hegel does think repetition, but not a pure non-productive one, not a 'mechanical' repetition which just strives for more of the same: his notion of repetition always involves sublation; in other words, through repetition, something is idealised, transformed from an immediate contingent reality [in]to a notional universality (Caesar dies as a person and becomes a universal title); or, at least, through repetition, the necessity of an event is confirmed (Napoleon had to lose twice to get the message that his time was over, that his first defeat was not just an accident). (Žižek 2012, 455)

What is missing in Hegel is repression and the return of the repressed (in the distorted and contingent form of the 'symptom') as we find it in Freudian psychoanalytic theory. Hegel supplants repression with supersession (*Aufhebung*); not the negation which presses something into the unconscious but only inadequately, across a porous border which will allow the negated to rise again in the mechanical repetition or bad infinite that characterises neurotic and psychotic madness (Žižek 2012, 456f, cf. 18, 491ff et al.).

In this critique, Žižek is perhaps influenced by Alenka Zupančič (2008, 149ff), but in Hegel's defence, we should consult the third of Žižek's 'troika', Mladen Dolar (2017) and his reading of the very beginning of the *Science of Logic* in which, it seems, Hegel himself might be said to envisage a certain bad infinite.

Here we might also recall Derrida's assertion of an irreducible bad infinite in Levinas, which Derrida is wary of positing simply at the expense of the true infinite, since he considers this latter to be just as irresistible a telos. It is as if philosophy and reason (the Same) were just as necessary as unreason and madness (the Other), which is to say, an excess with respect to the logical after the manner of the bad infinite — for Derrida, it seems that an absolute outside *and* its internalisation (which is to say, sublation, *Erinnerung*) are equally inevitable.

And yet, Catherine Malabou has gone so far as to affirm that the bad infinite is the *only* infinite which Derrida himself ultimately believes in (cf. Malabou 2013, 11'25"), but this is perhaps less a point justified by Derrida's own texts than a necessary (and retrospectively posited) precondition for Malabou's own critique of the deconstructive trace. In *Changing Difference*, the trace is presented as repeatedly thwarting the attainment of full presence, in a way that remains identical each time, never growing weak or tired or changing its strategy, which is to say that the trace is not thought in a fully *plastic* manner (Malabou 2011 [2009], 120–22/137–39).

Rodolphe Gasché has written what should perhaps by rights have become the canonical text on Derrida's notion of infinity (Gasché 1994, 129–49).

34. Indifference has come increasingly to preoccupy philosophy in recent years. Schuster goes so far as to ask, rhetorically, 'is not our "generational problem" much better captured by the term "indifference" [than that of "difference"], which expresses a generalised disorientation and malaise that is the flipside of the empty celebration of "differences"? Today indifference ought to become a matter of thought' (Schuster 2016, 143).

And sure enough there are signs that this is taking place in a number of different yet related areas:

The idea of nature as indifferent ('indifferent to difference' [Chiesa 2016, 62], the differentiality which is introduced by the signifier or 'language'), as opposed to the 'ontology of difference' which ultimately relies upon a contrast with the 'One', a unified totality of Nature, which from a Lacanian standpoint does not exist, has been developed by Lorenzo Chiesa (2016, 60ff) and deployed in another way by Frank Ruda (2016).

Malabou had already gone some way towards a conceptualisation of indifference in the slightly different context of 'destructive plasticity', in which certain forms of trauma lead to the indifference of apathy (Malabou 2012 [2009], 14/21, 18/24 et al.).

The becoming-indifferent or undifferentiated of the oppositions that define metaphysics is a central thesis of Agamben's work. Matthew Calarco has drawn attention to the significance of this notion of 'indistinction' in the context of the relation between man and animal (although he suggests that in the end his position stands more under the influence of Donna Haraway than Agamben, and asserts a jointly Deleuzian heritage of the idea) (Calarco 2015, 48ff).

And before all of this, Charles Scott had devoted a whole monograph to the issue of indifference (2007).

Finally, in the still earlier work of Heidegger, although far from being the first to note the distinction between inauthenticity and indifference with respect to *both* inauthenticity *and* authenticity, prior to their very differentiation, the author of the present work has nevertheless devoted some time to the concept (Lewis 2005). And we could continue to cite . . .

35. When it comes to the notion of a workless work we shall always be indebted to Georges Bataille and the notion that stands on the margins of philosophy in its Kanto-Hegelian guise, *désœuvrement*, the failure or refusal to produce a work (*œuvre*) following the sabotage of the dialectical machine. This invention is sometimes attributed to Maurice Blanchot (see 1982 [1955], 46/39, for one of the earlier occurrences of this term, translated into English as 'lack of work' or 'inertia'; and later: 1993 [1969], 424/622), but the earliest reference to such a notion that we have been able to locate, expressed in terms of 'unemployed negativity' (*négativité sans emploi*), even if we do not find the exact word, is in a letter Bataille addressed to Alexandre Kojève, whose work was the occasion for this coinage, on 6th December 1937 (cf. Hollier 1988 [1979], 90/171 and Agamben 2004 [2002], 7/14). Denis Hollier avows the notion to be an invention of Bataille's (Hollier 1988 [1979], 87/165). William Allen, however, gives a more nuanced reading of the word which suggests that it is only with Bataille that the word acquires a narrow technical usage, perhaps under the influence of Kojève, but this risks obscuring the more commonplace signification that it assumes in Blanchot, whatever the chronology (Allen 2015, 65–66).

But our focus here is Bataille, and we might recall here the epigraph to Bataille's *Accursed Share*, a telling line from William Blake's 'Proverbs of Hell' from *The Marriage of Heaven and Hell* — 'Exuberance is beauty' (Blake 1948 [1793], 185). 'Exuberance' is one of Bataille's names for an expenditure without profit, a negation without determinate product, a pervasive entropy or loss, which the sovereign is capable of sustaining (let it be noted that this employment of the notion of 'entropy' is indebted to Nick Land's account of Bataille [1992]). This negation is to be liberated from its devaluation by philosophy and incorporated into a more 'general economy', with which Bataille proposes to replace the 'restricted economy' that operates only in terms of exchange, calculating an action's value and the energy it is worth expending upon it by examining what will be received *in return*.

The relation to Kojève becomes apparent in the way that Bataille relates these two economies to the master and the slave from Hegel's *Phenomenology of Spirit*, the episode of which Kojève made so much: 'servile' sublation, theoretical and practical labouring — the conceptual 'labour of the negative' and the production of a work — as opposed to masterful or sovereign expenditure, loss without compensation, the destruction or refusal of all works, the abstract and absolute negation characteristic of annihilation rather than the determinate and productive negation which characterises sublation. Thus the dialectic amounts to the victory of the slave at the expense of the master, and Bataille stages the revenge of a Nietzschean master upon the once triumphant Hegelian slave.

It is as if with the sovereign, all concern for dialectic vanishes into indifference. At least to this extent we might be said to be adopting a Bataillean position in relation to philosophy in the present work, in our selfish and perhaps undialectical fixation upon our beloved animals. Would the beast then be sovereign too, or rather, never having had the capacity for dialectic, would it remain indifferent to the opposition between master and slave, non-dialectical sovereign and dialectical progress?

Here I am once again indebted to Timofeeva's attempt to present an alternative reading of Bataille according to which the animal — and not just the human — may properly be characterised as sovereign. Timofeeva is led, with the support of certain of Bataille's less well-known works — less well-known to *philosophers*, at least — on the prehistory of man, to suggest that the working animal is only pretending to be under our yoke and may at any moment decide to run off (Timofeeva 2012, 107, cf. Plutarch 1957, 502–5). Following Timofeeva, Schuster postulates that, of all the animals, the cat is the most sovereign in this sense: it enjoys 'the mastery of a power [according to Deleuze] that is not defined by opposition and negation but goes its own way, coolly indifferent to any external viewpoint[,] including that of one's own self. [. . .] The only way to really be a master is not to care if one is' (Schuster 2016, 130).

Perhaps Schuster's last point anticipates our own position, for we depart — albeit ever so slightly — from Timofeeva's extremely revealing reading of Bataille in our suggestion that the animal might in fact *elude* the opposition between master and slave altogether, and in such a way as to explain how the *human* might be said to achieve the sovereign vision. This would be in keeping with the predominant reading of Bataille's text except that on our account the *animal* is what opens the sovereign vista *for* the human, while standing aloof from both mastery and slavery. This is what we can learn from our experience of the animal's sincerity, and indeed its sincere performance of natural functions: we learn a new sense of the 'functional' from the way functionality appears to us in the animal.

Let it be said, finally, that on this point we are inspired, in general, by Derrida's work on the relationship between animality and sovereignty, and also the polemic he opens up with Agamben in the first volume of *The Beast and the Sovereign*.

I owe all these notes to Will Stronge's faith in my ability to write something of value on Bataille, and to his continued enthusiasm and support.

CHAPTER 1. THE ANIMAL'S SINCERITY: WITTGENSTEIN, LEVINAS, LACAN

1. Quoted by Paul Davies in 'Sincerity and the End of Theodicy' (2002, 163), which ascribes to the dog an impersonal pronoun, 'it', while Wittgenstein's original translator, Elizabeth Anscombe gives 'he'. The German reads '*er*', but all Austrian and German dogs are male, and so one might ponder for some time this differing sexuation of the animal, the dog in particular, which may be related to either or both of the historical moment and the authors' own sex and predilections, whether charmed or repelled.

2. And not only here: my general and immeasurable debt to Paul Davies — philosophical but not only philosophical — must be acknowledged. To him I owe the broadly phenomenological idea that 'doing justice' to a phenomenon, an act of something like 'mere description', is an essential task for philosophy, and, at least until quite recently, for him quite indifferent to all kinds of naturalism and natural science; at the same time, Paul taught us that one should feel no guilt in writing (philosophy) about something that one loves, for writing needs no further

justification. In that sense, this book is a gift I address to him, and in general an autobiographical record, not just of the author's loves, but of his changing relation to philosophy. This is why I have often tried to mark, discreetly, the names of those who made these veerings possible.

3. Bentham speaks of the 'insuperable line' that separates those upon whom pain may be inflicted with impunity and those not, a line drawn by *metaphysics* between the animal and the human. Bentham goes on to perform an exemplary deconstruction of this opposition, first of all assigning reason and speech (*logos*) to animals, or rather, to *certain* animals in comparison with certain humans (a gesture Derrida will insist upon), before changing the terrain altogether and speaking of a capacity to suffer which encompasses (most) human beings and (most) animals:

> The French have already discovered that the blackness of the skin is no reason why a human being should be abandoned without redress to the caprice of a tormentor. It may come one day to be recognised, that the number of the legs, the villosity of the skin, or the termination of the *os sacrum*, are reasons equally insufficient for abandoning a sensitive being to the same fate. What else is it that should trace the insuperable line? Is it the faculty of reason, or, perhaps, the faculty of discourse? But a full-grown horse or dog is beyond comparison a more rational, as well as a more conversable animal, than an infant of a day, or a week, or even a month, old. But suppose the case were otherwise, what would it avail? the [*sic*] question is not, Can they *reason?* nor, Can they *talk?* but, Can they *suffer?* (Bentham 2007 [1780/1823], 311n)

4. The similarities between Jews and animals in philosophy's depiction of them have not gone unnoticed. Before us, Peter Atterton will have noted this connection in the Levinassian text (Atterton and Calarco 2004, 55). In general, however, we would not closely associate our attempt to read Levinas with his since all too often Atterton seems more keen than is just to indict Levinas for having 'equivocated' (ibid., 58), rather than attempting to understand the movement of the text as embodying a deliberate strategy designed to communicate something that an isolated thesis could not. As if Levinas had merely, stupidly, 'contradicted himself', as if the principle of non-contradiction were ever simply in effect in texts of this kind or in post-Hegelian philosophy in general.

In a similar way, Atterton speaks of Levinas's relation to Darwin (and Heidegger) as 'ambiguous' — rather ingenuous given how explicitly and technically thematised the notions of 'ambiguity' and 'equivocation' are in Levinas, and how important a role they so often play in his textual strategy of uncovering the trace of the sincere Saying in the equivocal Said (ibid., 60).

An uncharitable strategy allows one to draw rather harsh conclusions that in the end reflect rather badly on the author's own hermeneutic strategy and even on their intentions.

5. Thereby, does the dog itself become dignified? Levinas's text is not without ambiguity — 'the dog will attest to the dignity of its person [*la dignité de la personne* — Séan Hand's translation seems to assume that this is the person of the dog, but it could also refer to the dignity of any person, the dignity of personhood as such. Then again, and as if to settle the matter, Levinas continues:] [. . .]. There is a transcen-

dence in the animal! [*Une transcendance dans l'animal* — and this supports Hand's version, suggesting in Sartrean terms a certain freedom on the part of the animal and hence a dignity to be accorded]' (DF, 152/215). That said, Llewelyn seems to read this 'dignity' as referring to the humans recognised *by* the dogs (cf. Llewelyn 1991, 51). But does the very ability to *recognise* the dignity of personhood imply that the one recognising is also possessed of the same personhood? It does for Hegel. And yet does Levinas want anything to do with Hegel here? We are speaking of a *Kantian* animal, a *pre-* or *non-*Hegelian beast. Nevertheless, the ambiguity we have noted in the preceding passage suggests that a Hegelian notion of reciprocal recognition might be at work here, which would imply that dignity must also be bestowed upon the animal on pain of rendering worthless the recognition which it gives; such an acknowledgement from the animal would be analogous to the slave's ineffectual recognition of his master's freedom. If this is the case, and if Levinas will ultimately *not* vouchsafe the animal this dignity, then we could read the adjective 'Kantian' as taking a pejorative sense, relegating the animal to a *pre-*Hegelian and pre-*human* stage.

6.

> The sublime in general is the attempt to express the infinite, without finding in the sphere of phenomena an object which proves adequate for this representation [*Darstellung*]. Precisely because the infinite is set apart from the entire complex of objectivity as explicitly an invisible meaning devoid of shape and is made inner, it remains, in accordance with its infinity, unutterable and sublime above any expression through the finite. (A, 363/467)

7. Llewelyn is not alone in his disquiet over the apparent humanism of Levinas's thought. Robert Bernasconi, Veronique Fóti, and Silvia Benso progressively push Levinas's discourse beyond its actual limits to wonder whether first animals and then non-sentient 'things' might not have a face in some analogical or non-analogical sense.

To cite our own earlier account: 'Levinas even entitled one of his books, *Humanism of the Other {Humanisme de l'autre homme}* but he does oscillate in this regard. At times he is quite explicit: "it is only man who could be absolutely foreign to me [*il n'y a que l'homme qui puisse m'être absolument étranger*]" (TI, 73/71). "The dimension of the divine opens forth from the human face [*le visage humain*]" (TI, 78/76). And yet even in a relatively early essay he is already beginning to ask, "[c]an things take on a face?" (IOF, 10/EN, 23). Later, perhaps under the sway of Heidegger's later works, he becomes more assertive: "The face [*Visage*] is thus not exclusively a human face [*la face de l'homme*]" (PP, 167/344)' (Lewis 2007, 165).

One should supplement this with certain crucial passages of an interview from 1986, where Levinas states that the human face and even human suffering must be known *before* any such thing can be attributed to animals and that a 'more specific analysis' would be needed in certain cases to decide upon this later attribution. (But are these analyses of an empirical-scientific or a phenomenological kind? Levinas, unsurprisingly perhaps, opts for the latter, speaking in the same place of 'a specific *phenomenological* analysis' [Levinas 2004 {1986}, 49, emphasis added], and indeed later in the same interview he sets himself in opposition to Darwin, who, incidentally, is spoken of in the same breath as Heidegger, of all people (in the name of a certain Spinozist 'persistence in being' on the part of the individual).

The exclusion of a scientific analysis of the continuity between man and animal perhaps goes some way towards explaining Levinas's position according to which animal and man are indeed opposed up to a certain point in that any ethical characteristics assigned to animals would be posited only on the basis of a prior experience of man.) 'One cannot entirely refuse the face of an animal [. . .]. Yet the priority here is not found in the animal, but in the human face. [. . .] In the dog, in the animal, there are other phenomena. [. . .] But it also has a face' (ibid., 49). 'I cannot say at what moment you have the right to be called "face". The human face is completely different and only afterwards do we discover the face of an animal. I don't know if a snake has a face. I can't answer that question. A more specific analysis is needed' (ibid.).

Reiterating the priority of the human in relation to the possibility of an ethical imperative concerning animals, Levinas affirms that, 'the ethical extends to all living beings [. . .]. But the prototype of this is human ethics. Vegetarianism, for example, arises from the transference to animals of the idea of suffering. The animal suffers. It is because we, as human, know what suffering is that we can have this obligation' (Levinas 2004 [1986], 50).

Levinas then repeats his earlier statement, 'I cannot say', in the form of an 'I do not know', as to when one can *rightfully* describe another entity as having a face, which he seems to understand as the 'moment the human appears' (ibid., 50). Here the priority seems to be epistemic rather than ontological, as if it were possible that animals could indeed in themselves have a face, but the question is how we come to *know* and *speak* of it.

The context of this second utterance bestows a new meaning upon the first, for here Levinas directly asserts that there cannot be a 'gradualist' account of the emergence of man from the animal. More precisely, any account which stresses the Spinozist *conatus*, the Darwinian struggle for life, or the Heideggerian human's concern for its own being, will not capture the essence of man, since this involves a concern for the life of the *other* human being prior to any 'instinct for self-preservation' and easily capable of outweighing it — an *ethical* relation to the Other 'earlier' than the *ontological* relation to the self: 'with the appearance of the human — and this is my entire philosophy — there is something more important than my life, and that is the life of the other' (ibid., 50). This ability raises the human by an abrupt leap beyond the animal kingdom, and beyond any Heideggerian or Darwinistic explanation of human beings and their behaviour.

That said, even this account is rendered less straightforward by Levinas's very last words, which return to the metaphysical definition according to which man is the animal possessed of reason and language only to reverse it: '[m]an is an unreasonable animal' (ibid., 50). But an animal nevertheless? How would one construe this animality? Or does this inversion of the metaphysical definition so radically affect metaphysics' distinction between man and animal that we can no longer understand 'animality' here to be some sort of pre- or non-human substrate to which a specifying predicate would be attached? Is a new thinking of the animal, even if only in the form of a reworking of the evolutionary account of man, called for in Levinas's text? Are we to 'explain' the 'emergence' of the human from the animal at all, in the sense of identifying an impetus on the side of animality and nature? Or should we simply attend to an 'election' and 'elevation' that derives from the divine and the other man, towards which Levinas would almost always seem to be more inclined?

Derrida will distance himself from Levinas here and identify an all too humanistic trait that situates Levinas within the same filiation as the preponderance of metaphysical philosophers and supposedly post-metaphysical thinkers, however much his approach deviates from the history of metaphysics and its surmounting in a history of being (of which Heidegger would be the author), because this moment of continuity and the concomitant possibility of a 'more specific' *scientific* account are ruled out. The restoration of an immanent continuity is the very first stage of a deconstruction, the flattening of a field once furrowed by a trench that divided it in two, as a prelude to any number of alternative taxonomies and differentiations.

Let us note in passing that this moment of deconstruction, which erases the oppositional barrier and restores pure immanence, makes it all the more surprising that a commentator of David Wood's stature should affirm that Derrida is 'suspicious of continuity theses' (Wood in Atterton and Calarco 2004, 134), although he later specifies that he has in mind primarily 'homogeneous *biological* continuities' (ibid., 138, emphasis added) and makes it somewhat clearer that he is speaking of the ultimate *outcome* of a deconstruction, which for him is not, at least in general, an undifferentiated continuity.

In light of this, it is worth stressing the fact that there is nothing to prevent the new taxonomy from being continuistic, or indeed oppositional. Derrida is quite explicit on this point in a conversation with Elisabeth Roudinesco: 'Like you, I believe that there is a radical discontinuity between what one calls animals — primates in particular — and man. But this discontinuity cannot make us forget that between different animal species and types of social organisations of living beings there are other discontinuities' (Derrida and Roudinesco 2004 [2001], 72–73/121–22). How many people suspect that the *outcome* of a deconstruction can in fact be something so close to a binary opposition?

Despite this, Wood's text, 'Thinking with Cats', is illuminating in a great many ways, perhaps as much for its 'autobiographical' anecdotes as for its theoretical manoeuvres.

To conclude this excursus on Derrida and Levinas, and the latter's supposed humanism, we should recall the primal scene of Derrida's animal book, which reveals itself to be a direct challenge to those moments in the Levinassian text where the philosopher hesitates to attribute a face to the animal: Derrida's book begins with a cat gazing inscrutably at a naked philosopher.

8. As a recent somewhat ham-fisted translation of an already not terribly funny joke has it:

> *Two Jews meet in a railway carriage at a station in Galicia. 'Where are you travelling?' asks the one. 'To Cracow', comes the answer. 'Look what a liar you are!' the other protests. 'When you say you're going to Cracow, you want me to believe that you're going to Lemberg. But I know that you're really going to Cracow. So why are you lying?'* (Freud 2002 [1905], 112/129–30)

174 *Notes*

The interlocutor sees through what they perceive to be a double bluff, and indeed, if the joke is funny, it is partly because we assume that this perception embodies an *excess* of scepticism and mistrust, since there might not be a double bluff going on here.

Freud comments:

> this powerful technical device — absurdity [*Widersinn*] — is coupled with another technique, representation by the opposite [*Darstellung durch das Gegenteil*], for according to the unspoken assertion of the first Jew, the other is lying when he is telling the truth, and telling the truth with a lie. [. . .] Is it truth when we describe things as they are, without bothering about how our listener will understand what we have said? Or is this only a jesuitical truth, and does not genuine truthfulness rather consist in taking the listener into account and conveying to him a true likeness of our own knowledge? (ibid., 112/130).

Freud assigns witticisms which invoke the intersubjective situation to a special category all their own, '*"sceptical"* jokes' ('skeptische' *Witze*), a philosophical formulation which mirrors Freud's description of such *Witze* as 'attacking [. . .] the very certainty of our knowledge itself, one of our speculative goods [*spekulativen Güter*]' (ibid., 112–13/130).

Lacan recounts this joke in his Seminar on 'the formations of the unconscious', which is to say, the symptomatic manifestations of repressed unconscious desire: jokes, dreams, and slips in word and deed. The translation we are using, by Cormac Gallagher, reads as follows:

> once we bring the signifier into play [. . .] that renders my behaviour no longer luring, but provocative [*ma conduite n'est plus leurrante, mais provocatrice*] [. . .] [in that] even [lying] must appeal to the truth [*le mensonge doit faire appel à la vérité*] and can make of the truth itself something that does not appear to belong to the register of the truth [*la vérité elle-même peut sembler ne pas être du registre de la vérité*] [/]. Remember this example: '*Why [are you telling] me you are going to Cracow so that I'll think you're going to Lemberg when you're really going to Cracow?*' This can make of the truth itself something that is required by the lie, and taking things further makes the qualification of my good faith depend, at the moment when I put all my cards on the table, on the judgement of the other, in that he thinks he has discovered my game precisely when I am trying to show it to him, and which subjects the discrimination of bluff and trickery [*la bravade et de la tromperie*] to the mercy of the bad faith of the other [*la mauvaise foi de l'Autre*]. (Lacan, *Seminar V*, 1957–58, Session of 11th December 1957, translation modified; cf. Lacan 2017 [1957–58], 94–95/105)

Thus Lacan agrees with us that the humour of the joke derives from the excess of scepticism involved in taking for a double bluff what, in all likelihood, is a straightforward statement of fact. Such a redoubling is possible only thanks to the intervention of the symbolic order.

Many thanks to Maria (Masha) Kochkina for her help in obtaining the French text of this seminar.

9. Derrida quotes from this passage at least three times in *The Animal That Therefore I Am* (Derrida 2008 [2006], 127/174–75, 129–30/176–78, and 131/179–80). In the course of interpreting it he devotes the greater part of his attention to the final

possibility denied to the animal by Lacan, which Derrida apparently reads as the *complete* erasure of a trace: 'he [Lacan] maintains "the animal" within the first degree of pretence (pretence without pretence of pretence [*feinte sans feinte de feinte*]) or, which here amounts to the same thing, within the first degree of the trace: the capacity to trace, to leave a track [*de pister*] and to track [*de dé-pister*], but not to distract the tracking or lead the tracker astray [*mais non de dé-pister le dé-pistage*] by *erasing* [effacer] its trace or covering its tracks' (ibid., 128/176).

Perhaps the reason for focussing on this part of Lacan's account is that it remains the most deconstructible: for Derrida, an erasure is itself a trace, a making of a mark, and hence no effacement is ever complete, even when it is carried out by the logical animal, man: one never erases a text; one only constitutes a more or less legible palimpsest. If even the *human being* cannot erase the trace, then the opposition which Lacan posits between man and animal will not hold.

And yet has Derrida himself been sent off course in his pursuit of Lacan? It seems to us that there is no real warrant in Lacan's text for the suggestion that, on his account, erasure can be total. The passage in fact relates a ruse to deceive the pursuer with an *imperfectly erased* trace, left on the assumption that the one following will *assume* that it was an attempt at *total* erasure and thus part of a strategy designed to disguise the direction the quarry was taking. If the trace that remains is intended to make the one who reads it assume that its erasure was meant to be absolute, has Derrida's reading of Lacan not fallen into the same trap?

Let us expand upon this important point of disagreement. For Lacan, there are at least two kinds of redoubling that the symbolic order allows: the first is that of pretending to pretend — to present a signifier in the expectation that it will be taken for its opposite. The second is to imagine that the entire order in which marking and effacing take place could be destroyed: an erasure of (the very order of) erasure. This latter duplication is the doubling of erasure: one can erase a trace and then erase the very system in which that erasure took place, thus effacing the (first) effacing. This would be an absolute forgetting without the possibility of remembrance, the forgetting *of* forgetting.

It seems possible that Derrida is conflating these two redoublings, but may ultimately intend the second. While he takes Lacan to believe in the latter, Derrida himself remains doubtful, insisting that the erasure of a trace — even of the complete 'archive' — will always leave a mark and thereby remain legible. The *fact* of erasure will be manifest, and thus, an altogether successful wiping of memory is impossible — forgetting can never entirely be forgotten. Derrida thus refuses — or deconstructs — the opposition between a system of traces and a supposedly pure outside of this system in which there would be no trace, no recording, no differentiality, and no memory — such indeed would be a moment of pure presence, or pure absence, which deconstruction sets itself to hunt down.

In an earlier passage, but partly on the basis of the same text, and in the course of establishing the dominance of the *metaphysical* strands within Lacan's text, Derrida invokes another aspect of the distinction between the imaginary and the symbolic, which is made in 'the most dogmatically traditional manner' (Derrida 2008 [2006],

122/168) and constitutes the 'most Cartesian' moment of Lacan's discourse (ibid., 124/171): the opposition between 'reaction' and 'response' — the animal-machine's automatic and programmed reactions, in contrast with the human being's freely given (or withheld) response.

We have already encountered this distinction in the context of Levinas. The animal is a machine in that a specific reaction is involuntarily triggered by a certain signal emanating from its environment: there is a 'stimulus' and a 'response [i.e., a reaction]', and in general the animal enjoys a one-to-one or bi-univocal relation with its finite world, whether these stimuli are atomic or Gestalt. A properly human *response*, on the other hand, involves the possibility of delay and in the meantime the production of a multiplicity of possible thoughts, words, gestures, and deeds, which includes the response of deliberately *refraining* from responding to what naturally demands a response, and indeed responding in such a way that, thanks to the intervention of the symbolic order, deceives by telling the truth.

About this opposition, Derrida tells us candidly, 'we are not concerned with erasing every difference between what we are calling *reaction* and what we commonly name *response*. [. . .] My hesitation concerns only the purity, the rigor, and the indivisibility of the frontier that separates — already with respect to "us humans" ["*nous-les-hommes*"] — reaction from response' (Derrida 2008 [2006], 125/171–72). How are we to establish that an animal, or rather *certain* animals, do not also double bluff? And indeed, how can we be so sure that all humans are always incapable of an absolute sincerity?

10. To bolster Lacan's case for a distinction between humans and animals in terms of redoubling, one might consider animal techniques and their 'artefacts' in the theory of animality which Karl Marx has bequeathed us.

The animal can use tools, but it cannot perform the exponential redoubling which would allow it to *use* these tools to make *new tools* — tools to the second power — not to speak of the yet further redoubling which would involve using these tools to produce the *means* to produce new tools, constructing thereby the very 'means of production'. Human beings, on the other hand, can do all this, and as a result, in their case we can isolate the following three levels: (1) tools used to produce (2) tools which produce (3) tools. This doubling, or tripling, this production of (the means of) production, is not available to the animal, and in an analogous way the tools which the latter employs can be used only to satisfy its needs and those of its kin; they cannot be produced as (or be used to produce) goods which are in themselves surplus to requirement and therefore need not be *used* but may instead be *exchanged* for other tools or indeed for other *non*-functional goods. This is itself a kind of redoubling — the tool seen as a means to acquire other tools (or other goods), in a relation of exchange.

Exchange, and the production of goods destined to be exchanged, is restricted to the human world and human activity, which from that point onwards may be understood as 'labour'. A certain gap separating human labour from the vital needs of the species gradually widens to the point at which the human being is able to treat as an object of exchange not just the products of its labour but that very labour itself. Thus the gulf separating man from animal becomes even more gaping: no animal can rent out its own life-activity as 'labour-force' to another animal — its living 'praxis' cannot become a 'labour' that would be alienable on a market.

We might deploy this Marxian insight to argue in a new way, after Hegel, that animals are confined to nature or the 'imaginary' and are prevented from crossing the threshold into history or the 'symbolic'. History for Marx is the history of technical and technological innovation — a new epoch in history is sparked by a revolutionary change in the means of production, the tools or machinery by means of which men produce artefacts, or by a change in the ownership of such means. Even if animals use tools, they cannot be involved in radical alterations with regard to *which* tools they use, and, as a result, history in the strict sense is withheld from them (cf. Lewis 2007, 134ff).

11. Apart from some of his very earliest accounts of Lacan, Derrida always demonstrates an initial charitability towards his texts and acknowledges their progressive (deconstructive) character, the fact that they speak from a place other than metaphysics. But then, in a second moment, these same texts are shown to fall short in certain respects. In *The Animal That Therefore I Am*, Derrida clearly repeats this double gesture in stating that the texts under consideration, 'it seems to me, announce *at the same time* a theoretical mutation and a stagnant confirmation of inherited thinking, its presuppositions, and its dogma' (2008 [2006], 120/165). The 'theoretical mutation' involves in part 'the taking into account of a specular function in the sexualisation of the animal, as early as 1936, in "The Mirror Stage"' (ibid., 120/165), in other words, the idea that, '"the maturation of the gonad in the hen-pigeon" relies on the "sight of a fellow creature [*congénère*]", that is to say, another pigeon of either sex. And that is true even to the extent that a simple mirror reflection will suffice' (ibid., 121/166, quoting Lacan 2006 [1966], 77/95). Lacan's novelty, then, seems to reside in his invocation of the Imaginary, in the earliest days of the Gestalt theorisation of perception and animal ethology more generally.

We have analysed the potential blind spots of Derrida's reading of Lacan, which are not without relation to the real, nature, and the animal, along with the undue emphasis it consequently places on the metaphysical elements of Lacan's work, in *Derrida and Lacan: Another Writing* (Lewis 2008).

To demonstrate that we might not even need Derrida's deconstruction in order to undercut the metaphysical strand in the Lacanian text, we could reread Lacan's own frank admission that this whole vision of the animal as radically opposed to man may be nothing more than a perspectival distortion: 'There is no unconscious except for the speaking being [man]. The others, who possess being only through being named [animals] — even though they impose themselves from within the real — have instinct, namely the knowledge needed for their survival. Yet this is so only for our thought, which might be inadequate here' (Lacan 1990 [1974], 5/15). As if to press the point, Lacan immediately adverts to a third moment, *between* animal and man — the *domestic* animal: 'This still leaves the category of *homme*-sick animals, thereby called domestics [*d'hommestiques*], who for that reason are shaken, however briefly, by unconscious, seismic tremors' (ibid.).

Even if Derrida were right about Lacan's solidarity with metaphysics, we should perform here the same type of operation that we are carrying out in the case of

Hegel's two infinites: accepting the metaphysical distribution of man and animal while giving it a new value.

12. Here the necessity of considering the differences between a wild animal and a domestic pet becomes pressing. Schuster has brought to our attention a vivid analysis from Sartre concerning the way in which a dog's relationship with human beings and their culture alters its very nature, in a passage which bears more than a passing resemblance to Lacan's account of the dog at dinner (Schuster 2016, 148–49):

> It seems clear that household animals are bored; they are homunculae, the dismal reflections of their masters. Culture has penetrated them, destroying nature in them without replacing it. Language is their major frustration: they have a crude understanding of its function but cannot use it; it is enough for them to be the *objects of speech* — they are spoken to, they are spoken about, they know it. This manifest verbal power which is denied to them cuts through them, settles within them as the limit of their powers, it is a disturbing privation which they forget in solitude and which deprecates *their very natures* when they are with men. I have seen fear and rage grow in a dog. We were talking about him, he knew it instantly because our faces were turned toward him as he lay dozing on the carpet and because the sounds struck him with full force as if we were addressing him. Nevertheless we were speaking to *each other*. He felt it; our words seemed to designate him as our interlocutor and yet reached him *blocked*. He did not quite understand either the act itself or this exchange of speech, which concerned him far more than the usual hum of our voices [. . .] and far less than an order given by his master or a call supported by a look or gesture. Or rather — for the intelligence of these humanised beasts is always beyond itself, lost in the imbroglio of its presence and its impossibilities — he was bewildered at not understanding what he understood. [. . .] This dog passed from discomfort to rage, feeling at his expense the strange reciprocal mystification which is the relationship between man and animal. But his rage contained no revolt — the dog had summoned it to simplify his problems. Once calmed, he went off to the next room and returned, much later, to frolic and lick our hands.
>
> This example sufficiently demonstrates that for the animal, culture, at first a simple ambience [*milieu*], an ignored lacuna, becomes under the guise of training the pure negation *in itself* of animality. It is a *fission* that leads the beast both above and below his familiar level, raising him toward an impossible comprehension just when his misplaced intelligence is collapsing in a daze. Nothing is bestowed by culture, but something is taken away; without ever achieving a reflective schis-iparity [*sic* — *la scissiparité*, an explicit self-relation, which presupposes an initial split between I and myself, a fissure in the immanence of 'being-in-itself'], the immediacy of what is experienced is cracked, questioned. By nothing — therefore no hope of mediation; a shadow of distance separates life from itself, renders nature less natural. As a consequence, peaceful immanence is changed into self-consciousness. The transformation is never complete, it is pure movement; but this renewed questioning, this injection of the human as a denied possibility is translated by a kind of pleasure — the dog *feels alive, he is bored*. His boredom is life tasted as the impossibility of becoming man and as the perpetual collapsing of the desire to transcend the self in the direction of the human. [. . .] Without culture the animal would not be bored — he would live, that is all. (Sartre 1981 [1971], 137–38/144–46)

In a passage which seems to have gone largely unnoticed (Derrida being the exception — [cf. Derrida 2008 {2006}, 158/215–16]) from his great treatise on animality,

Heidegger raises the question of the domestic animal, and once again a dog is sitting down to dine with the philosopher. In keeping with the unusual gaiety of these lectures, in the course of recounting this convivial meal, Heidegger even seems to venture a pun:

> Let us consider the case of domestic animals [*Haustiere*] as a striking example. We do not describe them as such simply because they turn up in the house but because they belong to the house, i.e., they serve the house in a certain sense. Yet they do not belong to the house in the way in which the roof belongs to the house as protection against storms. We keep domestic pets [*Haustiere*] in the house with us, they *'live' with us* ['leben' mit uns]. But we do not live with them if living means: *being* in an animal kind of way. Yet we *are with* [sind *wir* mit] them nonetheless. But this being-with [*Mitsein*] is not an *existing-with*, because a dog does not exist but merely lives [*ein Hund nicht existiert, sondern nur lebt*]. Through this being with [*Mitsein*] animals we enable them to move within our world. We say that the dog is lying underneath the table or is running up the stairs and so on. Yet when we consider the dog itself — does it comport itself toward the table as table [*Tisch als Tisch*], toward the stairs as stairs [*Treppe als Treppe*]? All the same, it does go up the stairs with us. It feeds with us — and yet [*nein*], we do not really 'feed' [*fressen*]. It eats with us — and yet [*nein*], it does not really 'eat'. Nevertheless, it is with us! [*er ißt nicht. Und doch mit uns!*] A going along with . . . , a transposedness, and yet not [*und doch nicht*]. (Heidegger 1995 [1929–30], 210/308)

CHAPTER 2. KANT AND THE ANIMAL'S CHARM

1. I recall here a talk by Davide Tarizzo, at a conference which helped foster the development of a number of our concerns here, in which the relation between man and animal was compared to a door, or more precisely, it was suggested that man alone is familiar with doors, as distinct from the thresholds upon which they stand (Tarizzo 2011, cf. 2015).

For this way of comparing Kant and Hegel's visions of the dialectic, I am also indebted to a presentation by Daniel Steuer at the University of Brighton on Adorno (c. 2011) and his debate with Paul Davies immediately afterwards.

2. On the presentation of an earlier version of this work at the European University at St. Petersburg (2015), Artemy Magun raised some doubts regarding this translation: perhaps 'touching' as an adjective would be more apt; our fancy is 'tickled' by the cherished animal.

In §371 of Hegel's *Philosophy of Nature*, '*Reiz*' is translated by Michael Petry as 'irritation' in the sense of an excitation, a tickling, and a susceptibility to such affections: 'Disease is not an irritation [*ein Reiz*] incommensurate with the susceptibility [*Reizempfänglichkeit*] of the organism' (PNIII, 194/521). Elsewhere (§354), the Latinate '*Irritabilität*' is preferred but defined in terms of '*Reiz*', here translated as 'stimulation': '*Irritability* [Irritabilität] is stimulation [*Reizbarkeit*, stimulability] by an other, and the reaction of self-preservation in the face of this; conversely and to an equal extent, it is active self-preservation, and in this it submits itself to another'

(PNIII, 112/439). So rather than 'charm', 'being-affected by . . . ', or having an alien presence penetrate the enclosure of one's impressionability.

The notion of irritability indicates a certain impossibility of 'disinterest', which up to a point is useful for our exposition. This is perhaps the sense in which an animal is always watchful and never entirely at rest, catnapping rather than properly sleeping.

Tina Röck has pointed out that the word '*Reiz*', in the adjectival and adverbial form of '*reizend*', oscillates between the two extremes of charm and irritation but can also remain stationary at the midpoint of this opposition where it signifies simply a neutral form of 'being-affected' as in the '*Reiz-Reaktion Modell*' ('stimulus-response model'), to which we will so often have seen the animal's perceptual and motor systems confined.

Thus, if one restores to the term '*Reiz*' its ambiguity so as to include this kind of affectability, and ultimately an auto-affection prior to the cognitive self-relation of consciousness, a self-'touching', we might say that it installs not just a phenomenological but an ontological borderland, an unregulated zone in which man and animal can freely interact.

Apart from the author's own personal experience of such places, in particular the lake by the wood at the University of Warwick, I am thinking of Derrida's *On Touching* (2005 [1998]), which finds in Edmund Husserl's *Ideas II* and Maurice Merleau-Ponty's work, *inter alia*, a moment of self-affection prior to reflective self-consciousness. This 'auto-affection' deconstructs the metaphysical opposition between man and animal in terms of 'self-consciousness' understood as the exclusive province of the former.

In this connection, we should also read Daniel Heller-Roazen's fascinating book, *The Inner Touch* (2007), which devotes itself exclusively to this matter, although curiously — and perhaps deliberately — it does not refer to Derrida's text. It opens with a chapter on E. T. A Hoffmann's cat from *The Life and Opinions of the Tomcat Murr*, one of the prototypes of so many books from more recent times in which the animal itself, and more often than not the cat, begins to write and to write of *itself*, displaying in the process all of the supposed flaws of its kind — vanity and a not infrequent contempt for its 'owners' first among them (Sarah Kofman has devoted a whole book to Hoffmann's text and its implications for both autobiography and the relation between them and us: 'The cat's writing is plucky [*déplumante*] because he seizes the quill [*plume*], a privilege of man, in order to cross out [*raturer*] the opposition between man and animal' [Kofman 1980 {1976}, 4/91–92]).

In a related way, *Old Possum's Book of Practical Cats* opens with a poem concerning the (human) naming of cats (cats are said already to have a secret name that we do not know and which they appear to have given themselves) and ends with a poem entirely given over to a cat who writes and speaks to us (Eliot 1998 [1939]).

Finally, we might also cite a book which could have been influenced by Heller-Roazen in certain of its theses: Giorgio Agamben's *Use of Bodies* (2016 [2014]).

3. Between being and the Other, being and that which is 'otherwise than being', totality and infinity, reason and madness: Derrida's position is often expressed in these terms in his earlier works, and in particular, 'Violence and Metaphysics' (1964)

(2001 [1967c]) and 'Cogito and the History of Madness' (1963) (2001 [1967c]). To say that we are 'between two infinities' is to cite a part of the subtitle of a later work on Hans-Georg Gadamer and Paul Celan: *Rams: Uninterrupted Dialogue — Between Two Infinities, the Poem*, although these infinities are not obviously related.

4. To take account of even a fraction of the secondary literature on Kant's third critique and the critical project as a whole would be to engorge the text to a hypertrophic extent. Such scholarly completeness, while probably impossible, is at the same time hardly necessary here — although its absence risks impugning any claim to 'originality'. This is a personal work, an essay that is also a kind of 'autobiography' in something like the sense which Derrida gives to the word in his own book on animals.

That said, a certain scholarly spirit still haunts some out of the way corners, and this is also autobiographical in another respect.

5. We shall largely discount the astonishing Analytic of the Sublime, given our focus on beauty, but it will already have forced its head above water and will continue to do so at various intervals as the mighty Leviathan surfaces on occasion to remind us of just how indifferent to humankind nature can be.

6. The two parts of the third Critique are not isomorphic with the distinction between the sensible and the intelligible in that each part on its own displays something like an intrusion of the intelligible into the sensible. Since beauty and animality are *each already* in themselves a certain coincidence of nature and freedom, the question is: what precise alchemy occurs when these two instances fall together?

7. On 'joy' in beauty, or more precisely, 'rejoicing' (*erfreuen*), see CJ, 23f/184.

8. Strictly speaking this is a simplification, as everything generally is, since the deliverances of the senses are for Kant *already* 'formed', by space and time, the a priori necessary 'forms of intuition'.

9. This reading is in general indebted to Martin Heidegger's gesture in *Kant and the Problem of Metaphysics* (1929) along with everything it entailed in the history of continental philosophy in the twentieth century (cf. Heidegger 1997 [1929], 139/198–99).

10. The connection between nature and freedom by way of the 'free play' of the imagination goes some way to explaining Kant's name for the type of beauty he is exclusively concerned with in the Critique of Aesthetic Judgement: 'free beauty' (*freie Schönheit*), an experience or judgement which 'does not presuppose a concept of what the object is [meant] to be', and hence a freedom *from* the restriction of a single concept (CJ, 76/229).

11. For this is what aesthetic pleasure ultimately is. Agamben himself makes the connection between his own (Benjaminian) notion of a pure 'means' and Kant's third critique (Agamben 2000 [1996], 59/52) (thanks to German Primera for this reference). Naturally this would lead us to the notion of a suspended dialectic without Parousia in Kant's pre-Hegelian work, in the precise context of a judgement of beauty, a dialectic we might also find in Agamben (in *The Time That Remains* in particular). Our own question throughout the present work may be condensed in this idea of a stalled dialectic without consummation or production, without an *end*: it is the question asked by Ludwig Feuerbach and perhaps by Søren Kierkegaard as soon as Hegel proposed the

idea: why and by what right is the dialectical engine started at all, and once it is, what keeps it running? — at what point, if any, are we justified in stopping it?

12. In an earlier text, the *Observations on the Feeling of the Beautiful and Sublime* (1764), Kant had unequivocally joined together the two things which he would later strive to keep apart: 'the beautiful *charms* [*das Schöne* reizt]' (Kant 2011 [1764], 16/209).

13. The beautiful must involve disinterest, and we are too interested in the continued existence of something we favour so; and yet at a certain level, we must distinguish the interest we take in animals from that which we take in human beings, for the former can never truly be a desire for possession, erotic or otherwise. It is a unique kind of love and one which, indirectly, our exploration of charm is approaching — an intensely passionate love, which draws us together more closely than *philia* but without becoming entangled in *eros* and the strife (*neikos*) which must accompany it. The collapse of beauty and charm, disinterest and interest, in the animal experience may go some way towards explaining the peculiar nature of this love.

14. Heidegger might have had this botanist and the general movement of subtraction we are beginning to trace in the back of his mind when he wrote, in the context of nature and the artistic account of it, '[t]he botanist's plants are not the flowers of the hedgerow, the river's "source" ascertained by the geographer is not the "source in the ground"' (Heidegger 2010 [1927], 70/70). And again, much later:

> There is a tree in the yard. We state: the tree is well-shaped. It is an apple tree. This year it did not bear many apples. The birds [*Singvögeln*] like it. The apple-grower has still other things to say about it. The scientific botanist, who conceives of the tree as a plant, can point out a variety of things about the tree. And finally there comes along a strange and curious human being [*ein seltsamer Mensch*] and says: the tree is. (Heidegger 1968 [1951–52], 173/177)

Michael Marder analyses this passage with respect to the tree in *The Philosopher's Plant* (2014, 173ff).

15. But at what point does the infinite conceptualisability of the wallpaper's twirls and arabesques pass over into the vertiginous spiralling of the infinite divisibility of the *sublime*, the infinity of the unconditioned which only *reason* — as distinct from the understanding which remains securely anchored in sensory experience and its finite capacity — can think? What ultimately is the difference between the crustacean and the whale, the most sublime of all animals, or, if we must think a closer analogy, the countless workers in an ant-colony, decorating their mound? Does the animal, in its ability to span both extremes, encompass beauty *and* sublimity? At a certain almost indefinable point, the calling of birds becomes a tormenting hysterical screech, and the flocking in the trees a sinister Hitchcockian swarm.

On the question of sublime animals: in a private discussion, Matt Lee — to whom I dedicate this note — responded to a description of the present work by pointing out that it had what he took to be a much narrower focus than I was imagining: did it not focus exclusively on *domestic* animals — creatures small, furry, and unthreatening to us in either their size or their power (*Macht*)? His concern, tactfully implicit, seemed to be that in this case the work would fall victim to a certain anthropomorphism of animals which was not, I think, to his taste. Perhaps this passage from Gilles Deleuze and Félix Guattari was in his mind:

> We must distinguish three kinds of animals. First, individuated animals, family pets, sentimental, Oedipal animals each with its own petty history, 'my' cat, 'my' dog. These animals invite us to regress, draw us into a narcissistic contemplation, and they are the only kind of animal psychoanalysis understands [. . .]: *anyone who likes cats or dogs is a fool*. And then there is a second kind: animals with characteristics or attributes: genus, classification, or State animals; animals as they are treated in the great divine myths, in such a way as to extract from them series or structures, archetypes or models [. . .]. Finally, there are more demonic animals, pack or affect animals that form a multiplicity, a becoming, a population, a tale . . . . Or once again, cannot any animal be treated in all three ways? There is always the possibility that a given animal, a louse, a cheetah or an elephant, will be treated as a pet, my little beast. And at the other extreme, it is also possible for any animal to be treated in the mode of the pack or swarm; that is our way, fellow sorcerers. Even the cat, even the dog. . . . (Deleuze and Guattari 1988 [1980], 240–41/294, quoted in Atterton and Calarco 2004, 89–90)

Well, we are not entirely sure that our proud cat has ever been part of a swarm, and one might presume that it is against precisely this kind of passage that Derrida writes when he invokes his own cat. But then again, it is not certain that a cat is ever truly domesticated, seeming rather to breach the walls of the human *oikos* and to problematise its exclusion of the outside. If cats are often wild, what packs might they not after all join in their nocturnal wanderings?

In a certain way, by narrowing our remit to include only cats and their like, if such there be — perhaps birds and even fish, with their mysterious non-human elements of air and water, are secretly kin to their deadly feline enemy: they are certainly all among the chief protagonists of this book — we are focussing in on something which resists assimilation to the human world and displays a rather magnificent indifference to it. There is little of narcissism here. With their pawprints, cats obscure human boundaries, and first among them the central border of Western culture, between the inside and the outside of a house, the extent of our 'property' — including the garden if we are lucky enough to have one (although its growth and need of constant pruning are endlessly troubling).

Perhaps, in the passage cited previously, Deleuze and Guattari are charting something like the movement from the charming to the sublime, from the home to the great outdoors. But the 'domestic' animals that interest us the most stand on the threshold. It is important that they occupy the house since we are interested in the deviant ways that they have of inhabiting the same space, utilising our furnishings and equipment in unaccustomed ways — it is as if they had brought something of the uncultured and the wild in from the outside, like a dead mouse used as a gift.

16. Buildings most characteristic of St. Petersburg, in fact, where these lines were first spoken.

17. '[W]e may regard *natural beauty* as the *exhibition* [Darstellung] of the concept of formal (merely subjective) purposiveness, and may regard *natural purposes* [organisms] as the exhibition of the concept of a real (objective) purposiveness' (CJ, 33/193).

18. The ontological argument was a proof for the existence of god supposedly refuted by Kant as part of his critique of metaphysics (of which rational or apriori theology was a part), and frequently attributed to St. Anselm of Canterbury (fl. 1033–1109). The argument affirms that it would be contradictory to the concept and hence to the essence of an infinite being for it to lack any single property, including that of existence (cf. Anselm, *Proslogion*, chs. 1–3). And yet, despite Kant's refutation, it is as if the self-caused cause would reappear in nature in the form of the animal.

19. Teleological judgement is 'the power to judge the real (objective) purposiveness of nature by understanding and reason' (CJ, 33/193).

20. And perhaps this is why we need to make distinctions between particular types of animal, especially the beautiful and the sublime, for the Leviathans of the deep risk detaining us at the level of a moral — or otherwise awed — respect for nature in its otherness, in contrast to the specific sense of kinship bestowed upon us by the experience of beauty.

CHAPTER 3. HEGEL AND NATURE

1. In response to those who propose that philosophy must cede its place to science, or that on topics such as nature and animality, at least, it must defer to natural-scientific insight, we would respond in two ways:

First, conciliatory: this text *does* partake of a general movement that attempts slowly and cautiously, partly deconstructively, to open philosophy to some degree to the data provided by the natural and human sciences. It is a small but precious part of a broader project which attempts in its own way to track the course of a development within philosophy, which began with Heidegger if not (long) before, in which the division between the transcendental and the empirical, metaphysical and physical, begins to collapse in various ways.

Second, less conciliatory, and perhaps this is the traditionally phenomenological aspect of the present work: what can science tell us about *beauty*, and in particular about the *meaning* and *experience* of beauty?

One can quite easily point to a great many of the central disciplines of philosophy, from ethics to politics, aesthetics, perhaps law, which would not automatically succumb to scientific reason even if metaphysics had somehow been supplanted by physics in the modern age. Above all, the sciences deal with what *is*, but philosophy addresses both this *and* what *ought* to be but *is not*. And, if one follows Heidegger, the underlying reason for this is that philosophy ultimately addresses being, which is precisely *not* an entity.

This allows us to take a step further, and to make a point of principle: philosophy should begin with an attempt to defend a rationalist or idealist project, and not least because empiricism and naturalism are so spontaneously adopted by the pre- or non-philosophical 'mindset', but perhaps even more because this is how philosophy itself — as metaphysics — begins, phylogenetically, so to speak, by passing beyond all particular entities to ask about their being. It is only later on that things will become more complicated.

Once, at Warwick, Paul Davies — in a conversation, not strictly speaking with me — suggested that naturalism was the spontaneous presupposition of analytic philosophy, while for continental philosophy it first needed to be argued for.

2. Or later than twilight. Deleuze and Guattari elegantly describe Kant's *Critique of Judgement* as 'an unrestrained work of old age', like the question, 'what is philosophy?', 'a question posed [. . .] at midnight, when there is no longer anything to ask' (Deleuze and Guattari 1994 [1991], 1–2/7).

3. And the author of that form of *Naturphilosophie* which is today considered most our contemporary, as the work of Iain Hamilton Grant confirms (along with that of Adrian Johnston and Slavoj Žižek) (cf. Grant 2006, x–xi).

4. Perhaps in the end this comes quite close to the question of whether this philosophy will be properly naturalistic or whether it will permanently prevent itself from attaining this standpoint, coming to rest on the side of idealism. Hegel's dialectic would be a genetic or developmental account which was not simply a naturalistic one.

5. This contrasts with a certain way of taking Heidegger's famous statement, 'science does not think', which seems to position Heidegger firmly on the side of the transcendental-empirical account of philosophy and science that we have just presented. Nevertheless, if one perseveres with the passage in question, it becomes apparent that Heidegger's *later* position at least is more complex than it might seem (Heidegger 1968 [1951–52], 8/9). The transition from the earlier to the later Heidegger is frequently understood as a move from a Kantian to a Hegelian position, and his relation to science is no exception.

For Hegel, what allows us to describe physics as a form of thinking is that it comprehends not particulars but universals (PNI, 196–97/15 §246), albeit — in the case of physics — the universal 'as it presents itself in a determinate form' (PNI, 197/15 §246). Among such universals of nature Hegel lists, 'forces, laws, [and] genera' (PNI, 197/15 §246). But physics assumes that these structures have no necessity; the philosophy of nature, on the other hand, attempts to bring out a necessity implicit within these universals and hence displays the extent of their coherence with a conceptual order (PNI, 197/15 §246).

This necessity is understood by Hegel to mean that the universal structures of nature may be derived from the very *concept* of nature. He describes this as the universal's *determining* itself, autonomously generating its own particular forms. Nature must contain, according to its very idea, a certain number of features: for instance, its division into physical, chemical, and biological levels. In this sense, the universal concept, 'nature', the general '*form*' of nature, spontaneously produces certain of the more particular *contents* of this concept, and it does so of necessity. Thus many natural features may be deduced rationally, and certain parts of empirical nature insofar as they correspond to these features may be said to be logically necessary.

At the same time, we should note that this 'implication' does not describe a movement of *thought* which would simply be distinct from reality. Entities themselves, insofar as they are what they are, which is to say insofar as their reality lives up to their notion, unfold in the way of the concept. Thus, the notion of 'generation' has a much more literal, physical sense than we might have imagined. Thought and being, logic and ontology — reason and nature — are not separated in the way of the bad infinite and the finite, for Hegel. All such oppositions, bequeathed to us by Kant and the history of philosophy, will be overcome.

While physics thinks inasmuch as it deals with universals, it does not allow itself to become fully aware of this thoughtfulness, since it does not understand the universal immanently to generate its own particular contents. Thus contrary to its frequent claims, in Hegel's terms, the universals of the natural sciences are 'abstract' rather than 'concrete'. The word, 'concrete' is here being used in the literal sense of *concrescere*, to grow together, to overcome the opposition between form and content, universal and particular, by showing how the former necessarily generates the latter, concretising or particularising *itself*. All of this should allow us to gain a preliminary idea of how important Kant's notion of the organism as a self-actualising concept will be for Hegel. In physics, universal and particular appear to be external to one another, and as a result, the particularities in nature lack intrinsic connection: they just happen to have turned out that way — such is the meaning of 'contingency' (PNI, 202/21 §246A).

All of this remains intimately related to the notion of the infinite in Hegel, which has guided our discussion from the start: we might say that the relation between the universal and the particular as it stands in the sciences assumes the form of the relation between the *bad* infinite and the finite, while the philosophy of nature rethinks it according to the *true* relation between the infinite and the finite, their opposition overcome.

This is one of the ways in which philosophy 'presupposes and is conditioned [*Voraussetzung und Bedingung*] by empirical physics' (PNI, 197/15 §246R). It does not ignore or discount the actual empirical experience of nature, but in philosophy itself, 'it is no longer *experience*, but rather the *necessity* of the *Notion*, which must emerge as the foundation [*Grundlage*]' (PNI, 197/15 §246R, emphases added). In philosophy there is always another sense of priority, distinct from chronological earliness, the priority of the concept which can render intelligible the experienced phenomenon: 'only the Idea, because it has returned into itself and is therefore being in and for self, subsists eternally. In time nature comes first, but the absolute prius [first] is the Idea. This absolute prius is the finis [*das Letzte*, the last], the true beginning [*Anfang*], alpha is omega' (PNI, 211/30 §248A). Logically (which is to say in the order of derivation or presupposition), the idea comes first; but time does not exist in the realm of the idea, the eternity within which god's mind operates — the order in which relations of derivation are forever true. Time is a part of *nature*: it is created along with it, just as history is created with spirit. Therefore we cannot say that logic is *temporally* earlier than nature, and yet it is in a truer sense first and indeed all-pervasive, unfolding itself and nothing but itself throughout nature and the spirit which is its ripest fruit.

The relation between physics and philosophy that we have outlined implies that one cannot say that the concept has its ideal order and if real nature fails to conform to it then 'so much the worse' for nature: 'in the procedure of philosophic cognition, the object has not only to be presented in its *Notional determination* [*Begriffsbestimmung*], [but] the *empirical* appearance corresponding [*entspricht*] to this determination also has to be specified, and it has to be shown that the appearance does in fact correspond to its Notion' (PNI, 197/15 §246R).

6. And Kant was not the first to see conceptuality in nature: Hegel identifies among the philosophical predecessors of the Philosophy of Nature, Aristotle's *Physics*, which for him stands closer to the philosophy of nature than it does to contemporary physics (PNI, 193/11 §Introduction): '*Aristotle* had already noticed this notion of purpose in nature, and he called the activity the *nature of a thing*. This is the true teleological view, for it regards nature in its proper animation [*Lebendigkeit*] as free, and is therefore the highest view of nature' (PNI, 196/14 §245A).

7. 'Man must have eaten of the tree of knowledge of good and evil, he must have gone through the labour and activity of thought in order to be what he is, i.e. the subjugator of the separation [*Überwinder dieser Trennung*] of what is his, from nature' (PNI, 200/18 §246A). This is what Hegel means by 'sublation' (*Aufhebung*), the *retroactive* overcoming of an opposition: one must have left paradise behind, in order, with a parting glance, to know what it was. We cannot begin to understand from the beginning but only from the end, at dusk. Philosophy would then model its behaviour upon the Owl of Minerva, which takes flight only when all is said and done:

> One word more about giving instruction as to what the world ought to be. Philosophy in any case always comes on the scene too late to give it. As the thought of the world, it appears only when actuality is already there cut and dried after its process of formation has been completed [*die Wirklichkeit ihren Bildungsprozeß vollendet*]. The teaching of the concept, which is also history's inescapable lesson, is that it is only when actuality is mature that the ideal first appears over against the real [*das Ideale dem Realen gegenüber erscheint*], and that the ideal apprehends this same real world in its substance and builds it up for itself into the shape of an intellectual realm [*in Gestalt eines intellektuellen Reichs*]. When philosophy paints its grey in grey, then it has a shape [*Gestalt*] of life grown old. By philosophy's grey in grey it cannot be rejuvenated but only understood [*erkennen*]. The owl of Minerva spreads its wings only with the falling of the dusk. (PR, 12–13/28)

8. Eckart Förster has suggested, in an important talk on the philosophy of nature in Hegel and Goethe, that Petry's 'reconstitute' is less apt than 'reuse in a different way', while in a later, personal communication (Wednesday 18th January 2017), he proposed 'transform (and use in a different way)'.

9. We should recall here Hegel's subtle distinction between the concept (*Begriff*) and the idea (*Idee*), which develops Kant's distinction between Understanding and Reason, knowing and thinking, the respective vessels of which are precisely concept and idea. Hegel departs from Kant in affirming that the idea *can* find a correlate in empirical reality, while for Kant an idea is a concept *without* a (sensory) intuition, for that ('unconditioned' or infinite) thing which it thinks exceeds objective experience. Indeed, in Hegel, 'idea' is the title of an empirically real entity which lives up to its concept and therefore exists most truly: 'The Idea is the *adequate Notion* [*Die Idee ist der* adäquate Begriff], that which is objectively *true*, or the *true as such*' (SL, 755/462). And 'subjective truth is the correspondence [*Übereinstimmung*] between sensuous representation [*Vorstellung*] and the object [*Gegenstande*], objective truth

is the correspondence of the object [*Objekts*], of the fact [*Sache*], with itself, so that its reality is in conformity with its Notion' (PNI, 204/23 §246A).

In the *Science of Logic*, Hegel expands upon the connection between the Idea and reality: '[We shall] [r]eserv[e] then the expression "Idea" [*Idee*] for the objective or real Notion [*objektiven oder realen Begriff*] and distinguish [. . .] it from the Notion itself and still more from mere pictorial thought [*bloßen Vorstellung*]' (SL, 755/463).

> [T]he Idea is the unity of the Notion and objectivity [*Objektivität*], is the true [. . .], we must recognise that everything actual [*alles Wirkliche*] *is* only in so far as it possesses the Idea and expresses it. It is not merely that the object, the objective and subjective world in general *ought to be congruous* with the Idea, but they are themselves the congruence of Notion and reality [*die Kongruenz des Begriffs und der Realität*]; the reality that does not correspond [*entspricht*] to the Notion is mere *Appearance* [Erscheinung], the subjective, contingent, capricious element that is not the truth. (SL, 756/464)

10. That said, the position of Hegel's *Logic* as *prior* to the *Philosophy of Nature* might complicate matters, unless one adopts a retrospective view of that as well and assumes that what was always at stake was a conceptualisation which need not be understood as present in the beginning. We address this in more detail elsewhere.

11.

> The animal organism is the microcosm, the centre of nature which has become for itself. Within it, the whole of inorganic nature has recapitulated itself [*zusammengefaßt*], and is idealised [*idealisiert*] [. . .]. As the animal organism is the process of subjectivity [*Prozeß der Subjektivität*] which is self-relating in the midst of externality, the rest of nature is present [*vorhanden*] here, for the first time, as something external, for animal being [*das Animalische*] preserves itself in this relationship with that which is external to it. (PNIII, 108/435–36 §352A)

Animality is the determinate negation of those parts of nature which remain less sentient, and this means that the animal attains a kind of subjectivity and hence an awareness. The animal resumes within it all that has gone before, and precisely thereby it becomes *different* from everything else. Thus an *opposition* is retroactively installed between the inorganic and the organic only *after* the latter has emerged. The animal is the site at which the whole of (inorganic) nature becomes 'aware' of itself, 'for itself' (*für sich*).

12.

> The Idea is itself the pure Notion that has itself for subject matter [*Gegenstande*, its object] and which, in running itself as subject matter through the totality of its determinations, develops itself into the whole of its reality [*Realität*], into the system of the science [of logic — Miller's addition], and concludes by apprehending this process of comprehending itself, thereby superseding [*aufzuheben*] its standing as content and subject matter and cognising the Notion of the science. [. . .] [T]his Idea is still logical, it is enclosed within pure thought, and is the science only of the divine *Notion*. True, the systematic exposition is itself a realisation of the Idea but confined within the same sphere. Because the pure Idea of cognition is so far confined within subjectivity, it is the *urge* [Trieb] to sublate [*aufzuheben*] this, and pure truth as the last result becomes also the *beginning* [Anfang]

of another sphere and science. [...] [/] The Idea, namely, in positing itself as absolute *unity* of the pure Notion and its reality and thus contracting itself [*zusammennimmt*] into the immediacy of *being*, is the *totality* in this form — *nature* [*als die* Totalität *in dieser Form* — Natur]. (SL, 843/572–73)

13. At this point, Hegel refers us back to the first volume of the *Philosophy of Nature*, §270A and is presumably thinking of the following passages on Kepler's laws: 'It was his unshakeable belief in the inherent rationality of the facts [*er hatte den absoluten Glauben, Vernunft müsse darin sein*] that led him to his discovery' (PNI, 271/96 §270A). But the crucial material appears some ten pages later, where Hegel urges us in fact to remain modest in our search for rationality amongst facts:

> Philosophy has to proceed on the basis of the Notion, and even if it demonstrates [*aufstellt*] very little, one has to be satisfied. It is an error [*Verirrung*] on the part of the philosophy of nature to attempt to face up to all phenomena [*Erscheinungen*]; this is done in the finite sciences, where everything has to be reduced to general conceptions [*Gedanken*] (hypotheses). (PNI, 281/106 §270A)

Thus, strangely enough, the insult of 'panlogicism' might ultimately be more appropriate to science than to philosophy.

Hegel goes on to account for this discrepancy between science and philosophy in such a way as to explain why the philosophy of nature can afford to be patient in its quest for reason in nature:

> In these sciences the empirical element [*Das Empirische*] is the sole confirmation of the hypothesis, so that everything has to be explained. Whatever is known [*erkannt*] through the Notion is its own explanation and stands firm [*steht fest*] however, so that philosophy need not be disturbed if the explanation of each and every phenomenon [*Phänomene*] has not yet been completed. (PNI, 281/106 §270A)

This is how Hegel views the status of his own *Philosophy of Nature* as he has so far found himself capable of elaborating it (at least in the realm of Mechanics):

> Here I have merely traced the foundations [*Anfänge*, rudiments, beginnings] of a rational interpretation, as this must be employed in the comprehension [*Begreifen*] of the mathematical and mechanical laws of nature within the free realm of measures. Specialists do not reflect upon the matter, but a time will come when the rational concept [*Vernunftbegriffe*] of this science will be demanded! (PNI, 281/106 §270A)

14. The notion of nature's 'weakness' has been taken up at length by Adrian Johnston (2012 et al.).

15. Here, the danger of an idealism difficult to justify at least to modern eyes threatens from another direction, in this gesture of comparing and in a certain way *judging* nature against the concept, and in particular, the most flagrantly idealist assertion that nature's falling short is actually *responsible* for one of its primary characteristics, as if the concept and an entity's discrepancy with respect to it had an actual ontological effect.

(I can almost see Ray Brassier's nostrils flaring as he recounted a presentation on Hegel's Philosophy of Nature at Middlesex University, some time in the mid- to late 2000s.)

In deference to such worries, one might concede that this profusion should be read in terms of what the subject *sees* in nature, and assert that this profusion would indeed *be* there in some sense but might not be recognised as such if there were no creatures capable of deploying concepts. Such would accord with the thoroughly retrospective character of the philosophy of nature's 'return path'. But this smacks of the amelioration that so much of the best Hegelian scholarship today has come to repudiate as the worst.

16. I must salute my teacher, Stephen Houlgate, for all that he has imparted of Hegel, and in particular this point concerning viruses, which stands out very clearly in my memory even though it was only the briefest of interventions at a talk — I no longer remember which — almost a decade ago.

17. Another feature of the living thing which straddles the Philosophy of Nature and the Philosophy of Spirit is habit. Analogous to the way in which the self-determination of autonomy enters nature in the form of the animal soul, in habit the mechanism of matter potentially gives way to a movement possessed of skill and grace, with the ability to liberate the body from automatism, to adapt freely and ultimately to act spontaneously: a capacity denied to the inorganic world. A full account of the notion of habit must wait until it becomes necessary to relate Hegel's discourse to the psychoanalytic account of drive and desire, which has already shown itself to be important in distinguishing man from animal on the topic of the bad infinite.

18. It is with this natural and final cessation in mind that Hegel identifies nature itself with death (PNI, 216/36 §251).

19. Frank Ruda has written some remarkable passages on this transition (Ruda 2017, 100ff).

20. Cf. Malabou 2005 [1996], 145–46/199–200 et al. on the prefiguration of sublation in nature, specifically in the form of (Aristotle's conception of) habit, to which we shall return.

21. For Hegel's discussion of the organism's unity in plurality and the passages on metabolism and dialectic, which we cite next, see PNIII, 102f/430f §350–A.

22.

> [W]e can tell those who assert the truth and certainty of the reality of sense-objects that they should go back to the most elementary school of wisdom, viz. the ancient Eleusinian Mysteries of Ceres and Bacchus, and that they have still to learn the secret meaning of the eating of bread and the drinking of wine. For he who is initiated into these Mysteries not only comes to doubt the being of sensuous things, but to despair of it; in part he brings about the nothingness of such things himself in his dealings with them, and in part he sees them reduce themselves to nothingness. Even the animals are not shut out from this wisdom but, on the contrary, show themselves to be most profoundly initiated into it; for they do not just stand idly in front of sensuous things as if these possessed intrinsic being, but, despairing of their reality, and completely assured of their nothingness, they fall to without ceremony and eat them up. And all Nature, like the animals, celebrates these open Mysteries which teach the truth about sensuous things. (PhG, 65/91 §109)

Metabolism, swallowing and digesting, transforming raw matter into fuel for some more ideal mental or spiritual activity often seems to anticipate the properly rational-spiritual gesture of sublation.

The *Philosophy of Nature* repeats in a more scientific form what the *Phenomenology* had already stated: the animal is not entirely self-contained, still somewhat dependent and lacking the free-standing character of man — it is essentially related to an environment of a different character than itself, 'an inorganic nature, an external world' (PNIII, 102/430 §350A). But despite this, the organism is not only capable of maintaining its unity in the face of its inherent plurality, it can also retain its (self-) identity despite and indeed thanks to the existence of *otherness* in the form of the externality of the environment. The organism is able to assimilate this alterity into the loop of its subjectivity — in some cases, if not all, by way of metabolism.

It seems that this assimilation, rendering same what is other and yet standing in a relation of mutual dependence with this otherness, is precisely that organic process which presages the dialectical idealisation: 'animal subjectivity consists of bodily self-preservation [*sich selbst zu erhalten*] in the face of contact with an external world, and of remaining with itself [*bei sich selbst zu bleiben*] as the universal. As this supreme point of nature, animal life is therefore absolute idealism' (PNIII, 102/430 §350A).

23. Which is the analogical term in such a sentence? Is reason a form of organic activity, or organic activity an inchoate form of reason? Where does one begin? The question is of retroactivity, once again.

CHAPTER 4. BEAUTY IN NATURE — HEGEL'S AESTHETICS

1. '*Ahnen*', here 'foreshadowing', is elsewhere translated as 'presentiment' (*ahnt sich*) (PNI, 194/12 §Introduction), and earlier in this section of the *Aesthetics*, as 'divination' (A, 129/173–74).

2. One might note in passing that this beauty is *not* manifest to the animal itself, and so, in order for there to be beauty, the human being must also have arrived on the scene. Thus we find in Hegel a hint of the way in which we shall ultimately rethink the essence of the human: as the one capable of appreciating the beauty of the animal.

3. Then horses, insects, and finally cats: 'cats purr [*schnurren*] when they are pleased' (PNIII, 105/433 §351A). Timofeeva has commented on this passage in the course of an exceptionally rich engagement with the Hegelian menagerie (Timofeeva 2012, 80–81).

4. Derrida has devoted many important passages to the status of sound, the voice, and their proximity to thought, in Hegel in particular, in 'The Pit and the Pyramid' and elsewhere (cf. 1981 [1972], 88ff/101ff).

5. This is how the mediævals sometimes spoke of their universals — 'a voice that is merely breath', a mere word without any real referent. Such would be the 'nominalist' position on universals, stemming from Roscelin and running through William of Ockham, right up to Nietzsche, one might argue. We present such a genealogy,

in the context of an elucidation of certain passages from Heidegger, in another text (Lewis 2018).

6. When we spoke of weeding the garden earlier, we paid scant regard to the poor weeds themselves, and in this gesture remained perhaps unwittingly Hegelian. For Hegel, the animal is the uprooted plant which does not die. Perhaps the closest the plant itself gets to this state is the remarkable tumbleweed.

Michael Marder has recently gone much further in the attention he has paid to 'vegetal being' and 'plant-thinking' (cf. Marder and Irigaray 2016; Marder 2013).

7. Nietzsche, in his opposition to the spirit of gravity (*Geist der Schwere*), which he was perhaps all too ready to associate with Hegel himself, chose rather the butterfly than the bird (and the inorganic but remarkable structure of the airborne soap-bubble) (1969 [1885], 68/49), although birds do feature in his work, as in this clear echo of Hegel's *Philosophy of Right* with its grey old owl, painting its own stripe on the already faded memories of an ageing past:

> Alas, and yet what *are* you, my written and painted thoughts! It is not long ago that you were still so many-coloured, young and malicious, so full of thorns and hidden spices you made me sneeze and laugh — and now? You have already taken off your novelty and some of you, I fear, are on the point of becoming truths: they already look so immortal, so pathetically righteous, so boring! And has it ever been otherwise? For what things do we write and paint, we mandarins with Chinese brushes, we immortalisers of things which *let* themselves be written, what alone are we capable of painting? Alas, only that which is about to wither and is beginning to lose its fragrance! Alas, only storms departing exhausted and feelings grown old and yellow! Alas, only birds strayed and grown weary in flight who now let themselves be caught in the hand — in *our* hand! We immortalise that which cannot live and fly much longer, weary and mellow things alone! And it is only your *afternoon*, my written and painted thoughts, for which alone I have the colours. (1990 [1886], 221/239–40)

One might also recall another bird that soars through the texts of philosophy: the dove 'cleaving the air' which Kant employs as a metaphor for free-floating speculation, 'on the wings of the ideas' — although in his case this particular form of thought is precisely what stands in need of Critique, and which, appropriately enough given the shared analogy, for Hegel is to be rehabilitated differently (CPR, A5/B8–9).

But to return to Nietzsche's butterfly for a moment: one should here reread Miran Božovič's marvellous account of the place of butterflies and their metamorphosis in the history of philosophy (Božovič 2000, 15–23). With half an eye on our own preoccupations, it should not escape our notice that this text also contains a remarkable passage on the animal gaze in a form we have not considered: 'By means of eyespots, tiny dark dots on their wings, certain insects such as butterflies and moths are able to return the gaze' (ibid., 16). The animal stares back not at us but at its predators, and, as Božovič points out, this is not strictly the animal's own gaze but the (imaginary) gaze of their predator's *own* predator.

The example he chooses is that of a moth, menaced by a rat, whose wings, when unfurled, cast back to its pursuer the 'gaze of an owl' (ibid., 17).

Many thanks to Oxana Timofeeva for calling the relevance of this book to my attention.

8. Here, once again, Derrida will have been right in his assertion that Heidegger is at his most Hegelian when it comes to the animal: one merely has to recall his notion of the animal's 'disinhibiting ring', penetrated by an unknown other — an entity, and yet not (Heidegger 1995 [1929–30], 273/396, cf. 273/396 & 243/353).

9. For Hegel, the animal does not undergo individuation in the same way a human being does; it remains entirely subordinate to its genus, identical with it, and yet, despite this identity, no individual animal can ever perfectly embody its genus — individual and genus are to this extent opposed: the singular animal is 'the individual opposed to itself [*gegen sich*] as the genus [*Gattung*] with which it is implicitly identical [*an sich identisch*]' (PNIII, 108/436 §352A). This difference and identity seem to be opposed to one another as life is to death: 'In life, the animal certainly maintains itself in the face of its inorganic nature and its genus [*Gattung*], but in the long run the universality [*Allgemeine*] of the genus retains its supremacy' (PNIII, 210/536 §375A). The fact that no one animal can be fully adequate to its type means that the individual creature must lay down its life for its species — become sick and perish: 'The *original disease* of the animal, and the inborn *germ of death*, is its being inadequate to universality' (PNIII, 209/535 §375).

The individual animal may be said to contain something like a contradiction in that the organism is an individuated entity but one which also embodies a universal with which it is not identical and that no individual animal can ever exhaust — there is never a perfect horse. Animals must keep dying one after the other, in a bad infinite chain, in the hope of one day matching up to the universal (a hope that, in truth, is only satisfied when, one fine day, a curious animal named 'man' arises).

10. This rejoining of self and other in non-alienation is the reason why art, along with its progeny, religion and philosophy, are instances not of 'objective spirit' but of '*absolute* spirit'.

11. Hence Hegel's claim that '*Wesen ist Gewesen*', which we might idiosyncratically translate as 'the essence of an entity is what it will (always) have been': 'The German language has preserved *essence* in the past participle of the verb *to be* [*Die Sprache hat im Zeitwort* sein *das Wesen in der vergangenen Zeit,* "gewesen", *behalten*]; for essence is past — but timelessly past — being [*das Wesen ist das vergangene, aber zeitlos vergangene Sein*]' (SL, 389/13).

CHAPTER 5. FOSSILS AND THE FOSSILISATION OF THE DIALECTIC

1. Quentin Meillassoux has attempted to generalise the notion of the fossil beyond its literality to encompass anything that existed prior to the emergence of humanity or sentient life (he occasionally oscillates on this point, between thought and feeling, or 'sapience' and 'sentience' as is sometimes, unappealingly, said today), and of which traces remain — the generalisation is marked by the prefix used to create the neologism, '*archi*-fossil' (Meillassoux 2008 [2006], 10/26).

Meillassoux's aim is to overcome a philosophical tendency to equate *being* with *givenness*, which he names 'correlationism'. Correlationism, by affirming the identity of being and the given, asserts the inaccessibility of any *non*-correlated thing-in-itself, a Being which would not appear *to* any form of consciousness. Meillassoux attempts vividly to lay the flaws of correlationism open to intuition by asking us to imagine a time prior to the very *existence* of consciousness, and challenging us to say how we are to make sense of statements concerning such a time.

For drawing a great deal of philosophical attention to the fossil, in whatever guise, we owe a substantial debt to Meillassoux's work. Where we differ is in taking fossils *literally*. For Meillassoux, the archi-fossil *is not* and *cannot be* a literal 'fossil' — it cannot itself have been a living creature since it is the trace of a time in which there *was* no sentient life, and this is precisely what allows the archi-fossil to put in question the correlation of being and givenness. Here, I am interested in the philosophical implications of *literal* fossils, the stone remnants of life — petrified vitality — and the metaphorical transplantation of such a fossil to the dialectic.

Let us note in passing that Ted Toadvine has responded to Meillassoux's critique of phenomenology as one particular form of correlationism, largely on behalf of Maurice Merleau-Ponty, by considering the literal fossil, noting as he does so that, '[p]henomenology has generally avoided the fossil' (Toadvine 2014, 271). Merleau-Ponty does indeed provide us with a brief but striking account of fossils, very similar to our own in certain ways, in the course of attempting to describe the manner in which the human body involves us in a relation with the deep past:

> Evolution, embryogenesis: The body-object is only a *trace* — Trace in the mechanical sense: present substitute of a past that no longer is — the trace for us is more than the present effect of the past. It is a survival of the past [*une survie du passé*], an enjambment. The trace and the fossil: ammonite [*La trace et le fossile: l'ammonite*]. The living thing is no longer there but it is almost there; we have the negative of it, which is related to it, not as the sign is related to the signification, the effect or the cause, but something for itself. And the mineral, reoccupying the hollow, remakes the animal *in quasi*. But hollowed fossils are more striking: there is nothing between them and the very animal — the trace of the footstep [*trace de pas*] — [. . .]. The body is not comprehensible in the actual (actualism). Thickness of the past. (Merleau-Ponty 2003 [1956–60], 276/343–44, cf. 260–61/326–28)

I must thank Tom Greaves for alerting me to Toadvine's essay and for his many helpful comments on the manuscript of the present work. And thanks to Dylan Trigg for locating the passages cited from Merleau-Ponty's course on *Nature*.

2. Naturally, throughout this passage, I have in mind Derrida's *Of Grammatology* (1997 [1967b], 95ff/143ff).

3. Maurice Blanchot, without thinking that he might be speaking of fossils, describes the 'first writer' scoring a mark upon a surface of stone or wood, carving out an emptiness or void in the real. This is construed as the very precondition of what we today call 'writing':

> But the first one to write, the one who cut into stone and wood under ancient skies, was hardly responding to the demands of a view requiring a reference point and giving it a meaning; rather, he was changing all relations between seeing and the visible. What he left behind was not something more, something added to other things; it was not even something less — a subtraction of matter, a hollow in relation to a relief. Then what was

it? A gap in the universe [*Un vide d'univers*]: nothing that was visible, nothing invisible. (Blanchot 1993 [1969], 422/620)

With thanks to Paul Davies and William Allen for this reference, and to Lilian Peter for her help in obtaining the French text.

4. The reading of fossils may thus be taken as a way to describe the successive stages of anthropogenesis: I am thinking of something André Leroi-Gourhan says regarding the ability of early man to appreciate decorative items, non-functional but beautiful, and the way this very appreciation might be said to be consummated in the scientific gaze of the completely elaborated science of palæontology (Leroi-Gourhan 1993 [1965], 367ff/212ff).

5. In terms of the 'intention' behind fossil writing, Nathan Brown provides a similar description of the fossil as a 'radically unintentional inscription or trace of a biological body' in his work, *The Limits of Fabrication* (Brown 2017, 172).

6. Derrida writes of this contrast between a 'divine or natural writing and the human and laborious, finite and artificial inscription [. . .][,] the theme of God's book (nature or law, indeed natural law)' in *Of Grammatology* (1997 [1967b], 15–16/27).

7. In this connection we are indebted to Martin Hägglund's texts on the relation between Derrida and Darwinism, which have in a general way formed part of the conditions for the possibility of the present work (cf. Hägglund 2011a & 2011b). Hägglund's reading of Derrida's archi-writing as a primitive form of 'recording' has made it much easier to translate writing into the vocabulary of the living, as memory and the formation of habits. This facilitation of communication between deconstruction and biology has been essential to our own account (such a communication is also pursued by Francesco Vitale and Mauro Senatore, in other ways).

In passing, let us note that Edmund Husserl invokes the fossil as a kind of written trace, and more precisely as an example of the 'indicative' sign, which Derrida in *Voice and Phenomenon* will treat in terms of the 'indication' most important to him — writing, but in a much broader sense than is usually assigned to it: 'the concept of an indication extends more widely than that of a mark. We say the Martian canals are signs of the existence of intelligent beings on Mars, that fossil vertebrae [*fossile Knochen*] are signs of the existence of antediluvian animals etc.' (Husserl 1970/2001 [1900/1913], 184/24, translation modified) (cf. Derrida 2011 [1967a], 15/17ff and esp. 23/28f, although here, while citing the other examples, Derrida elides the reference to the fossil).

8. Catherine Malabou attempts to criticise deconstruction for the tirelessness it appears to attribute to the trace, the latter's continuous and unflagging resistance to the formation of a stable moment of presence, such as a fully determinate signified meaning: 'writing is not really exposed, it is not fragile enough. To elude "essence", the trace makes itself tireless, always elsewhere, always rebelling against its capture, always other. But as a result of this "always", since it denies all plasticity, writing never grows old, writing never changes' (2011 [2009], 120–21/137–38).

We would agree but then go somewhat beyond Malabou, since here we have a living entity which *loses* its plasticity altogether and has grown so old that it has turned to stone: a tiring *of plasticity itself* — every child knows that plasticine goes hard, losing all malleability if it is left for too long.

9. Agamben makes the tantalising suggestion that in (old) photographs, entities are revealed to us as they will appear on the Last Day, frozen and judged for all time from the perspective of the end of time (2007 [2005], 23/25). The death mask may be considered a similar, though more primitive technology: it is a voluntary fossil, without the immense delay preceding the construction of the actual cast, a lapse of time which is potentially mirrored in the latency of the photographic negative.

10. Heidegger, but also Derrida, and a number of others will have developed a certain type of negation in this graphic fashion. For an excellent account of the speculative sentence, see Malabou 2005 [1996], 169–83/227–44; Žižek 1989, 206ff (on the 'infinite judgement' expressed in such a sentence), and Jean-Luc Nancy's foundational text, *The Speculative Remark* (2001 [1973], 73ff/95ff et passim).

11. Let us salute Derrida here, without whom it is unlikely we would have dared to make so much of these moments in Hegel: 'how could a here-now pass through writing unscathed? Perhaps we interpret today more effectively, with or without Hegel, the intervention of a written trace (in the ordinary sense) in the chapter of the *Phenomenology of Spirit* on sense certainty and its here-now' (Derrida 1995 [1992], 11/19).

12. The connection between the movement from singularity to universality in the Sense-Certainty dialectic and the founding decision of metaphysics in Aristotle is due largely to Giorgio Agamben (1991 [1982]).

13. Hence the poignancy of those gravestones which bear nothing but the name of the deceased and the dates of their birth and death, or, as is common in England at least, a bench with a memorial plaque. In Hegelian circles, an example often cited is that of the survival of Julius Caesar in the form of the title, 'Caesar', which becomes a general term for the (Roman) Emperor, a common noun rather than a proper name — the king's being dead as a singularity, long live the King in his immortal body as a general idea which can be passed on to the title's inheritor (Žižek 2003, 17; Žižek 2012, 455; cf. PR, 181ff/444ff §279). One might also consult Derrida on Bataille's response to Hegel in relation to the immortal renown of a name, in 'No Apocalypse, Not Now' (2007 [1984], 407/384).

14. Given Hegel's immediate proximity to Kant on the question of beauty and nature, and animality in particular, we have confined ourselves to speaking of Kant and Hegel alone, but a sojourn in Bristol, the home of British Schellingianism and the philosophy of nature in general, will have taught us the indelible lesson that a reading of Schelling would need to be interpolated here.

I dedicate this note — a promissory one — to Iain Grant, in gratitude for all of the Kant, Schelling, Nature, and Geology he was able to impart, and which, simply by osmosis in such a place, one could not fail to imbibe.

15. The promise of saying much and then not, is made, unwittingly, by the wonderfully helpful book of Alison Stone's on Hegel's Philosophy of Nature (2005). Not only is it titled precisely '*Petrified Intelligence*', but the book's front cover appears to feature a menagerie of fossils. A closer inspection disappoints our rush of expectation for it proves to be a detail from Ernst Haeckel's *Art Forms in Nature* (Haeckel 1900, 68–69) and the creatures depicted seem to be *Cristellaria siddalliana*, a form of *globigerina*, a marine plankton. In an analogous way, the book itself does not in the end

speak of the stone animal, deeming it unnecessary for its purposes. Stone, despite her name, thus evades the question of whether fossils might not be a somewhat different case, that would compel us to rethink the philosophy of nature itself.

In truth, the remarkable animal depicted on the covers that enclasp the book is so venerable a survivor that it has indeed been found in fossil form, and certain of these forms closely resemble the ammonites we first, in our haste, took them to be.

16. The point stands even though the index of the single-volume translation by A. V. Miller, which gives pp. 281 (p. 19 in Petry), and 292–93 (pp. 31–33 in Petry, but here the word 'fossil' is apparently not given; hence these pages are not included in Petry's more literal index), misses out at least three instances, on p. 286 (translated by Petry as 'oryctological objects' and hence not included in his index), p. 419 (p. 182 in Petry) and p. 421 (p. 184 in Petry). Petry in total offers three from the third volume of the *Philosophy of Nature*, pp. 19, 182, & 184, under the heading, 'fossil bone', although in these cases both Petry and Miller at times have recourse simply to 'fossil'.

The German edition I am using, like many continental works, dispenses with an index altogether.

17. In some of her more recent work, Catherine Malabou has examined the notion of the anthropocene as a geological epoch which she suggests must — from the other end of history — come to trouble the Hegelian division between nature and spirit, as the spiritual human animal becomes a 'force of *nature*' (Malabou 2015). The burning of fossils as fuel is an important part of this becoming.

We speak elsewhere of the possibility of fossils surviving the 'second death' of nature and culture, but perhaps we shall not be so fortunate: if such resources are finally exhausted, even fossils might become extinct.

18. Hegel himself compares the history of the earth to something like an evolutionary theory of organic life, in which '[t]he production of living being is generally envisaged [*stellt . . . dar*] as a revolution out of chaos, in which vegetable and animal life, organic and inorganic being, were together in a single unity' (PNIII, 22/349 §339A).

19. Iain Hamilton Grant, somewhat more violently than us, repudiates 'Hegel's stupefying judgement in the *Encyclopædia* (§339) that there is nothing philosophically pertinent in geology', a parting of the ways which will lead him away from Hegel and towards Schelling (Grant 2011, 41).

20. Hegel is not alone in thinking that the *ex nihilo* is more apt than evolution, when it comes to life, at least (cf. Lacan 1992 [1959–60], 115/139).

21. Here we would develop Michel Foucault's account of the fossil and the monster in the context of Natural History.

Foucault has written some exceptional passages on the topic in connection with the concept of nature in play in the Classical Age which extends from the end of the Renaissance in the mid-seventeenth century to the turn of the nineteenth century. The interpretation of the fossil is dictated by at least three features of this concept: continuity, tabulation ('taxonomy') and time.

First, the 'continuity [*continuité*] [. . .] of living beings' or the 'continuity of nature' amounts to the infinite number of possible varieties of animal, from the most simple to the most complex, with man generally taken to form the pinnacle of this ascending ladder of complexity, for pre-Darwinian notions of evolution at least (Foucault 1989 [1966], 155/168–69).

Time then supervenes on this continuity ('continuity [*le continu*] precedes time'), and over time there emerges a sequence of forms the possibility of which was delineated in advance.

This actualisation tends towards the achievement of a finite set of species laid out in the form of a *table*, the arrangement of a finite number of distinct entities — named and described by means of a *linguistic* representation — which exhibits nature's *ideal* form.

So, from continuum, through time, to the table.

That said, another tradition within the Classical Age, in fact closely allied to the first, takes continuity to be a characteristic of the table itself, as it places species in immediate juxtaposition with one another. In that case, we would find a *continuous tabulation*, with *time* supervening upon it.

Foucault describes these two traditions, in such a way as to reveal their hidden kinship, as 'evolutionism' and 'fixism':

> It will be seen how superficial it is to oppose, as two different opinions confronting one another in their fundamental options, a 'fixism' that is content to classify the beings of nature in a permanent tabulation, and a sort of 'evolutionism' that is supposed to believe in an immemorial history of nature and in a deep-rooted, onward urge of all beings throughout its continuity. The solidity, without gaps, of a network of species and genera, and the series of events that have blurred that network, both belong, at the same level, to the epistemological foundation that made a body of knowledge like natural history possible in the Classical age. (Ibid., 150/163)

But the existence of both a continuum of pre-given possibilities and their actualisation in time has two consequences: the existence of monsters and the remnance of fossils. Monsters are hybrids that indicate a *continuity* between the species which intermingle here, the abutment of species standing adjacent to one another in the table being exacerbated to the excessive level of hybridisation and the confusion of boundary.

And then there are in time the extinctions of certain species: 'if it is necessary for time, which is limited, to run through — or perhaps to have already run through — the whole continuity [*continu*] of nature, one is forced to admit that a considerable number of possible variations have been encountered and then erased' (ibid., 155/169). According to Foucault, this fact allows us to work our way back from an infinite continuum of possible forms to a 'table' of species which are finite in number, or at least clearly divided from one another and not monstrous: 'the proliferation of monsters without a future is necessary to enable us to work down again from the continuum [*continu*], through a temporal series, to the table' (ibid., 156/169).

And while some species will have vanished without trace, some will have survived in the form of the fossil. Foucault associates such remnants of extinction with what he calls 'resemblance' or 'similitude', defining characteristics of the order of knowledge in the Classical Age: 'the signs of continuity [*continuité*] throughout such a history can no longer be of any order other than that of resemblance. [. . .] [T]he living forms will be subjected [. . .] to all possible metamorphoses and leave behind them no trace of the path they have followed other than the reference points represented by similitudes' (ibid., 156/169).

What are we to understand by this resemblance? At first it seems that the resemblance is borne to *man*, the terminal point of an evolution, towards which the continuity of nature is tending in its temporal development. But perhaps more generally it refers to a kind of tempering of the monster's difference from the familiar and orderly table of species, which reassures us that nature does not tend towards the chaos of monstrosity and the transgression of boundaries but rather towards identifiable and stable species, the finitude of the taxonomic table. Monsters after all may be defined as monstrous only because they can be perceived as mixtures of *identifiable* species.

So, '[t]he fossil, with its mixed animal and mineral nature, is the privileged locus of a resemblance required by the historian of the continuum [*continu*]' (ibid., 156/169), while on the other hand, 'the space of the *taxinomia* decomposed it [the fossil] with rigour', which is to say that it revealed the monstrous intermingling of two species ultimately kept distinct by the table.

The monster and the fossil are contrasted as representatives of difference and identity, respectively, difference and resemblance: 'the monster ensures the emergence of [*fait apparaître*] difference. [. . .] The fossil is what permits resemblances to subsist throughout all the deviations traversed by nature' (ibid., 156/170). How does the fossil allow this? Is it by revealing the now eliminated existence of an intermediate stage between two species which would otherwise seem so different as to rend the continuum of nature? Fossils as mediators?

In this way, fossils exhibit both features of nature: infinite continuum and finite table, the former by having lived, the second by having (been forced) to die. Fossils would thus deconstruct not just the difference between animal and mineral, but the two competing elements within the concept of nature — the continuum and the tabulation:

> the monster and the fossil are merely the backward projection of those differences and those identities that provide *taxinomia* first with structure, then with character. Between table and continuum [*le continu*] they form a shady, mobile, wavering region in which what analysis is to define as identity is still only mute analogy; and what it will define as assignable and constant difference is still only free and random variation. (Ibid., 157/170)

In this way, the fossil and the monster demonstrate that the theories of 'natural history' which Foucault is considering (the 'historical a priori' of the Classical Age when it came to the study of nature [ibid., 158/171]) cannot properly conceive of a 'history of nature', a genuine becoming without any entities that have already been individuated in potential, which simply become one another, passing from one pre-given identity to the next, given either by the continuum or by the table:

> But, in truth, it is so impossible for *natural history* to conceive of *the history of nature*, the epistemological arrangement delineated by the table and the continuum is so fundamental, that becoming can occupy nothing but an intermediary place measured out for it solely by the requirements of the whole. This is why it occurs only in order to bring about the necessary passage from one to the other [. . .]. Thus, against the background of the continuum the monster provides an account, as though in caricature, of the genesis

of differences, and the fossil recalls, in the uncertainty of its resemblances, the first buddings of identity. (Ibid., 157/170)

We are approaching fossils from the standpoint of a different historical a priori, that of the present age, whether Modern or somehow beyond — an a priori which we are attempting to understand by contrasting it with the one that held sway in the age of Kant and Hegel. It seems possible that the distinction between continuum and table may still be found in Hegel, in the opposition between contingency and (conceptual) necessity — and we would follow Foucault in affirming that the fossil also deconstructs this opposition.

Perhaps the theory of fossils which then emerges will be able to make good on the promise, broached by Foucault, of eliminating necessity within nature, and produce a genuine 'history of nature' in which the natural world is depicted as an absolutely contingent becoming.

The existence of the creatures preserved in the Burgess Shale prove that the line of evolution which we trace retrospectively from our terminal species to a primitive outset is not a *necessary* one and hence not the only *possible* one. In this regard, Stephen Jay Gould inveighs against two common images of nature: a ladder of progress and a 'cone of increasing diversity', from the simple old to the complex new. Rather, '[l]ife is a copiously branching bush continually pruned by the grim reaper of extinction, not a ladder of predictable progress' (Gould 2007, 361) and, speaking of his beloved snails, '[t]he data of the Burgess Shale falsify this central view of arthropod evolution as a continuous process of increasing diversification' (ibid., 365). In general, '[i]f humanity arose just yesterday as a small twig on one branch of a flourishing tree, then life may not, in any genuine sense, exist for us or because of us. Perhaps we are only an afterthought, a kind of cosmic accident' (ibid., 368).

What the Classical Age perhaps demonstrates is that the fossil can also be used to prove the exact opposite, as we imagine *Hegel*'s theory of fossils, had it been complete, would in fact have assayed: the fact that these species did *not* survive can be used to support the argument that one single line of progress was *destined* to unfold, and they did not belong to it. On this account, the fossils do present us with an alternative line, but only in order to demonstrate that this was not a *viable* alternative at all.

Gould retorts by describing this as:

> the stunning mistake of citing unsuccessful lineages as classic 'textbook cases' of 'evolution' [i.e. of being unfitted to survive]. We do this because we try to extract a single line of advance from the true topology of copious branching. In this misguided effort, we are inevitably drawn to bushes so near the brink of total annihilation that they retain only one surviving twig. We then view this twig as the acme of upward achievement, rather than the probable last gasp of a richer ancestry. (Ibid., 361)

22. Oscillating between petrifaction and its opposite, which still seems to predominate in 'calcareousness' or the quality of being limestone, Hegel affirms that:

> calcareousness expresses the transition to organic being, for it restrains the relapse into dead neutrality on one side, and into moribund abstraction and simplicity on the other.

These organic forms are still-born [*nicht zu betrachten*], and should not be regarded as having actually lived and then died. Some of them undoubtedly have lived, but it is not these that are being considered. [. . .] At this juncture nature therefore resembles the artist, who uses stone or a flat canvas in order to represent human and other shapes. The artist does not strike people dead, dry them out, pump them with petrifaction [*durchzieht sie mit Steinmaterie*], or press them into stone (although he can also do this, for he casts models into moulds). (PNIII, 33/360 §340A)

23. Petry elides the crucial phrase, 'that is one explanation . . . '

24. Like A. G. Cairns-Smith's hypothesis of the replication and complexification of inorganic crystals at the origin of life (cf. Brown 2017, 153ff). The question which this particular theory helps bring to light is posed by all explanations of the transition from the inorganic to the organic: how does *evolution itself* emerge? and how can it? We have raised an analogous question at the boundary between nature and spirit, and more starkly at the very beginning of Hegel's system as a whole: how can *dialectic* begin?

25. Miller gives: 'the rudimentary organic forms in the geological organism'.

26. The final indexed reference to fossilisation in the *Philosophy of Nature* shows us what philosophy can learn from the unfolding of chronology, which is otherwise philosophically insignificant: it refers to Georges Cuvier's attempt to reconstruct the totality of the organism on the basis of individual fossilised parts, the only remnants he had to go on: 'he was led to do so as the result of his having concerned himself with fossil bones [*fossilen Knochen*]' (PNIII, 182/505 §370A). And Hegel quotes a passage of Cuvier's which could have come straight from either Kant or Hegel: 'Every organised being forms a whole, a unified and closed system, all the parts of which mutually correspond, and by means of reciprocal action, contribute to a common purposive activity. None of these parts can alter without the others altering also; as the result of this, each of them, taken separately, implies and yields all the others'.

27. I take the liberty of referring the reader to my own, 'On Thinking at the End of the World' for a consideration of certain of the issues surrounding extinction and what it might afford to thought (2017). It is a notion which has understandably attracted a great deal of attention in recent years. Paul Davies has penned what is in some ways perhaps a response, of a vastly superior kind, in his 'Investment without return: On futures that will never be ours' (2017).

28. Thinking of our own destiny as humans, we might wonder if anything will come after us that will be capable of reading the spirit we set in stone, or even, if there is time, our own literally fossilised remains. Is our fate to embody a line of Friedrich Hölderlin's 'Mnemosyne' according to which man is a 'sign that is not read' (*Ein Zeichen* [. . .] *deutungslos*)? (cf. Heidegger 1968 [1951–52], 10/11). Or is the human not just unread, but unreadable, an illegible sign, a creature for whom there can be no judge come the Apocalypse? (Such is the impetus behind Zarathustra's faith in the Overman, a 'posthuman' future made possible by man's — technical? — tendency to surpass himself: to decipher the sign of man from a position which stands beyond it.) If we sit atop the pinnacle of nature, just as we are said to stand at the end of history, and if nature does not have time either to fossilise us or to generate another higher — terrestrial — reader before the sun swallows its children, then perhaps our fate is to

be the last animal capable of reading the signs of the animal, and, uniquely, we have no reader of our own. It is a question of the end or the ends of man.

That all imaginable traces of one's life be wiped out, leaving not the slightest remnant, thus putting an end not only to one's *natural* life but also to one's supposedly immortal 'spiritual' life, was the Marquis de Sade's ultimate wish — such would accord with the movement of nature itself on Sade's account, enunciated by the Pope in *Juliette* (Sade 1968 [1797], 766ff/870ff) and expanding upon a much shorter account in *Justine* (Sade 1991 [1791], 518ff/500ff). This wish was expressed in Sade's own Last Will and Testament (1806) (Sade 1991, 157) (cf. Schuster 2016, 39–42, although the pages referred to here appear to be erroneous).

Jacques Lacan makes much of this Sadean idea, under the heading of a 'second death', which would be the destruction of the symbolic order — the order of objective and absolute spirit — in which natural life would be memorialised. On this matter, one should consult Lacan's *The Other Side of Psychoanalysis* (Seminar XVII) (2007 [1969–70], 66–67/75–76) and *The Ethics of Psychoanalysis* (Seminar VII) (1992 [1959–60], 210–15/248–54).

29. Earlier on, we entertained the dire possibility that even *this* was not guaranteed, in light of the fact that human beings treat so many of the earth's fossils instrumentally, as *fuel*.

30. As we have attempted to suggest, discreetly, in turns of phrase throughout, there is nothing unaccustomed in speaking of a stone effigy as 'immortalising [an entity] in stone', indeed it is the only context in which the adjective 'immortal' becomes a verb that can be used transitively.

(Let it be acknowledged that we were put onto this way of expressing the matter with respect to the stone's deathlessness by Nathan Brown [2017, 52], even if his text has other purposes in mind).

31. When it comes to horror, we still have Žižek in mind, but when it comes to comedy we are thinking of the work of Gregor Moder and the inspirational texts of Alenka Zupančič (cf. Zupančič 2008, 173ff and 217–18).

32. The sheer depth of time which fossils evince led Kant to intimate that such things are not beautiful but *sublime*. In this context, Iain Hamilton Grant has drawn attention to Kant's invocation of a 'sublime of time', to supplement the mathematical and dynamic sublimes which he describes in the *Critique of Judgement* (Grant 2006, 18). Something of Toadvine's account of the experience of fossils may be taken as gesturing towards sublimity, as well:

> we are first motivated to provide an account of the fossil [. . .] precisely because it confronts us perceptually, viscerally, with an immemorial past that both invites and refuses us. [. . .] [W]hat makes it possible for me to resonate with this ancient past, to catch a marginal and brief glimpse of its abyssal expanse? How is such an incomprehensible time already sketched out within my own being such that it prepares me for this encounter? (Toadvine 2014, 272)

Toadvine responds to these questions by referring to, '[t]he sensibility, sedimented habits, and organic rhythms of our bodies', which 'offer the most proximal and constant encounter with the immemorial past — by which I mean an anonymous and asubjective prehistory' (ibid., 276). This leads him to a statement which echoes

Kant even more closely: 'The phenomenological encounter with *the vertigo of deep time*, of which I catch a glimpse in the fossil, is the echo within my body of an asubjective time of matter, of an unfathomably ancient passage [*sic*, rather, 'past']' (ibid., emphasis added).

But in light of what Meillassoux has taught us, this would be a hyperbolically sublime instance, if one could so describe it at all, since here we are called to imagine not just the capacity of reason to encompass what the faculty of understanding is unable to know and we to experience, but a time in which reason itself did not exist. Might the fossil then be said to transcend even sublimity? For the reasons we are gradually unfolding, we would rather say that the fossil provides us with an opportunity to construct a new concept of *beauty*, indebted to both Kant and Hegel but exceeding their accounts.

33. To speak of preserving darkness as dark, paradoxically illuminating this darkness without betraying it, evokes Heidegger's 'Origin of the Work of Art', in which the *earth* is preserved in its 'self-enclosure', its hiddenness revealed *as* hiddenness. This takes place in and as the 'material' from which the artwork is moulded (such as *stone*). 'It shows itself only when it remains undisclosed [*unentborgen*] [. . .] undisclosable [*Unerschließbare*]' (Heidegger 1971a [1936], 47/36).

34. The present book being something of an autobiographical work, and since we are speaking of a personal love, I might be indulged in giving way to a personal reminiscence. This terminal locution is a paraphrase of one of my earliest teachers in philosophy, to whom personally, for his kindness and support on so many occasions, I owe a lot — Greg Hunt, of the University of Warwick. He would be speaking, in a precise and ironic Australian, of the mediæval name for a certain logical law, perhaps *modus ponendo ponens*: 'what it means I haven't the faintest idea, *and I care even less . . .* '

Certain phrases, without any obvious profundity in some cases, can stay with us for a lifetime — like a poem one might have memorised at school without understanding it. It is as if at the end of history, when one runs through its moments again, one does not place them in an ideal, rationalised order as a Hegelian dialectical resumption would require; rather, one experiences them as random flashes of illumination and unrelated fragments which seem all the more significant for their mysteriousness — like the texts of the pre-Socratics, even the most banal.

If there were some reason why they should come to mind *now*, then our relation to this history would approach the 'dialectic at a standstill' we are preparing to invoke.

35. 'Perilous' presumably in the twin risks of appropriating the past (text) to the present without remainder, and of allowing the past wholly to dictate the terms in which we understand the present.

Since Benjamin's words can hardly be read often enough, we might gather up the following passages and thus piece together the other important facets of the notion:

From 'Paralipomena to "On the Concept of History"':

> History deals with connections and with arbitrarily elaborated causal chains. But since history affords an idea of the fundamental citability of its object, this object must present itself, in its ultimate form, as a moment [*Augenblick*] of humanity. In this moment, time must be brought to a standstill [*stillgestellt*]. [/] The dialectical image is an occurrence

of ball lightning that runs across the whole horizon of the past [*Vergangnen*]. (Benjamin 2003, 403/1233 [Vol. 1])

In the 'Theses on the Philosophy of History', Benjamin speaks of the theological underpinning of historical materialism as a theory of history:

> The true picture of the past flits by. [*Das wahre Bild der Vergangenheit huscht vorbei*, Agamben has pointed out that in the typescript of this text, the word '*h u s c h t*' is emphasised in the manner of being spaced out, indicating not just emphasis but an implicit *citation* that the printed version here manages to elide. Agamben postulates the text cited to be Martin Luther's translation of the messianic account of 1 Corinthians 7:31, according to which 'passing away is the figure of this world' (although this would not be a literal quotation since Luther's text reads, *das Wesen dieser Welt vergeht*) (Agamben 2005 [2000], 141/131f).] The past can be seized only as an image which flashes up at the instant when it can be recognised [*Augenblick seiner Erkennbarkeit*] and is never seen again. [. . .] [E]very image of the past that is not recognised by the present [*Gegenwart*] as one of its own concerns threatens to disappear irretrievably. (Benjamin 1999b, 247/695 [Vol. I])

'Historical materialism wishes to retain that image of the past which unexpectedly appears to man singled out by history at a moment of danger' (ibid.). This danger is that of being exploited by the ruling classes, or entirely obliterated from the archives: 'Only that historian will have the gift of fanning the spark of hope in the past [*Vergangenen*] who is firmly convinced that *even the dead* will not be safe from the enemy if he wins' (ibid.).

'A historical materialist cannot do without the notion of a present [*Gegenwart*] which is not a transition [*Übergang*], but in which time stands still [*Stillstand*] and has come to a stop. For this notion defines the present in which he himself is writing history' (ibid., 254/702).

'Thinking involves not only the flow of thoughts, but their arrest [*Stillstellung*] as well. Where thinking suddenly stops in a configuration pregnant with tensions, it gives that configuration a shock, by which it crystallises [*sic*, rather "is crystallised"] into a monad' (ibid., 254/702–703).

'A historical materialist approaches a historical subject only where he encounters it as a monad. In this structure he recognises the sign of a Messianic cessation of happening [*Stillstellung des Geschehens*], or, put differently, a revolutionary chance in the fight for the oppressed past [*Vergangenheit*]. He takes cognisance of it in order to blast a specific era out of the homogeneous course of history' (ibid., 254/703).

In light of this wealth one might reassess the opinion of the editor of *The Arcades Project*, Rolf Tiedemann, according to whom, 'Benjamin never brought himself to define these categories at length, yet they are the basis of all his thoughts on the *Passagen-Werk* [*Arcades Project*, 1999a], which he identified with the "world of dialectical images" and for which dialectic at a standstill was to be "the quintessence of the method" [. . .]. Although both concepts are absent from Benjamin's publications during his lifetime [. . .]' (Tiedemann in Benjamin 1999a, 1014n23. Cf. Benjamin 1999a, 865/1035 (from 'First Sketches'): 'Dialectics at a standstill — this is the quintessence of the method').

36. If the animal can form habits, why in this case do we speak of it as a mechanical entity caught in a bad infinite of repetition, as if it fell under the same unbreak-

able laws that govern the stone so absolutely? The apparent contradiction between an animal's ability to form habits and its being stuck in a rut may be resolved by distinguishing between the levels of species and individual, phylogeny and ontogeny. In this way we might think of habit-forming *phylogenetically* as something animals can do but stones cannot, as Aristotle pointed out in the *Nicomachean Ethics* (1103a), but *ontogenetically* speaking, the fixed instincts of animals prevent them from learning habits over the course of their individual lives in the way that human beings do. Human habit at the level of ontogeny may thus be said to involve an infinite plasticity which allows man to contradict his natural needs (with suicide and other activities harmful to the self) or overcome them (by means of technology and other spiritual products, including simply the subjective freedom of the will).

In this way, one might distinguish, as Aristotle did, between good and bad habits, those formative of good character and bad. The transition from habit to character is in Greek the transformation of *ethos* into *ēthos* (cf. ibid., 1103a ff). A bad habit is a bad infinity, of the kind we are trying to redeem, but when understood as the capacity to form new habits and break out of old ruts and automatic gestures, thus inspiring dead matter, the habit is good and acts as a presentiment of dialectical learning *in statu nascendi*.

37. I address in more detail the questions surrounding madness, habit, and anthropogenesis in 'Philosophical Anthropology from Kant and Hegel to the Present Day' (2019), which may be considered a companion to these passages.

38. For a much more subtle reading of the hindering of the instinct, we should consult Alenka Zupančič's *What Is Sex?* (2017, 9–10).

39. A similar role for boredom (*ennui*, in Sartre's terms) at the threshold of humanity has been identified by the generally clean-shaven Agamben in a brilliant reading of Heidegger's notion of *Langeweile* (Agamben 2004 [2002], 49ff/52ff).

CONCLUSION

1. Kelly Oliver and Brian Massumi have each in different ways approached the question of animals in terms of what they can *teach* us (Oliver 2009; Massumi 2014). Such might also be the lesson of Vinciane Despret's work, which insists that previous attempts to speak to the animals have in general posed the wrong questions, and in fact it is as if there were a kind of teaching involved in animal behaviour in the form of morals to be drawn from the 'scientific fables' with which they provide us (Despret 2016 [2012]). In becoming pupil rather than master, we experience a reversal of the traditional relation between man and animal and find ourselves humbled beneath their withering gaze.

2. In a reference to something like a work-less 'animal sincerity', Agamben speaks of 'the habitual dwelling in which the living being, before every subjectivation, is perfectly at ease. If the gestures and acts of the animal are agile and graceful [. . .], this is because for it no act, no gesture constitutes a "work" of which it is posited as responsible author and conscious creator', suggesting that the movement of animals seems to us so expert because they simply ignore the logic of the true infinite (Agamben 2016 [2014], 64/94–95).

Bibliography

Dates in square brackets refer to the original date of publication or delivery, whichever is the earliest. In the text, page references are given first to the English translation and then to the original.

Adorno, Theodor. (1973 [1966]). *Negative Dialectics*. Trans. E. B. Ashton. London: Continuum. *Negative Dialektik*. Frankfurt: Suhrkamp, 1966.
Agamben, Giorgio. (1991 [1982]). *Language and Death: The Place of Negativity*. Trans. Karen E. Pinkus with Michael Hardt. Minneapolis: University of Minnesota Press. *Il linguaggio e la morte: Un seminario sul luogo della negatività*. Turin: Einaudi, 1982.
———. (2000 [1996]). *Means without End: Notes on Politics*. Trans. Vincenzo Binetti and Cesare Casarino. Minneapolis: University of Minnesota Press. *Mezzi senza fine: Note sulla politica*. Turin: Bollati Boringhieri, 1996.
———. (2004 [2002]). *The Open: Man and Animal*. Trans. Kevin Attell. Stanford, CA: Stanford University Press. *L'Aperto: l'uomo e l'animale*. Turin: Boringhieri, 2002.
———. (2005 [2000]). *The Time That Remains: A Commentary on the Letter to the Romans*. Trans. Patricia Dailey. Stanford, CA: Stanford University Press. *Il tempo che resta. Un commento alla Lettera ai Romani*. Turin: Boringhieri, 2000.
———. (2007 [2005]). *Profanations*. Trans. Jeff Fort. New York: Zone. *Profanazioni*. Rome: Nottetempo, 2005 [Fourth edition, 2014].
———. (2016 [2014]). *The Use of Bodies*. (Homo sacer, IV, 2). Trans. Adam Kotsko. Stanford, CA: Stanford University Press. *L'uso dei corpi*. Vicenza: Neri Pozza, 2014.
Allen, William S. (2015). 'The Absolute Milieu: Blanchot's Aesthetics of Melancholy', *Research in Phenomenology* 45 (2015): 53–86.
Anselm. (1973). *The Prayers and Meditations of St. Anselm*. Trans. Benedicta Ward. Harmondsworth: Penguin.

Aristotle. (1932). *Politics*. Trans. H. Rackham. Cambridge, MA: Harvard University Press.
———. (1934). *The Nicomachean Ethics*. Trans. H. Rackham. Cambridge, MA: Harvard University Press.
Assiter, Alison. (2015). *Kierkegaard, Eve and Metaphors of Birth*. London: Rowman & Littlefield.
Atterton, Peter, and Calarco, Matthew. (eds.) (2004). *Animal Philosophy: Ethics and Identity/Essential Readings in Continental Thought*. London: Continuum.
Bataille, Georges. (1991 [1949]). *The Accursed Share: An Essay on General Economy. Volume 1: Consumption*. Trans. Robert Hurley. New York: Zone. *La part maudite*. Paris: Minuit, 1967 [First edition, 1949].
———. (1992 [1973]). *Theory of Religion*. Trans. Robert Hurley. New York: Zone. *Théorie de la religion*. Paris: Gallimard, 1973.
———. (1993 [1976]). *The Accursed Share. Volumes II (The History of Eroticism) & III (Sovereignty)*. Trans. Robert Hurley. New York: Zone. *Œuvres Complètes, VIII*. Paris: Gallimard, 1976.
Baudelaire, Charles. [n.d. {1866}], *Les Fleurs du Mal*. Brussels: Editions de la Toison D'Or, n.d. [1866].
———. (1909). *Baudelaire: The Flowers of Evil*. Trans. Cyril Scott. London: Elkin Mathews.
———. (1952). *Poems of Baudelaire*. Trans. Roy Campbell. New York: Pantheon.
———. (1954). *The Flowers of Evil*. Trans. William Aggeler. Fresno, CA: Academy Library Guild.
———. (1974). *Selected Poems of Charles Baudelaire*. Trans. Geoffrey Wagner. New York: Grove.
Benjamin, Walter. (1999a). *The Arcades Project*. Trans. Howard Eiland and Kevin McLaughlin. Cambridge, MA: Belknap Press of Harvard University Press. *Das Passagen-Werk*. Ed. Rolf Tiedemann. (Gesammelte Schriften, Band 5). Frankfurt: Suhrkamp, 1991 [First edition, 1982].
———. (1999b). *Illuminations*. Ed. Hannah Arendt. Trans. Harry Zorn. London: Pimlico. *Gesammelte Schriften, Band 1*. Eds. Rolf Tiedemann & Hermann Schweppenhäuser. Frankfurt: Suhrkamp, 1991.
———. (2003). *Selected Writings*, Vol. 4, 1938–1940. Eds. Michael W. Jennings, Marcus Bullock, Howard Eiland, Gary Smith. Cambridge, MA: Harvard University Press. (Gesammelte Schriften, Band 1).
Benso, Silvia. (2002). *The Face of Things: A Different Side of Ethics*. Albany: SUNY Press.
Bentham, Jeremy. (2007 [1780/1823]). *An Introduction to the Principles of Morals and Legislation*. Mineola, NY: Dover.
Berger, John. (2009). *Why Look at Animals?* London: Penguin.
Blake, William. (1948 [1793]). *Poetry and Prose of William Blake*. Ed. Geoffrey Keynes. London: Nonesuch Press [First edition, 1927].
Blanchot, Maurice. (1982 [1955]). *The Space of Literature*. Trans. Ann Smock. Lincoln: University of Nebraska Press. *L'Espace littéraire*. Paris: Gallimard, 1955.

———. (1993 [1969]). *The Infinite Conversation*. Trans. Susan Hanson. Minneapolis: University of Minnesota Press. *L'Entretien infini*. Paris: Gallimard, 1969/2009.
Božovič, Miran. (2000). *An Utterly Dark Spot: Gaze and Body in Early Modern Philosophy*. Ann Arbor: University of Michigan Press.
Brown, Nathan. (2017). *The Limits of Fabrication: Materials Science, Materialist Poetics*. New York: Fordham University Press.
Buber, Martin. (n.d. [1923]). *I and Thou*. Trans. Ronald Gregor Smith. Edinburgh: T. & T. Clark. *Ich und Du*. Stuttgart: Reclam, 1995 (11th edition) [First edition, 1923].
Buchanan, Brett. (2008). *Onto-Ethologies: The Animal Environments of Uexküll, Heidegger, Merleau-Ponty, and Deleuze*. Albany: SUNY Press.
Calarco, Matthew. (2008). *Zoographies: The Question of the Animal from Heidegger to Derrida*. New York: Columbia University Press.
———. (2015). *Thinking through Animals: Identity, Difference, Indistinction*. Stanford, CA: Stanford University Press.
Cazotte, Jacques. (1991 [1772]). *The Devil in Love*. Trans. Judith Landry. Sawtry, Cambs.: Dedalus. *Le diable amoureux*. Paris: Garnier-Flammarion, 1979.
Chiesa, Lorenzo. (2016). *The Not-Two: Logic and God in Lacan*. Cambridge, MA: MIT Press.
Coetzee, J. M. (2016 [1999]). *The Lives of Animals*. Ed. Amy Gutmann (with contributions by Marjorie Garber, Peter Singer, Wendy Doniger, and Barbara Smuts). Princeton, NJ: Princeton University Press.
Davies, Paul. (2002). 'Sincerity and the end of theodicy: three remarks on Levinas and Kant' in Simon Critchley and Robert Bernasconi (eds.), *The Cambridge Companion to Levinas*. Cambridge: Cambridge University Press.
———. (2017). 'Investment without return: On futures that will never be ours' in James Cullis, Vinita Damodaran, and Alexander Elliott (eds.), *Climate Change and the Humanities: Historical, Philosophical and Interdisciplinary Approaches to the Contemporary Environmental Crisis*. Basingstoke: Palgrave Macmillan.
Deleuze, Gilles, and Félix Guattari. (1988 [1980]). *A Thousand Plateaus: Capitalism and Schizophrenia*. Trans. Brian Massumi. London: Athlone. *Mille Plateaux: Capitalisme et Schizophrénie*, Vol. 2. Paris: Minuit, 1980.
———. (1994 [1991]). *What Is Philosophy?* Trans. Hugh Tomlinson and Graham Burchell. New York: Columbia University Press. *Qu'est-ce que la philosophie?* Paris: Minuit, 1991.
Derrida, Jacques. (1978 [1962]). *Edmund Husserl's* Origin of Geometry: *An Introduction*. Trans. John P. Leavey Jr. Ed. David B. Allison. New York: Nicolas Hays. *Introduction à 'L'Origine de la géométrie' de Husserl*. Paris: Presses Universitaires de France, 1962.
———. (1981 [1972]). *Dissemination*. Trans. Barbara Johnson. London: Athlone. *La Dissémination*. Paris: Seuil, 1972 ('Points' edition).
———. (1986 [1974]). *Glas*. Trans. John P. Leavey Jr. and Richard Rand. Lincoln: University of Nebraska Press. *Glas*. Paris: Galilée, 1974.
———. (1989 [1987]). *Of Spirit: Heidegger and the Question*. Trans. Geoffrey Bennington and Rachel Bowlby. Chicago: University of Chicago Press. *De l'esprit: Heidegger et la question*. Paris: Galilée, 1987.

———. (1995 [1992]). *Points . . . Interviews, 1974–1994*. Ed. Elisabeth Weber. Trans. Peggy Kamuf et al. Stanford, CA: Stanford University Press. *Points de suspension: Entretiens*. Paris: Galilée, 1992.

———. (1997 [1967b]). *Of Grammatology*. Trans. G. C. Spivak. Baltimore, MD: Johns Hopkins University Press. *De la grammatologie*. Paris: Minuit, 1967.

———. (1998 [1996]). *Resistances of Psychoanalysis*. Trans. Peggy Kamuf, Pascale-Anne Brault, and Michael Naas. Stanford, CA: Stanford University Press. *Résistances de la psychanalyse*. Paris: Galilée, 1996.

———. (2001 [1967c]). *Writing and Difference*. Trans. Alan Bass. London: Routledge. *L'Écriture et la différence*. Paris: Seuil, 1967.

———. (2005 [1998]). *On Touching — Jean-Luc Nancy*. Trans. Christine Irizarry. Stanford, CA: Stanford University Press. *Le Toucher, Jean-Luc Nancy*. Paris: Galilée, 1998.

———. (2007 [1984]). 'No Apocalypse, Not Now: Full Speed Ahead, Seven Missiles, Seven Missives' [1984]. Trans. Catherine Porter & Philip Lewis in Peggy Kamuf & Elizabeth Rottenberg (eds.), *Psyche: Inventions of the Other. Volume 1*. Stanford, CA.: Stanford University Press. *Psyché: Inventions de l'autre*. Paris: Galilée, 1987.

———. (2008 [2006]). *The Animal That Therefore I Am*. Ed. Marie-Louise Mallet. Trans. David Wills. New York: Fordham University Press. *L'animal que donc je suis*. Paris: Galilée, 2006 [1997].

———. (2009 [2001–2]). *The Beast and The Sovereign. Volume I (2001–2002)*. Eds. Michel Lisse, Marie-Louise Mallet, and Ginette Michaud. Trans. Geoffrey Bennington. Chicago: University of Chicago Press. *Séminaire. La bête et le souverain, Volume I (2001–2002)*. Paris: Galilée, 2008.

———. (2011 [1967a]). *Voice and Phenomenon: Introduction to the Problem of the Sign in Husserl's Phenomenology*. Trans. Leonard Lawlor. Evanston, IL.: Northwestern University Press. *La Voix et le phénomène*. Paris: Presses Universitaires de France, 1967.

———. (2011 [2002–3]). *The Beast and the Sovereign. Volume II (2002–2003)*. Eds. Michel Lisse, Marie-Louise Mallet, and Ginette Michaud. Trans. Geoffrey Bennington. Chicago: University of Chicago Press. *Séminaire. La bête et le souverain. Volume II (2002–2003)*. Paris: Galilée, 2010.

———, with Elisabeth Roudinesco. (2004 [2001]). *For What Tomorrow . . . A Dialogue*. Trans. Jeff Fort. Stanford, CA: Stanford University Press. *De Quoi Demain . . .* Paris: Fayard & Galilée, 2001.

Despret, Vinciane. (2016 [2012]). *What Would Animals Say If We Asked the Right Questions?* Trans. Brett Buchanan. Minneapolis: University of Minnesota Press. *Que diraient les animaux, si . . . on leur posait les bonnes questions?* Paris: La Découverte, 2012.

Dolar, Mladen. (2017). 'Being and MacGuffin', *Crisis and Critique* 4:1, *Hegel('s) Today*.

Eliot, T. S. (1998 [1939]). *Old Possum's Book of Practical Cats*. With decorations by Nicolas Bentley. London: Faber and Faber.

Feuerbach, Ludwig. (1972 [1839]). 'Towards a Critique of Hegel's Philosophy' [1839] in *The Fiery Brook: Selected Writings of Feuerbach*. Trans. Zawar Hanfi. New York: Doubleday. *Zur Kritik der Hegelschen Philosophie*. Berlin: Aufbau Verlag, 1955.

Fontenay, Élisabeth de. (1998). *Le silence des bêtes: La philosophie à l'épreuve de l'animalité*. Paris: Fayard.

———. (2011). 'A Golden Bough to Translate the Beasts'. Trans. Clodagh Kinsella. *Inaesthetics* 2, no pagination in online version, available at http://inaesthetics.org/index.php/main/issue/2/3 [accessed 7th February 2017].

———. (2012 [2008]). *Without Offending Humans: A Critique of Animal Rights*. Trans. Will Bishop. Minneapolis: University of Minnesota Press. *Sans offenser le genre humain: Réflexions sur la cause animale*. Paris: Albin Michel, 2008.

Förster, Eckhart. (n.d.). 'On Goethe's *Metamorphosis of Plants*', Unpublished Manuscript.

Fóti, Véronique. (1991). *Heidegger and the Poets: Poiēsis-Sophia-Technē*. Amherst, NY: Humanity.

Foucault, Michel. (1989 [1966]). *The Order of Things: An Archaeology of the Human Sciences*. Trans. A. Sheridan. London: Routledge. *Les Mots et les choses*. Paris: Gallimard, 1966.

———. (2008 [1961]). *Introduction to Kant's* Anthropology. Ed. Roberto Nigro. Trans. Roberto Nigro and Kate Briggs. Los Angeles: Semiotext(e). *Introduction à l''Anthropologie' de Kant*. Paris: Vrin, 2008 [Foucault's secondary doctoral thesis, University of Paris-Sorbonne, 1961].

Freud, Sigmund. (2001 [1914]). 'On Narcissism: An Introduction' in *The Standard Edition of the Complete Psychological Works of Sigmund Freud, Volume XIV* (1914–1916). Trans. James Strachey. London: Vintage. *Gesammelte Schriften*. Vol. 6. Leipzig: Internationaler Psychoanalytischer Verlag, 2016.

———. (2002 [1905]). *The Joke and Its Relation to the Unconscious*. Trans. Joyce Crick. London: Penguin. *Der Witz und seine Beziehung zum Unbewußten*. Frankfurt am Main: Fischer, 1992.

Gasché, Rodolphe. (1994). *Inventions of Difference: On Jacques Derrida*. Cambridge, MA: Harvard University Press.

Gould, Stephen Jay. (1990). *Wonderful Life: The Burgess Shale and the Nature of History*. London: Hutchinson Radius.

———, et al. (2007). *The Richness of Life: The Essential Stephen Jay Gould*. Ed. Paul McGarr and Steven Rose. London: Vintage.

Grant, Iain Hamilton. (2006). *Philosophies of Nature after Schelling*. London: Continuum.

———. (2011). 'Mining Conditions: A Response to Harman' in Levi Bryant, Nick Srnicek, and Graham Harman (eds.), *The Speculative Turn: Continental Materialism and Realism*. Melbourne: re.press.

Haeckel, Ernst. (1900). *Kunst-Formen der Natur*. Leipzig & Vienna: Bibliographisches Institut.

Hägglund, Martin. (2011a). 'The Arche-Materiality of Time: Deconstruction, evolution and speculative materialism' in Jane Elliott and Derek Attridge (eds.), *Theory after 'Theory'*. London: Routledge.

———. (2011b). 'Radical Atheist Materialism: A Critique of Meillassoux' in Levi Bryant, Nick Srnicek, and Graham Harman (eds.), *The Speculative Turn: Continental Materialism and Realism*. Melbourne: re.press.

Hegel, G. W. F. (1977 [1807]). *Phenomenology of Spirit*. Trans. A. V. Miller. Oxford: Oxford University Press. *Werke in Zwanzig Bände*, Vol. 3 (Abbreviation: PhG [references are given to the English and German pages and then to the standard section numbers, marked by §, to facilitate comparisons between various editions and translations.])

———. (1969 [1812/1831]). *Science of Logic*. Trans. A. V. Miller. Amherst, NY: Humanity Books. *Werke in Zwanzig Bände*, Vols. 5 and 6. (Abbreviation: SL)

———. (1970 [1827]). *Philosophy of Nature (The Second Part of the Encyclopædia of the Philosophical Sciences in Outline). Volume I.* Ed. and trans. M. J. Petry. London: Allen and Unwin. (Abbreviation: PNI [references throughout the Encyclopædia are given to the English and German pages and then to the standard section numbers marked by §])

———. (1970). *Philosophy of Nature. Volume III.* Ed. and trans. M. J. Petry. London: Routledge. (Abbreviation: PNIII)

———. (1970 [1830]). *Hegel's Philosophy of Nature: Being Part Two of the Encyclopædia of the Philosophical Sciences (1830). Translated from Nicolin and Pöggeler's edition (1959) and from the Zusätze in Michelet's Text (1847)*. Trans. A.V. Miller. Oxford: Clarendon. *Werke in Zwanzig Bände*, Vol. 9.

———. (1967 [1821]). *Philosophy of Right*. Trans. T. M. Knox. Oxford: Oxford University Press. *Werke in Zwanzig Bände*, Vol. 7. (Abbreviation: PR)

———. (1975 [1822–30]). *Lectures on the Philosophy of World History: Introduction*. Trans. H. B. Nisbet. Cambridge: Cambridge University Press. *Werke, in Zwanzig Bände*, Vol. 12, and, with a wider range of material, *Die Vernunft in der Geschichte*. Ed. Johannes Hoffmeister. Hamburg: Meiner, 1955. (Abbreviation: WH) (I refer to the Hoffmeister when it contains materials not [obviously] present within the Moldenhauer and Michel edition.)

———. (1975). *Aesthetics: Lectures on Fine Art.* Vol. 1. Trans. T. M. Knox. Oxford: Clarendon. *Werke in Zwanzig Bände*, Vol. 13. (Abbreviation: A)

———. (1993 [1886]). *Introductory Lectures on Aesthetics*. Trans. Bernard Bosanquet. Ed. Michael Inwood. London: Penguin. (Abbreviation: ILA)

———. (2007 [1824, 1827, 1831]). *Lectures on the Philosophy of Religion. Volume III. The Consummate Religion.* Ed. Peter C. Hodgson. Trans. R. F. Brown, P. C. Hodgson, and J. M. Stewart with the assistance of H. S. Harris. Oxford: Oxford University Press. *Vorlesungen über die Philosophie der Religion. Band 3: Die vollendete Religion*. Ed. Walter Jaeschke. Hamburg: Meiner, 1995. (I refer to the Jaeschke edition upon which this translation is based.) (Abbreviation: RIII)

———. (2008). *Lectures on Logic. Berlin, 1831.* Trans. Clark Butler. Bloomington: Indiana University Press.

———. (1969–). Georg Wilhelm Friedrich Hegel, *Werke in Zwanzig Bänden*. Eds. Eva Moldenhauer & Karl Markus Michel. Frankfurt am Main: Suhrkamp.

Heidegger, Martin. (1962 [1927]). *Being and Time*. Trans. John Macquarrie and Edward Robinson. Oxford: Blackwell. *Sein und Zeit*. Tübingen: Niemeyer, 1927/1979.

———. (1968 [1951–52]). *What Is Called Thinking?* Trans. John Glenn Gray and Fred Wieck. New York: Harper and Row. *Was heisst Denken?* Ed. Paola-Ludovika Coriando. Frankfurt am Main: Klostermann, 2002.

———. (1971a [1936]). 'The Origin of the Work of Art' in *Poetry, Language, Thought*. Trans. Albert Hofstadter. New York: Harper and Row. *Holzwege*. Frankfurt am Main: Klostermann, 1950.

———. (1971b [1950]). 'The Thing' in *Poetry, Language, Thought*. Trans. Albert Hofstadter. New York: Harper and Row. *Vorträge und Aufsätze*. Frankfurt: Klostermann, 2000.

———. (1971c [1951]). 'Building Dwelling Thinking' in ibid.

———. (1988 [1927]). *The Basic Problems of Phenomenology*. Trans. Albert Hofstadter. Bloomington: Indiana University Press. *Die Grundprobleme der Phänomenologie*. Ed. F.-W. von Herrmann. Frankfurt: Klostermann, 1975.

———. (1992 [1942–43]). *Parmenides*. Trans. André Schuwer and Richard Rojcewicz. Bloomington: Indiana University Press. *Parmenides*. Ed. Manfred S. Frings. Frankfurt: Klostermann, 1982.

———. (1995 [1929–30]). *The Fundamental Concepts of Metaphysics: World, Finitude, Solitude*. Trans. William McNeill and Nicholas Walker. Bloomington: Indiana University Press. *Die Grundbegriffe der Metaphysik: Welt-Endlichkeit-Einsamkeit*. Frankfurt: Klostermann, 2010 (pagination identical to Gesamtausgabe 29/30, 1983).

———. (1997 [1929]). *Kant and the Problem of Metaphysics*. Trans. Richard Taft. (Fifth edition). Indianapolis: Indiana University Press. *Kant und das Problem der Metaphysik*. Ed. F.-W. von Herrmann. Frankfurt: Klostermann, 1991.

———. (2010 [1927]). *Being and Time*. Trans. Joan Stambaugh, revised by Dennis J. Schmidt. Albany: SUNY Press.

Heller-Roazen, Daniel. (2007). *The Inner Touch: Archaeology of a Sensation*. New York: Zone.

Hoffmann, E. T. A. (1999 [1819–22]). *The Life and Opinions of The Tomcat Murr, together with a fragmentary Biography of Kapellmeister Johannes Kreisler on Random Sheets of Waste Paper*. Trans. Anthea Bell. London: Penguin. *Lebens-Ansichten des Katers Murr*. Berlin: Ferdinand Dümmler, 1819–22.

Hollier, Denis (ed.). (1988 [1979]). *The College of Sociology (1937–39)*. Trans. Betsy Wing. Minneapolis: University of Minnesota Press. *Le Collège de Sociologie (1937–1939)*. Paris: Gallimard, 1979.

Houlgate, Stephen (ed.). (1998). *Hegel and the Philosophy of Nature*. Albany: SUNY Press.

Husserl, Edmund. (1970/2001 [1900/1913]). *Logical Investigations. Volume 1*. Trans. J. N. Findlay. London: Routledge. *Logische Untersuchungen. Zweiter Band. I. Teil*. Tübingen: Niemeyer, 1968 (Fifth edition).

Johnston, Adrian. (2012). 'The Voiding of Weak Nature', *Graduate Faculty Philosophy Journal* 33:1: 103–57.

Kant, Immanuel. (1929 [1781/1787]). *Critique of Pure Reason*. Trans. Norman Kemp Smith. Basingstoke: Macmillan. *Kritik der reinen Vernunft*. Riga: Hartknoch, 1787. (Abbreviation: CPR)

———. (1987 [1790]). *Critique of Judgement*. Trans. Werner S. Pluhar. Indianapolis: Hackett. *Kritik der Urteilskraft* in Wilhelm Windelband (ed.), *Kants gesammelte Schriften*, Vol. 5 (First Introduction from Vol. 20). (Abbreviation: CJ)

———. (2011 [1764]). *Observations on the Feeling of the Beautiful and Sublime and Other Writings*. Trans. Paul Guyer et al. Eds. Patrick Frierson and Paul Guyer. Cambridge: Cambridge University Press. 'Beobachtungen über das Gefühl des Schönen und Erhabenen' in Paul Menzer (ed.), *Kants gesammelte Schriften*, Vol. 2. Berlin: Königlich Preußische Akademie der Wissenschaften, 1902– ['Akademie' edition].

Kofman, Sarah. (1980 [1976]). 'No Longer Full-Fledged: *Autobiogriffies*'. Trans. Winnie Woodhull. *Sub-Stance* 29 (1980): 3–22. *Autobiogriffures: Du chat Murr d'Hoffmann*. Paris: Galilée, 1984 [Second Edition; First Edition, Paris: Christian Bourgois, 1976].

Lacan, Jacques. (1957–58). *Seminar Book V: The Formations of the Unconscious* (1957–1958). Unpublished typescript. Unedited manuscripts translated by Cormac Gallagher. Available at http://www.lacaninireland.com/web/published-works/seminars/ [accessed 21st May 2016]. French texts of unpublished seminars available at http://ecole-lacanienne.net/en/bibliolacan/seminaires-version-j-l-et-non-j-l/ [accessed 25th February 2017].

———. (1961–62). *Seminar Book IX: Identification* (1961–62). Unpublished typescript. Unedited manuscripts translated by Cormac Gallagher.

———. (1988 [1953–54]). *Seminar Book I: Freud's Papers on Technique* (1953–1954). Trans. John Forrester. New York: Norton. *Le Séminaire, livre I. Les écrits techniques de Freud*. Ed. Jacques-Alain Miller. Paris: Seuil, 1975.

———. (1990 [1974]). *Television / A Challenge to the Psychoanalytic Establishment*. Trans. Denis Hollier, Rosalind Krauss, Annette Michelson, Jeffrey Mehlman, and Bruce Fink. Ed. Joan Copjec. New York: Norton. *Télévision*. Paris: Seuil, 1974.

———. (1992 [1959–60]). *Seminar Book VII: The Ethics of Psychoanalysis* (1959–60). Trans. Dennis Porter. Ed. Jacques-Alain Miller. New York: Norton. *Le Séminaire, livre VII. L'ethique de la psychanalyse*. Paris: Seuil, 1986.

———. (1998 [1957–58]). *Le Séminaire, livre V. Les formations de l'inconscient*. Ed. Jacques-Alain Miller. Paris: Seuil, 1998.

———. (1998 [1964]). *The Four Fundamental Concepts of Psycho-analysis*. Trans. Alan Sheridan. London: Vintage. *Le Séminaire, livre XI. Les Quatre Concepts Fondamentaux de la Psychanalyse, 1964*. Ed. Jacques-Alain Miller. Paris: Seuil, 1973.

———. (2006 [1966]). *Écrits: The First Complete Edition in English*. Trans. Bruce Fink in collaboration with Héloïse Fink and Russell Grigg. New York: Norton. *Écrits*. Paris: Seuil, 1966.

———. (2007 [1969–70]). *Seminar Book XVII. The Other Side of Psychoanalysis* (1969–70). Trans. Russell Grigg. New York: Norton. *L'Envers de la Psychanalyse*. Ed. Jacques-Alain Miller. Paris: Seuil, 1991.

———. (2017 [1957–58]). *Formations of the Unconscious: The Seminar of Jacques Lacan, Book V*. Trans. Russell Grigg. Cambridge: Polity.

Land, Nick. (1992). *The Thirst for Annihilation: Georges Bataille and Virulent Nihilism*. London: Routledge.

Leroi-Gourhan, André. (1993 [1965]). *Gesture and Speech*. Trans. Anna Bostock Berger. Cambridge, MA: MIT Press. *Le Geste et la parole [II]: La Mémoire et les rythmes*. Paris: Albin Michel, 1965.

Levinas, Emmanuel. (1969 [1961]). *Totality and Infinity: An Essay on Exteriority*. Trans. Alphonso Lingis. Dordrecht: Kluwer Academic Publishers. *Totalité et Infini*. The Hague: Martinus Nijhoff, 1971 (First published, 1961). (Abbreviation: TI).

———. (1996 [1951]). 'Is Ontology Fundamental?' [1951] in Adriaan T. Peperzak, Simon Critchley, and Robert Bernasconi (eds.), *Basic Philosophical Writings*. Bloomington: Indiana University Press, 1996 (Abbreviation: IOF). 'L'Ontologie est-elle Fondamentale?' in *Entre Nous: Essais sur le Penser-à-l'Autre*. Paris: Grasset, 1991. (Abbreviation: EN)

———. (1996 [1984]). 'Peace and Proximity' in *Basic Philosophical Writings, op. cit*. 'Paix et Proximité' in Jacques Rolland (ed.), *Les Cahiers de la Nuit Surveillée, no. 3: Emmanuel Levinas*. Lagrasse: Verdier, 1984. (Abbreviation: PP)

———. (1997 [1976]). *Difficult Freedom: Essays on Judaism*. Trans. Seán Hand. Baltimore: Johns Hopkins University Press. *Difficile Liberté*. Paris: Albin Michel, 1976 (3rd ed.) [First edition, 1963]. (Abbreviation: DF)

———. (1998 [1974]). *Otherwise Than Being, or Beyond Essence*. Trans. Alphonso Lingis. Pittsburgh: Duquesne University Press. *Autrement qu'être ou au-delà de l'essence*. The Hague: Martinus Nijhoff, 1974. (Abbreviation: OB)

———. (2004 [1986]). 'Interview' in Atterton and Calarco, *Animal Philosophy* (first published as 'The Paradox of Morality: An Interview with Emmanuel Levinas' (with Tamra Wright, Peter Hughes, Alison Ainley). Trans. Andrew Benjamin and Tamra Wright in Robert Bernasconi and David Wood (eds.), *The Provocation of Levinas: Rethinking the Other*. London: Routledge, 1988.

———. (2006 [1972]). *Humanism of the Other*. Trans. Nidra Poller. Urbana: University of Illinois Press. *Humanisme de l'autre homme*. Montpellier: Fata Morgana, 1972.

Lewis, Michael. (2005). *Heidegger and the Place of Ethics: Being-with in the Crossing of Heidegger's Thought*. London: Continuum.

———. (2007). *Heidegger Beyond Deconstruction: On Nature*. London: Continuum.

———. (2008). *Derrida and Lacan: Another Writing*. Edinburgh: Edinburgh University Press.

———. (2017). 'The Relation between Transcendental Philosophy and Empirical Science in Heidegger's *Fundamental Concepts of Metaphysics*', *Cosmos & History: The Journal of Natural and Social Philosophy* 13:1 (2017): 47–72.

———. (2017). 'On Thinking at the End of the World: Derrida, Lyotard, Bataille' in Will Stronge (ed.), *Georges Bataille and Contemporary Thought*. London: Bloomsbury.

———. (2018). 'Breath in the History of Philosophy', *Philosopher* CVI:1 (Spring 2018).

———. (2019). 'Philosophical Anthropology from Kant and Hegel to the Present Day', in preparation.

Llewelyn, John. (1991). *The Middle Voice of Ecological Conscience: A Chiasmic Reading of Responsibility in the Neighbourhood of Levinas, Heidegger and Others*. Basingstoke: Macmillan.

Lorenz, Konrad. (1964 [1950]). *Man Meets Dog*. Trans. Marjorie Kerr Wilson. Harmondsworth: Penguin. *So kam der Mensch auf den Hund*. Vienna: Verlag Dr. G. Borotha-Schoeler, 1950. [Unfortunately, the English and German editions available to us by no means correspond: curiously, the English edition, when compared to the German, contains a good deal more material on cats.]

———. (1964 [1963]). *King Solomon's Ring. New Light on Animal Ways*. Trans. Marjorie Kerr Wilson. London: Methuen. *Er redete mit dem Vieh, den Vögeln und den Fischen. Tiergeschichten*. Munich: Piper, 1988 (E-book, no pagination). [First edition, 1963]

Malabou, Catherine. (2005 [1996]). *The Future of Hegel: Plasticity, Temporality and Dialectic*. Preface by Jacques Derrida (trans. Joseph D. Cohen). Trans. Lisabeth During. London: Routledge. *L'Avenir de Hegel*. Paris: Vrin, 1996.

———. (2008). 'Addiction and Grace: Preface to Félix Ravaisson's *Of Habit*' in Félix Ravaisson, *Of Habit*. Trans. Clare Carlisle and Mark Sinclair. London: Continuum.

———. (2011 [2009]). *Changing Difference: The Feminine and the Question of Philosophy*. Trans. Carolyn Shread. Cambridge: Polity. *Changer de différence*. Paris: Galilée, 2009.

———. (2012 [2009]). *Ontology of the Accident: An Essay on Destructive Plasticity*. Trans. Carolyn Shread. Cambridge: Polity. *Ontologie de l'accident: Essai sur la plasticité destructrice*. Paris: Léo Scheer, 2009.

———. (2013). Intervention in the discussion of Rebecca Comay and Frank Ruda, 'The Dash (I) and (II)', at the conference, *The Actuality of the Absolute: Hegel, Our Untimely Contemporary*, 10th–12th May 2013. Available at: http://backdoorbroadcasting.net/2013/05/the-actuality-of-the-absolute-hegel-our-untimely-contemporary/ [accessed 18th April 2017].

———. (2015). 'Anthropocene, a New History?' Presentation at the European Graduate School, Saas-Fee, Switzerland. Available at: https://www.youtube.com/watch?v=eDdTqr-5APg [accessed 30th July 2016].

Marder, Michael. (2013). *Plant-Thinking: A Philosophy of Vegetal Life*. New York: Columbia University Press.

———. (2014). *The Philosopher's Plant: An Intellectual Herbarium*. Drawings by Mathilde Roussel. New York: Columbia University Press.

Marder, Michael, with Luce Irigaray. (2016). *Through Vegetal Being: Two Philosophical Perspectives*. New York: Columbia University Press.

Martin, Wayne. (2007). 'In Defence of Bad Infinity: A Fichtean Response to Hegel's *Differenzschrift*', *Bulletin of the Hegel Society of Great Britain* 55 (2007): 168–87.

Marx, Karl. (1998). *The German Ideology* [1845], including the *Theses on Feuerbach* and the *Introduction to the Critique of Political Economy*. Trans. unknown. Amherst, NY: Prometheus.

Massumi, Brian. (2014). *What Animals Teach Us about Politics*. Durham, NC: Duke University Press.

Meillassoux, Quentin. (2008 [2006]). *After Finitude: An Essay on the Necessity of Contingency*. Trans. Ray Brassier. London: Continuum. *Après la finitude. Essai sur la nécessité de la contingence*. Paris: Seuil, 2006.

Merleau-Ponty, Maurice. (2003 [1956–60]). *Nature. Course Notes from the Collège de France*. Compiled and with notes by Dominique Séglard. Trans. Robert Vallier. Evanston, IL: Northwestern University Press. *La Nature. Notes, Cours du Collège de France*. Paris: Seuil, 1995.

Nancy, Jean-Luc. (2001 [1973]). *The Speculative Remark (One of Hegel's Bons Mots)*. Trans. Céline Surprenant. Stanford, CA: Stanford University Press. *La Remarque spéculative: (Un bon mot de Hegel)*. Paris: Galilée, 1973.

Nietzsche, Friedrich. (1969 [1885]). *Thus Spoke Zarathustra: A Book for Everyone and No One*. Trans. R. J. Hollingdale. London: Penguin. *Also sprach Zarathustra* (Kritische Studienausgabe, Band 4). Eds. Giorgio Colli and Mazzino Montinari. Berlin: de Gruyter, 1980.

———. (1990 [1886]). *Beyond Good and Evil: Prelude to a Philosophy of the Future*. Trans. R. J. Hollingdale. London: Penguin. *Jenseits von Gut und Böse* (KSA, Band 5). Berlin: de Gruyter, 1980.

Oliver, Kelly. (2009). *Animal Lessons: How They Teach Us to Be Human*. New York: Columbia University Press.

Piasentier, Marco. (2015). *The Dancing God. One Monotheism, Two Doctrines: Giorgio Agamben, Roberto Esposito, and Davide Tarizzo on the Philosophy of Biopolitics*. University of Kent/Italian Institute of Human Sciences, Naples, March 2015. Available at: http://ethos.bl.uk/OrderDetails.do?uin=uk.bl.ethos.646947 [accessed 19th February 2018, restricted access].

Plutarch. (1957). 'Beasts are Rational' (*Peri tou ta aloga logōi khrēsthai*). Trans. William C. Helmbold in *Moralia. Volume XII.* Trans. Harold Cherniss and William C. Helmbold. Cambridge, MA: Harvard University Press.

Rilke, Rainer Maria. (1984 [1921]). *Mitsou: Forty Images by Balthus*. Preface by Rainer Maria Rilke (bilingual edition). Trans. Richard Miller. New York: Metropolitan Museum of Art/Harry N. Abrams.

———. (2011). *Selected Poems (with Parallel German Text)*. Trans. Susan Ranson and Marielle Sutherland. Ed. Robert Vilain. Oxford: Oxford University Press.

Ruda, Frank. (2013). 'Heglove prve beside' [Hegel's First Words] in *Problemi* (2013): 29–82.

———. (2016). *Abolishing Freedom: A Plea for a Contemporary Use of Fatalism*. Lincoln: University of Nebraska Press.

———. (2017). 'The Beginning of Spirit as We Know It: Hegel's Mother', *Russian Journal of Philosophy and Humanities* 1:2 (2017): 91–114.

Sade, Marquis de. (1968 [1797]). *Juliette.* Trans. Austryn Wainhouse. New York: Grove Press. *Œuvres III.* Ed. Michel Delon with Jean Deprun. Paris: Gallimard, 1998.

———. (1991 [1791]). *Justine, Philosophy in the Bedroom and Other Writings.* Trans. Austryn Wainhouse. London: Arrow. *Œuvres II.* Ed. Michel Delon. Paris: Gallimard, 1995.

Sallis, John. (1994). *Stone.* Bloomington: Indiana University Press.

Sartre, Jean-Paul. (1981 [1971]). *The Family Idiot: Gustave Flaubert 1821–1857.* Vol. 1. Trans. Carol Cosman. Chicago: University of Chicago Press. *L'Idiot de la famille.* Paris: Gallimard, 1971.

———. (1989 [1943]). *Being and Nothingness: An Essay on Phenomenological Ontology.* Trans. Hazel E. Barnes. London: Routledge. *L'Être et le Néant.* Paris: Gallimard, 1943.

———. (2000 [1938]). *Nausea.* Trans. Robert Baldick. London: Penguin. (First edition, 1963). *La Nausée.* Paris: Gallimard, 1938/1972.

Schuster, Aaron. (2016). *The Trouble with Pleasure: Deleuze and Psychoanalysis.* Cambridge, MA: MIT Press.

———. (2017). 'Fasting and Method: Kafka as Philosopher', unpublished manuscript. Available at https://www.academia.edu/26950419/Fasting_and_Method_Kafka_as_Philosopher [accessed 7th January 2017].

Scott, Charles. (2007). *Living with Indifference.* Bloomington: Indiana University Press.

Senatore, Mauro. (2015). 'Of Seminal Difference: Dissemination and Philosophy of Nature' in *CR: The New Centennial Review* 15.1 (Spring 2015): 67–91.

Steeves, H. Peter (ed.). (1999). *Animal Others: On Ethics, Ontology, and Animal Life.* Albany: SUNY Press.

Stone, Alison. (2005). *Petrified Intelligence: Nature in Hegel's Philosophy.* Albany: SUNY Press.

Tarizzo, Davide. (2011). 'The Door: Between Humans and Animals. Lacan and Beyond', at the conference, *The Human Animal in Politics, Science, and Psychoanalysis.* KW Institute for Contemporary Art, Berlin, 16th–17th December 2011. Available at: https://vimeo.com/album/1816803/video/35368225 [accessed 7th January 2017].

———. (2015). 'The Door' in *Filozofski Vestnik* 36:3 (2015): 131–47.

Timofeeva, Oxana. (2012). *History of Animals: An Essay on Negativity, Immanence and Freedom.* Maastricht: Jan Van Eyck Academy. (Second Edition, London: Bloomsbury, 2018, titled *The History of Animals: A Philosophy*).

———. (2015). 'The Two Cats: Žižek, Derrida, and Other Animals' in Agon Hamza (ed.), *Repeating Žižek.* Durham, NC: Duke University Press.

Toadvine, Ted. (2014). 'The Elemental Past' in *Research in Phenomenology* 44 (2014): 262–79.

Wittgenstein, Ludwig. (1999 [1953]). *Philosophical Investigations.* Trans. G. E. M. Anscombe. Oxford: Blackwell.

Wolfe, Cary (ed.). (2003). *Zoontologies: The Question of the Animal.* Minneapolis: University of Minnesota Press.

———. (2013). *Before the Law: Humans and Other Animals in a Biopolitical Frame*. Chicago: University of Chicago Press.
Žižek, Slavoj. (1989). *The Sublime Object of Ideology*. London: Verso.
———. (1991). *For They Know Not What They Do: Enjoyment as a Political Factor*. London: Verso.
———. (2003). *The Puppet and the Dwarf: The Perverse Core of Christianity*. Cambridge, MA: MIT Press.
Žižek, Slavoj (with Markus Gabriel). (2009). *Mythology, Madness and Laughter: Subjectivity in German Idealism*. London: Continuum.
Žižek, Slavoj. (2011a). 'Hegel and Shitting: The Idea's Constipation' in Slavoj Žižek, Clayton Crockett, and Creston Davis (eds.), *Hegel and the Infinite*. New York: Columbia University Press.
———. (2011b). 'The Animal Does Not Exist', at the conference, *The Human Animal in Politics, Science, and Psychoanalysis*. KW Institute for Contemporary Art, Berlin, 16th–17th December 2011. Available at: https://vimeo.com/35590714 [accessed 25th October 2016]. Reworked in *Less Than Nothing*.
———. (2012). *Less Than Nothing: Hegel and the Shadow of Dialectical Materialism*. London: Verso.
———. (2014 [1982]). *The Most Sublime Hysteric: Hegel with Lacan*. Trans. Thomas Scott-Railton. Cambridge: Polity. *Le plus sublime des hystériques. Hegel avec Lacan*. Paris: Presses Universitaires de France, 2011 (an edited version of Žižek's doctoral thesis, 'Philosophy Between the Symptom and the Fantasy', Department of Psychoanalysis, University of Paris-VIII, 1982).
Zupančič, Alenka. (2008). *The Odd One In: On Comedy*. Cambridge, MA: MIT Press.
———. (2017). *What Is Sex?* Cambridge, MA: MIT Press.

Postscript

Like the kitten whose heart will always have been yours, you lie curled up, tucked into yourself, bound together in a perfect circle — creature of paradise and eternity's return unto itself, but also a beast of tangents, rubbing up against us and walking alongside for a while before padding off into the darkness.

Cats have their own world and their own business — they belong to no one and are only ever our visitors. They stay in the house that was once ours just as long as they choose: we were immeasurably lucky that she chose to stay with us for so long. Cats will always remain strangers in this world they temporarily make their own, but in the inestimable honour they do us by lying down in our midst, these wild creatures vouchsafe us a glimpse into theirs. For those few moments, I had the feeling we were in paradise.

The main character of this book will never have lived to see its publication, although she got to rub her whiskers against the manuscript.

She was ill, and I thought the last year of her life might have begun. It turned out she was about to enter the last week of it. I had the feeling at the beginning of that week, weighed down with grief that was heightened by the slipping away of another from whom I had learned something of how to see into this world, that in the end this was to have been a book written in paradise, and that our Eden was now fast passing from sight.

But it is not certain that we will have fallen so very far, and difficult to believe that something so alive can ever truly die — even now, I think I sense her, just out of sight, in a shadow that sits just across an obscure threshold, a rustle in the darkness nearby, and the light of a sunburst scattered on the surface of a river.

This book was always dedicated to her. It came more easily than one has any right to expect, and surely because it was written out of the most sincere love. Now it stands as a monument to that paradise we shared, and into which you have wandered away.

To the memory of Bandit, 2003–2017.

Index

Absolute Idealism, 78, 191
Absolute Spirit, 90, 106, 193, 202
Abstract Negation, 149
Adorno, Theodor, 166, 179
Aesthetic Judgement, 39–42, 45–46, 53, 56, 181
Aesthetics, 47, 79, 81–83, 85, 87–91, 122, 184, 191
Agamben, Giorgio, 142, 152–154, 161, 165–169, 180–181, 196, 204–205
Animation, 78, 82–83, 187
Anthropocene, 119, 197, 216
Anthropogenesis, 2, 13, 131, 134, 195, 205
Anthropology, 132, 134, 205
Anthropomorphism, 87, 182
Aporia, 38–39
Archi-writing, 94–95, 98–99, 102–103, 195
Aristotle, 84, 107, 187, 190, 196, 205
Art, 27, 47, 53, 81, 84, 89–90, 148, 164–165, 193, 196, 203
Artificial Beauty, 79
Assiter, Alison, 144
Aufhebung, 8, 145, 150, 166, 187
Autobiographical, 12, 143–144, 170, 173, 181, 203
Autobiography, 180–181

Automatic, 13, 31, 132, 135, 176, 205
Automatism, 131, 135, 190

Bad Faith, 140–141, 174
Bad Habit, 14, 121, 131, 133, 137–138, 141, 146, 205
Bad infinite, 3–7, 10–14, 18, 27, 37–39, 46, 50, 52, 60, 69, 89–90, 120–121, 127–129, 135–137, 139–141, 145–146, 149, 166–167, 186, 190, 193, 204
Bataille, Georges, 141, 152, 168–169, 196
Baudelaire, Charles, vi, 158, 161
Beauty, 1, 17–18, 38–42, 45–59, 71, 73–75, 79, 81–85, 87–91, 122–125, 128, 139–140, 142–143, 147–148, 156, 168, 181–184, 191, 196, 203
Beautiful, 1, 14, 17, 19, 39–42, 45–55, 57–62, 73–75, 79, 82–83, 87–91, 93, 104, 109, 120, 122–124, 126–127, 129, 138, 140, 152, 154, 156, 182, 184, 195, 202
Beloved, 51, 104, 151, 168, 200
Benjamin, Walter, 127–128, 203–204
Benommenheit, 139, 160
Bird, 1, 48–50, 53–54, 78–79, 83–86, 133, 153, 182–183, 192

223

Birdsong, 48, 50–51, 84, 86, 88
Blanchot, Maurice, 168, 194–195
Boredom, 2, 145, 178, 205
Botanist, 53–55, 182
Botany, 57
Božovič, Miran, 192
Breath, 52, 57, 66, 73, 84–85, 88, 99, 171, 191, 216
Breathing, 45, 56, 99, 104
Brown, Nathan, 195, 201–202
Buber, Martin, 159

Captivation, 139, 160
Casts, 119, 128, 201
Cat, vi–vii, 1, 4–5, 11–13, 15, 18–19, 29–30, 37, 120, 137, 140–143, 145–148, 151–154, 157–159, 161–165, 169, 173, 180, 183, 191
Categorical Imperative, 27
Charm, vi, 1, 5–6, 13, 16–18, 21, 35, 37–41, 43, 45, 47–53, 55, 57, 59, 90–91, 121, 125–127, 129, 137–140, 142–143, 146–147, 153–154, 161, 163, 179–180, 182
Charming, vi, 2, 5–6, 12, 14–17, 19, 21, 37–38, 40, 47–48, 50–52, 59, 74–75, 88, 118, 121, 123, 126–127, 129, 141–142, 144, 156–157, 183
Child, 13, 21, 24, 31, 114, 132, 147, 152–154, 157–158, 195, 201
Childhood, 138, 152–153
Clearing, 46, 139, 160
Coelacanth, 91, 93, 109
Comedy, 121, 202
Concept, 5, 8–9, 13, 17, 39, 41, 44–46, 51, 53–58, 60, 62–67, 72–76, 78, 81–83, 85–86, 89, 94–98, 103–104, 108, 114, 122, 128, 131–132, 144–145, 155, 160, 168, 181, 183–187, 189–190, 195, 197, 199, 203–204
Conceptuality, 45, 54, 57, 65, 72–73, 159, 187
Consciousness, 9, 15, 63, 66, 70, 72, 76, 88–89, 105–106, 130, 132, 134, 148–150, 158, 178, 180, 194

Contingency, 19, 43, 63, 67, 69, 71–73, 87, 89, 113, 122–123, 125, 186, 200
Continuum, 58, 198–200
Contradiction, 69, 73, 105, 130–131, 170, 193, 205
Counterpart, 31, 66, 70
Creation, 69, 71, 87, 90, 100, 113, 149, 153, 158
Critique of Judgement, 16–17, 38–40, 49, 51, 55, 81, 185, 202
Critique of Practical Reason, 18
Critique of Pure Reason, 42
Culture, 3–6, 9–10, 13, 15, 31, 39, 49, 61, 67, 76, 107, 119–120, 134–135, 138, 145, 147, 178, 183, 197

Darwin, Charles, 165, 170–171
Davies, Paul, 22–23, 169, 179, 185, 195, 201
Deactivation, 153
Death, 8, 10–11, 50, 77, 99–100, 104, 107–108, 118–121, 134–135, 144, 148, 150–153, 157–158, 190, 193, 196–197, 202;
Drive, 119, 121, 134–135;
-drive, 121, 134;
mask, 104, 119, 196

Deleuze, Gilles, 144, 169, 183, 185, 209
Derrida, Jacques, 15–16, 23, 31, 33–34, 38–39, 84, 94–95, 98–99, 102–104, 130, 139, 147, 151–152, 154–161, 165–167, 169–170, 173–178, 180–181, 183, 191, 193–196
Desire, 1, 17, 30, 34–35, 37, 47, 120, 134–137, 158, 174, 178, 182, 190
Désœuvrement, 129, 168
Determinate Negation, 8–9, 78, 83, 106, 119, 149–150, 188
Determinative Judgement, 41, 44, 53–54, 56
Dialectic, 9–10, 13, 16, 19, 30, 37–38, 61, 78–79, 83, 90–91, 93–97, 99, 101, 103–107, 109, 111, 113–119,

121–123, 125–131, 133, 135–143, 146–147, 150, 166, 168, 179, 181, 185, 190, 193–194, 196, 201; at a standstill, 203–204
Dialectics, 16, 62, 68; at a standstill, 127–128, 204
Dignity, 5, 24–26, 144, 170–171
Disinterest, 17, 47–48, 50, 52, 124–125, 180, 182
Diversity, 40, 42–43, 45, 48–51, 73–74, 200
Dog, 21, 23–29, 33–35, 146–147, 161, 169–172, 178–179, 183
Dolar, Mladen, 134, 166
Domestic, 5, 35, 58, 146, 151, 153, 161, 177–179, 182–183
Domesticated, 5, 37, 146–147, 159, 183
Domestication, 60, 146
Doubling, 175–176
Drive, 13, 27, 72, 112, 119, 121, 134–135, 190
Duplication, 32, 175

Earth, ix, 7, 77, 86, 100, 108, 110–114, 119, 126, 197, 202–203; organism, 112, 114
Eden, 53, 151, 221
Efficient Causality, 39, 44
Effigy, 104, 120, 125, 202
Eliot, T.S., 148, 161, 180
Ennui, 4–5, 53, 136, 142, 205
Environment, 78, 123, 139, 160, 176, 191, 209
Eternal Recurrence, 7
Eternal Return, 2, 18
Ethics, 23, 27–29, 47, 172, 184, 202, 205, 208, 214–215, 218, 225
Evolution, 93, 112–113, 194, 197–201, 212
Extinction, 107, 119–120, 198, 200–201

Feint, 32, 34
Feuerbach, Ludwig, 130, 181, 211, 217

Fiat, 44, 69, 149
Final Cause, 39, 44, 55–56
Finality, 44–45
Fish, 11–13, 54, 83, 85, 109, 137, 140, 152, 183
Fixation, 131–132, 137, 168
Fossil, 75, 77, 87, 91, 93–105, 107–115, 117–127, 129–131, 133, 135, 137, 139–140, 159, 193–203; record, 94–95, 98; writing, 94–98, 100, 102–103
Foucault, Michel, 197–200
Functional, 5, 19, 137, 141, 152, 169, 176, 195

Garden, 3–4, 48–49, 141, 151, 183, 192
Gaze, 15–16, 19, 28, 71, 89, 91, 139–140, 142, 147–148, 155–163, 192, 195, 205, 209
Genera, 43, 55, 185, 198
Genet, Jean, 130–131
Genus, 11, 75, 183, 193
Geology, 77, 110–114, 196–197; Geological, 98, 100, 104, 110–112, 114, 117–118, 197, 201
German Idealism, 18, 38–39, 57, 62
God, 6–8, 44, 69, 71, 90, 100, 148–150, 157, 184, 186, 195
Gould, Stephen Jay, 200
Grant, Iain Hamilton, 144, 185, 196, 197, 202
Gravestone, 107, 118, 196
Guattari, Félix, 183, 185

Habit, 2, 11, 14, 87, 93, 102, 119, 121, 131, 133–138, 140–141, 146, 190, 195, 202, 204–205
Hägglund, Martin, 195, 212
Hegel, G. W. F., 3, 6–12, 14–18, 25, 27, 37–39, 52, 59–79, 81–91, 96–98, 104–106, 108–118, 122–123, 125, 127, 129–134, 138, 140–141, 145–146, 148–152, 166, 168, 171,

177–179, 181, 184–193, 196–197, 200–201, 203, 205
Heidegger, Martin, 11, 39–40, 121, 139, 142, 151–152, 155, 157, 159–161, 166–167, 170–171, 173, 179, 181–182, 184–185, 192–193, 196, 201, 203, 205
Heller-Roazen, Daniel, 180
Hindsight, 64, 87, 90, 116
History, 4, 6, 9–11, 16–17, 19, 27, 37, 66, 72, 77, 91, 93–95, 104–107, 109–114, 118–119, 128, 131, 134, 140, 143–146, 149, 155–156, 160, 165, 173, 177, 180–181, 183, 186–187, 192, 197–201, 203–204
Hoffmann, E. T. A., 180
Hölderlin, Friedrich, 201
Horror, ix, 121, 163–164, 202
Horse, 54, 74, 170, 191, 193
House, 5, 23, 30, 34–35, 37, 54, 146, 152, 163, 179, 183
Husserl, Edmund, 180, 195

Idea, 1, 37, 44, 51–52, 57, 65–66, 68–69, 71–73, 76–77, 82, 87–88, 98–100, 102–103, 106, 110–111, 115–117, 126, 128, 132–134, 142, 144–145, 148, 151–152, 167, 169, 172, 177, 180–181, 185–189, 192, 196, 202–203
Idealism, 18, 38–39, 57, 62, 65–66, 71–73, 78, 82, 185, 189, 191; of Life, 82
Idealist, 65, 73, 82, 184, 189
Imaginary, 30–34, 175, 177, 192
Imagination, 42, 46–47, 51, 56–58, 181
Immortal, 21, 76, 119–122, 135, 192, 196, 202
Immortality, 112, 118–121, 127
Indifference, 15, 18–19, 72, 91, 118, 120, 129, 141–142, 154, 166–168, 183
Indifferent, 12, 16, 18–19, 27, 62, 69, 71–72, 90, 93, 127, 129, 135, 142, 148, 167–169, 181

Infinity, 2–3, 6–7, 9–11, 13, 93, 127, 130, 133, 137, 149, 166–167, 171, 180–182, 205
Instinct, 31, 134–135, 147, 160, 172, 177, 205
Interest, 8, 16–17, 19, 33, 47–48, 50, 52, 61, 109–114, 128, 137, 146, 153, 182–183
Intuition, 41, 107, 147–148, 181, 187, 194
Irritability, 179–180
Irritation, 179–180

Judgement, 16–17, 32, 38–42, 44–47, 49, 51–58, 81, 121, 160, 174, 181, 184–185, 196–197, 202; of taste, 41, 46–47, 54, 57–58

Kafka, Franz, 148, 157, 161
Kant, Immanuel, 6–7, 14–18, 26–27, 37–55, 57–64, 67, 70, 72–74, 76, 78–79, 81, 86, 88, 122, 125, 140, 143–144, 147–148, 155, 166, 179, 181–182, 184–187, 192, 196, 200–203, 205
Kierkegaard, Søren, 144, 166, 181
Kofman, Sarah, 180
Kojève, Alexandre, 168

Lacan, Jacques, 21, 23, 25, 27, 29–35, 37, 120, 122, 135–137, 154–155, 169, 174–178, 197, 202
Language, 15, 21–23, 29–31, 33–35, 37, 85, 99, 105, 107, 119, 149, 155, 159, 167, 172, 178, 193
Langue, 22, 30, 33, 35
Levinas, Emmanuel, 21–31, 33, 35, 37, 122, 135, 155, 159, 166–167, 169–173, 176
Life, 3, 8, 11, 72, 75–78, 82–85, 87–89, 91, 98–99, 102–104, 107–108, 112, 115–123, 126–127, 130–131, 135, 145, 148, 150–151, 157, 160, 172, 177–180, 185, 187, 191, 193–194, 197, 200–202, 205

Living, 1, 11, 13, 17, 24, 45, 55–57, 59, 65, 72, 76–78, 82–84, 86, 89, 93, 98–100, 102–104, 107–108, 110–111, 113–114, 116, 118–124, 137, 146, 157, 162, 172–173, 177, 179, 190, 194–195, 197–198, 205
Llewelyn, John, 23, 26, 28–30, 171
Logic, 7, 67–68, 73, 78–79, 90, 149, 151, 166, 185–186, 188, 205
Lorenz, Konrad, 146–148, 152–153
Love, 2, 8, 51–53, 59, 71, 73, 124, 131, 136, 143, 147, 152, 162–165, 169–170, 182, 203

Machine, 38, 50, 60, 79, 90–91, 127, 135, 137, 155, 165–166, 168, 176
Madness, 91, 121, 130–137, 166–167, 180, 205
Malabou, Catherine, 131–132, 134, 151, 167, 190, 195–197
Marder, Michael, 145, 182, 192
Marx, Karl, 176–177
Matter, 41, 44, 46–48, 51, 55, 76, 82, 85–86, 98, 110–116, 120, 133, 145, 147, 149, 167, 170, 180, 188–191, 194, 202–203, 205
Maxwell, Gavin, 145
Mechanism, 86, 133, 135, 190
Meillassoux, Quentin, 94–95, 193–194, 203, 211–212
'Mere life,' 76, 91, 130
Merely life, 76, 89
Merely lives, 91, 179
Merleau-Ponty, Maurice, 180, 194
Metabolism, 190–191
Metaphysical, 15, 28–30, 33–34, 37, 40, 58, 60, 65, 98–100, 102–104, 155–156, 158–160, 172–173, 175, 177–178, 180, 184
Metaphysics, 15–17, 34, 40, 65, 99–100, 102–104, 113, 154–158, 160, 166–167, 170, 172–173, 177, 180–181, 184, 196
Mirror, 8–9, 31, 67–71, 85, 88–89, 91, 124, 136, 174, 177

Monster, 74–75, 83, 197–199
Monstrosity, 74, 199
Myth, 113, 183

Narcissism, 13, 88, 154, 183
Natural Beauty, 53, 79, 81, 83, 88–90, 140, 183
Natural History, 109–112, 197–199
Naturalism, 169, 184–185
Naturalistic, 185
Nature, 2–7, 9–11, 13, 16–18, 24, 31, 38–46, 48–79, 81–83, 85, 87–91, 93–95, 98, 100–102, 105, 108–120, 122–125, 127–128, 131–136, 138, 144–145, 147–149, 151–154, 159, 163, 165–167, 173, 177–179, 181–182, 184–191, 193–202
Necessity, 5, 17, 28, 38, 44, 47, 49, 56, 58, 62–70, 72, 76, 102, 107, 111–112, 123, 129, 135, 166, 178, 185–186, 200
Negation, 2, 8–10, 21, 78, 83, 106, 119, 121, 149–150, 152, 166, 168–169, 178, 188, 196
Neurosis, 130, 136–138
New Use, 153
Nietzsche, Friedrich, 144, 160, 166, 191–192

Objective Idealism, 82
Objet petit a, 136
oikos, 183
Ontogeny, 113, 205
Ontologist, 160
Ontology, 86, 167, 185, 215–216, 218
The Open, 10, 156–157, 160
Organic, 17, 69, 76–79, 93, 104, 110–111, 114, 116–117, 122, 128, 132–133, 188, 191, 197, 200–202
Organism, 16, 39, 45, 51–52, 55–57, 63–66, 72, 75–79, 81–82, 85–87, 108, 110–112, 114, 116–117, 119, 122–123, 129, 132–133, 135, 179, 183, 186, 188, 190–191, 193, 201
Otherness, 31, 68–69, 71, 184, 191

Otter, 145
Owl, 11, 85, 151, 187, 192

Painting, 2–5, 13, 192
Paradise, 53, 70, 187, 221–222
Parole, 22, 30, 32–33, 35
Perfect animal, 1, 13, 86–87, 91, 122
Perfect, 1, 7, 10, 13, 54, 66, 74, 86–87, 90–91, 93, 107–108, 122, 129, 138, 145, 165, 193, 221
Perfection, 1, 10, 16–17, 54, 57, 84, 88, 90–91, 93, 127, 129, 132, 148
Pet, 12, 35, 178–179, 183
Petrifaction, 114–117, 200–201
Petrification, 108, 115, 117, 121
Phenomenology, 79, 105–107, 156, 161, 168, 191, 194, 196
Philosopher, vi, 3, 14, 19, 83–84, 91, 116, 129, 144, 148, 154–157, 159–160, 163–164, 169, 173, 179, 182
Philosophical, 3, 6, 10, 16, 18, 23, 27, 39, 67, 70, 94–95, 105, 107, 110–111, 114, 116–117, 130, 134, 139–140, 153, 159–160, 169, 174, 187, 193–194, 205, 209, 212, 215–216, 218, 225
Philosophy, 1, 3, 6–7, 9, 14–19, 29, 37–40, 43–44, 52, 57, 60–72, 74–79, 81–82, 88, 90, 93, 96–99, 104, 106–119, 122, 127–130, 132, 134, 139–147, 149, 151–161, 166–170, 172, 179, 181, 184–193, 196–197, 201, 203–204; of History, 106–107, 204; of Nature, 7, 16, 43, 61–67, 69–71, 74–77, 79, 81–82, 88, 90, 108–118, 122, 127, 134, 151, 179, 185–191, 196–197, 201;
of Spirit, 67, 76, 132, 134, 190
Phoenix, 11, 79, 107, 119–120, 151
Photograph, 104, 128, 137, 196
Phylogeny, 113, 133, 205
Plant, 53–54, 57, 64, 69, 85, 110–111, 113, 117, 133, 138, 145, 182, 192
Plutarch, 155, 169
Poetry, 143, 148, 154, 157–158, 160–161

Porphyry, 55, 138
Posthuman, 201
Pretence, 30, 32, 175
Purpose, 2, 4–5, 15, 19, 27, 39, 42, 44–46, 51–57, 63–64, 66, 122–123, 142, 146, 151, 153, 183, 187, 197, 202
Purposive, 45, 141, 201
Purposiveness, 44–45, 47, 51–52, 54–57, 142, 183–184
Purring, vi, 82, 146, 152, 191

Rationality, 17, 26, 28, 58–59, 61, 63–64, 66–67, 70–72, 74, 78, 93, 106–107, 112, 122, 189
Reaction, 26, 133, 155, 176, 179
Realism, 65–66
Realist, 65
Reason, 2, 7, 10, 15, 17–18, 27, 29–30, 38–46, 49–52, 56–57, 60, 62–63, 65–68, 70–72, 74, 78–79, 82–85, 87, 89, 91, 99, 104–105, 109, 111, 113, 121–122, 125, 128–132, 134, 145–146, 148, 152, 157, 167, 170, 172, 175, 177, 180, 182, 184–185, 187, 189, 191, 193, 203
Reflective Judgement, 40–41, 44, 47, 53
Repressed, 166, 174
Repression, 136, 138, 166
Response, 2, 5, 14, 22–23, 25–26, 28–29, 31, 133, 143–144, 152, 155–156, 176, 184, 196, 201
Resurrection, 8, 10–11, 76, 120–121, 127, 150
Retroactive, 187, 191
Retrospective, 62, 64, 75, 141, 188, 190
Rilke, Rainer Maria, 139, 147–148, 157–161
Ruda, Frank, 149, 166–167, 190, 216–217

Sade, Marquis de, 120, 202
Sartre, Jean-Paul, 2, 136, 144, 155, 178, 205

Index 229

Saying, 22–23, 27–28, 33, 35, 110–111, 152, 170, 196
Schelling, F. W. J., 18, 39, 62, 108, 196–197
Schematisation, 51
Schematism, 42
Schuster, Aaron, 147–148, 154, 161, 167, 169, 178, 202
Science of Logic, 149, 166, 188
Second Death, 118, 120, 197, 202
Self-consciousness, 9, 15, 63, 66, 70, 72, 76, 88–89, 106, 132, 134, 178, 180
Semblable, 31
Shaving, 2–5, 13, 136, 142
Sincere, 1–2, 5–6, 18, 21–22, 24, 26, 35, 37, 118, 129, 137, 152, 169–170, 222
Sincerity, 1–2, 5–6, 12–13, 15, 21–25, 27–35, 37–38, 59, 90–91, 121–123, 127, 129–130, 137–138, 142–143, 146, 153, 160, 166, 169, 176, 205
Soul, 40, 76–78, 81, 83–88, 90, 98–99, 190
Sovereign, 62, 141–142, 154, 156, 159, 168–169
Species, 3, 11, 33, 43, 49, 55, 65, 75, 83, 87, 109, 114, 119–120, 145–147, 151, 173, 176, 193, 198–200, 205
Spirit, 8–11, 18, 53, 61–64, 66–73, 75–78, 84–85, 87, 89–91, 94–95, 100, 105–106, 108–112, 114, 116, 118–119, 122, 127–129, 131–134, 138, 145–146, 149–151, 159, 168, 181, 186, 190, 192–193, 196–197, 201–202
St. Anselm, 184
Stone-animal, 75, 93, 118, 127
Subjectivity, 28, 43, 46, 69–70, 76–77, 84–85, 107, 155–156, 159, 188, 191, 219
Sublation, 7–10, 78–79, 88, 93, 104, 107–109, 118–119, 127, 129, 138, 145, 149, 166–168, 187, 190–191

Sublimation, 34, 135
Sublime, 27, 48–49, 52, 147–148, 171, 181–184, 202–203
Sublimity, 58, 121, 148, 182, 202–203
Supersession, 18, 61, 67, 129, 137–138, 145, 149, 150, 166
Symbolic, 27, 30–35, 37, 119–120, 174–177, 202
Symptom, 109, 132–134, 137, 166
System, 9, 14, 30–31, 38, 46, 51–52, 64, 67, 70, 72, 75–76, 99, 105–106, 111, 114, 118, 127, 166, 175, 180, 188, 201

Tame, 5, 58, 60, 146
Taste, 41, 46–51, 53–54, 56–58, 183
Teleological Judgement, 39, 45, 52–53, 56–58, 184
Teleological, 39, 45, 52–53, 56–58, 63, 78, 83, 184, 187
Teleology, 39, 45
Thing in itself, 37, 160
Thing-in-itself, 6, 46, 194
Threshold, 5, 13–14, 30, 34–35, 37, 75, 77, 93, 121–122, 130, 132, 136, 146, 148, 177, 179, 183, 205, 221
Timofeeva, Oxana, 16, 143, 156–157, 169, 191–192
Trace, 5, 23, 32, 72, 90, 94–100, 102–104, 107, 119–120, 122–123, 125, 127, 144, 167, 170, 175, 182, 193–196, 198–200, 202
Transcendental, 42–44, 54, 56–57, 62, 70, 141, 184–185
Tree, 55, 64, 117, 138, 182, 187, 200
True Infinite, 3–7, 10, 13, 16, 38–39, 50, 128–129, 139–140, 145, 149, 167, 205
Umwelt, 139, 160

Understanding, 6–9, 11, 15, 18, 24, 27, 39, 41, 43–44, 46, 49, 55–56, 58, 60, 63, 65, 71, 78, 83, 98, 104, 112, 122,

139, 144, 146, 151–152, 154, 160, 178, 182, 184, 187, 203
Utilitarian, 142

Weed, 10, 46, 49, 145, 192
Wild, 3, 5, 37, 43, 48–50, 74, 146–147, 152, 178, 183, 221;
Wilderness, 4, 18, 51, 129, 147, 161;
Wildness, 147

Wittgenstein, Ludwig, 21–23, 25, 27, 29–31, 33, 35, 37, 122, 169
Writing, 15, 94–100, 102–109, 114, 116, 118–119, 122, 125, 152, 169, 177, 180, 182, 194–196, 204

Žižek, Slavoj, 13, 16, 121, 132–135, 150, 156, 166, 185, 196, 202
Zupančič, Alenka, 134, 166, 202, 205

About the Author

Michael Lewis is the author of *Heidegger and the Place of Ethics*, *Heidegger Beyond Deconstruction: On Nature*, *Derrida and Lacan: Another Writing*, and, with Tanja Staehler, *Phenomenology: An Introduction*, along with articles on Agamben, Bataille, Derrida, Esposito, Lacan, Stiegler, and Žižek, among others. Educated in philosophy at the University of Warwick and the University of Essex, he has taught philosophy, film, psychoanalysis, and philosophical anthropology at the University of Sussex (2007–2009, 2011), the University of Warwick (2010), and the University of the West of England (2011–15). He is Lecturer in Philosophy at the University of Newcastle upon Tyne.

www.ingramcontent.com/pod-product-compliance
Lightning Source LLC
Chambersburg PA
CBHW021825300426
44114CB00009BA/325